SHOT IN THE TOWER

By The Same Author

The Hood Battalion
Leo Cooper, 1995

For God's Sake Shoot Straight,
Leo Cooper, 1996

SHOT IN THE TOWER

The Story of the Spies executed in the
Tower of London During the First World War

by
LEONARD SELLERS

LEO COOPER
LONDON

First Published in Great Britain in 1997 by
LEO COOPER
an imprint of
Pen & Sword Books Ltd 47 Church Street Barnsley South Yorkshire S70 2AS

ISBN 0 085052 553.5

A catalogue record for this book
is available from the British Library

Typeset by Phoenix Typesetting, Ilkley, West Yorkshire
Printed in England by Redwood Books, Trowbridge, Wiltshire

*This book is dedicated to the memory of all those
who worked in the detection of spies who threatened the
well-being and life of this nation.*

Contents

Introduction

At the extremes of human experience, the Tower of London stands supreme in England in the scale of human suffering. For centuries the outspoken, the out of favour, the adulterous, traitorous and subversive have been confined, tortured and executed there. It has an aura that few other places possess: the pull of the macabre is the same for British citizen and foreign tourist alike. The Crown Jewels that glitter and shine in all their glory in their new home near the Martin Tower hold a secret. Few know or suspect that a short distance from where they admire the nation's royal treasure, eleven spies in the First World War were shot at dawn by detachments of Guards, having been brought before a court martial or civil court for service to Germany. (One spy was executed in the Tower during the Second World War – his case is detailed in brief in the Appendix.)

The timeless stones of the Tower of London reek of history, dating back to its founder, William the Conqueror. The Traitor's Gate and the ravens, the many towers, crypts, chapels and torture chambers, all combine to add to the strange feeling of unease that can envelop the soul – particularly at dusk, dawn, or on a dank, dark winter's day. The list of those confined in the Tower reads almost like an 'A to Z' of British History. Queens Anne Boleyn and Katherine Howard, Lady Jane Grey, Sir Walter Raleigh, the Earl of Essex, and many, many more waited through the night for the executioner's blade.

But by the time of the First World War the water had ebbed and flowed in the River Thames for some 150 years without an execution taking place in the Tower. Times had changed and such horrors were the story of bygone days. Few expected the need would arise again. But after the declaration of war, if there was the necessity for an execution, the Tower of London was considered the only suitable place in the capital to carry out the task. One of the reasons for this was its reputation, which it was hoped would place a chill in the heart of a potential enemy agent and a doubt in the mind of all but the most committed spy.

On being transferred to the Tower the spies of the First World War were often guarded at 29 The Casemates, bomb-proof buildings with embrasures for guns. Most of the executions took place in the miniature rifle range, situated between the Martin and Constable Towers. You can view the area by crossing Tower Bridge from the south side of the river along Tower Bridge Approach. As you get to Tower Hill, the turning to the left, stop and look towards the Tower of London. Over the now grassy moat and the curtain wall at the corner is the Martin Tower, and the next tower back towards the river is the Constable Tower. Between the two the spies met their maker. The Martin Tower, built in the reign of Henry III and modernized by Christopher Wren, was originally the Jewel House from where Colonel Blood stole the crown in the days of Charles II Tradition has it that Anne Boleyn was for a time held here. The Constable Tower was at one time the residence of the Constable, as the name implies. Between these two towers is the rampart called Northumberland Walk.[1]

The Tower was in 1914 under the control of three officers, the Constable, the Lieutenant, and the Major, also known as the Resident Governor. The Constable of the Tower, an office of great honour, dates back to just after the Norman Conquest. The Constable had long ago ceased to reside within the curtilage, handing over most of his duties to the Lieutenant of the Tower. In 1914 the Constable was Field Marshal Sir Evelyn Wood, the 134th person to have the rank.[2] The Lieutenants of the Tower had not resided there since 1689; like the Constable, they retired to the comfort of private residences. From 1912 until 1917 the Lieutenant was Lieutenant General the Honourable Sir Frederick Stopford.[3] The resident officer is known as the Major of the Tower and Governer, an office dating from the reign of William and Mary. In 1909 Major General Henry Pipon CB took up the post, which he was to hold until 1923.[4]

Apart from the court martial of Carl Hans Lody, all the rest were held in camera, so the opinions and observations of the press are not available for this narrative. There was good reason for this, as the enemy could gain useful information from an unfettered but well-informed journalist or onlooker. In the First World War the President of the courts martial was in most cases Lord Cheylesmore, born on 25 January, 1848, the third Baron. Being over 65 years of age, he had retired, but was recalled for service because it was felt that it was essential that the jurisdiction of the courts martial should not be open to challenge he was ordered back to duty on full pay to avoid the possibility of the legality of the constitution of the court being questioned.[5] He had been educated at Eton and passed directly into the army from there, joining the Grenadier Guards in 1867. He was later to command the 2nd Battalion of the Grenadier Guards. He contested the parliamentary seat of Coventry in 1887 upon the elevation of his father to the peerage, but was beaten by just 16 votes. Later he became chairman of both the National Rifle Association and the LCC.[6]

In writing this account I have been to some extent hampered by the fact that in a few cases the court-martial files cannot be found; according to the Lord Chancellor's Department they must have been destroyed some years ago.[7] As a result I wrote to Prime Minister John Major,[8] asking that consideration be given for me to be allowed access to the security services' (MI5's) private papers. The reply I received on the behalf of the Director General was that domestic records of the security and intelligence agencies are currently withheld under the provisions of the Lord Chancellor's 'blanket'![9]

So there it rests: I could get no other help. I have attempted to tell the story, using in many cases the words of the spy himself and the others involved. By taking this course I have endeavoured to capture the atmosphere of the times and tried to bring the characters to life, highlighting their thinking, motivation and explanations when on trial for their lives. Some were brave, some cowardly. Their motives ranged from the patriotic to the mercenary. But all the spies were widely different in their outlook and background and are part of the rich tapestry of the histories of both Germany and Britain.

CHAPTER 1

German Spies in Britain

In June, 1908, at Potsdam in Germany, the Kaiser held a secret council which the chief of the army and navy, as well as representatives of the leading Federal States, attended. He said during his two-hour speech:

> Do you remember, my Generals, what our never-to-be-forgotten Field Marshal Gebhard Lebrecht von Blücher exclaimed, when looking from the dome of St Paul's Cathedral upon the vast metropolis at his feet? It was short, and to the point. 'What a spendid city to sack!'[1]

This was pure fiction on the part of William Le Queux, an author who was very influential in Britain with his stories of German spies in England and invasion scares. Many people were fearful that a vast network of German spies had infiltrated among the thousands of German nationals who lived and worked in Britain. This threat was in fact greatly exaggerated, but there was some truth behind the alarm, as already a few German spies were scattered around Britain. Furthermore, Germany had taken up the gauntlet in the race to build Dreadnoughts. When Germany looked at Britain, concern was not for her army, which she considered small and insignificant, but her naval power and domination over the seas. So these intelligence gatherers were to concentrate mainly on the nautical, as to be forewarned is to be forearmed. Should war break out, such information could redress the balance of sea power, if used to strike an early and decisive blow.

On the other hand, in the early years of the 20th century, many British authorities did not take the threat of German espionage in Britain too seriously. A state of disbelief and indifference was prevalent in a certain type of politician, journalist and judge.

1

Speak gently to your German spy
And never seek to spurn him.
Nay, let a tear bedim your eye
If you must needs intern him.
For, though his calling may appear
To have a nasty flavour,
We ought to take his presence here
As something of a favour.

In other lands, of course, we knew
There had been lots of spying –
Which, from the German point of view,
Was highly gratifying.
Spies doubtless hastened Antwerp's fall,
They were so slim and clever;
But that was Belgium, after all.
And here in England? Never!

The German did his bit in France.
We saw his work too clearly.
But let us give him every chance
Of hurting us severely.
Let us admit his every claim
To our consideration,
And if there's anyone to blame
Let's blame the British nation.[2]

But it slowly became clear to the Imperial Defence Committee that the activities of enemy agents were causing grave concern to the directors of naval and military intelligence and that a system of counter-epionage was required.

Colonel James Edmonds suggested that it was necessary to find a suitable applicant who would be entrusted with forming an effective organization to check this now dangerous threat. Captain Vernon Kell was approached, and was amazed to hear that his name was being put forward. He knew that, should he accept the job which was seriously offered to him, he would be running a great risk. He would have to retire, on paper though not in fact, to enable him to remain at the War Office without being moved from one place to another, which in the ordinary course of a solder's life was inevitable. He might be a failure, and what then? He would be left jobless, and to what else could he turn, as jobs were not easy to find?

However, he accepted, and began his task with just one man. After a while he was joined by a second, a clerk, the request for whom was greeted with surprise by the authorities, who viewed it as an extravagance!

Soon things began to take shape and the foundations of what was to become a great department were laid. By the autumn of the year 1909 Vernon Kell had left his ordinary army career and had started to collect information vital to a number of official departments. He gradually but surely gained the confidence and goodwill of those he worked for. At first it was very uphill work, for it took much time and patience to sift what came in, and everything had to be absolutely foolproof before he could ask the authorities to give warrants for the police to make arrests: those in authority had to be fully convinced that such arrests were essential in the interests of the state.

Among the first few cases to be brought to trial was a Lieutenant Helm, who in 1910 was found near Portsmouth sketching details of the defences of the area.

Kell had to move cautiously, as he was aiming at gradually building up the channels by which a central network could be created. He was often told by his friends that he would find himself thrown over if he were to make the slightest slip. He kept a watchful eye on such places as Plymouth and Portsmouth, but at that time he had to investigate entirely alone.

A turning point was the arrest of a man named Schultz, who spoke English with a very guttural accent and was the owner of a small yacht, *The Egret*, in which he appeared to enjoy sailing the River Yalm and round the coast near Falmouth. Nobody bothered about him until some of the people he was constantly entertaining began to wonder why he seemed so interested in local naval and military matters. Investigation showed that he was receiving large sums of money from an agent employed by the German secret service. He was arrested, tried and convicted.

Things began to move after Schultz's arrest, and Kell soon required an assistant. Captain Frederick Stanley Clark was the first officer to be posted, followed later by Captain Reginald John Drake, a most able man, very quick-witted and a successful sleuth. There would be little hope for anyone who fell into his net. Later, in January, 1913, Captain Eric Holt-Wilson reinforced the staff. He was to prove a genius at intricate organization. But the number of suitable men who wished to join the staff of what was called the Security Service, or MO5, and later MI5, was necessarily somewhat restricted.

Vernon Kell was by now always referred to as 'K' and his department was rapidly increasing in importance. It was evident that he needed the services of an expert legal adviser to keep them all working strictly legally and create the fabric on which the whole legal side of the work would have to rest. Walter Moresby, son of Admiral John

3

Moresby, was a very astute barrister and under his guidance the many legal pitfalls that might have trapped them were avoided.

'K' was finding it necessary to engage an increasing number of clerks and women to run a registry where a system of card indexing was gradually producing an enormous collection of material. He had a firm feeling that there were only a few years in hand before war. He showed a wonderful flair for organizing, coupled with a gift for making people work happily together. He became known as 'the man with the golden tongue', as he had to be diplomatic and tactful to an unusual degree. He always seemed to know how to time his requests to the various heads of department. And he had much to ask, as his was a very new department, but he was never refused. Towards the end of 1913 Kell was promoted to major; MO5 was now thoroughly established.

Many cases were investigated, such as that of a German marine captain who had been convicted of fraud in the Far East. The Germans made full use of naturalized English people who were originally German. Another method used by German agents was to offer small weekly sums to men in the British services to report quite harmless small-talk in their barracks in the hope that more confidential information would be forthcoming. It was discovered that messages were sometimes concealed under postage stamps; others were written in invisible inks and between lines in letters and newspapers in code, requiring a great deal of ingenuity to discover them. One rather curious telegram read, 'Father dead, await instructions', which was turned into 'Father deceased, what action'. Back came the wire 'Father dead or deceased, please explain'. Evidently some of the messages were puzzling even to the intended recipients!

Another method involved using a map of a well-known town, along the tram routes of which a message was written in Morse, further complicated by the alphabet being used in shifting positions – the first letter being altered to the fifth or sixth position, and so on.

When war was declared on 4 August, 1914, 'K' left his home in Weybridge and based himself permanently in London, initially sleeping in his office with many telephones round his bed.[3]

Before 1911 the law regarding espionage had been confused and somewhat defective. But the passing of the Official Secrets Act that year made things clear and extended protection so as to embrace every possible mode of obtaining and conveying to the enemy any information which might be useful in time of war. By 8 August, 1914, new and more stringent powers for dealing with espionage were approved with the Defence of the Realm Act being passed by the Home Secretary through the House of Commons and receiving Royal Assent. Orders in Council could be made under its terms. Espionage was made a military offence, triable by court martial, and if tried as a war crime the punishment of death could be inflicted.

Other defensive measures were taken against the spy. All persons who kept carrier or homing pigeons had to be registered, and the importation and conveyance of these birds was prohibited. With the assistance of the National Homing Union it was felt that the steps taken would be effective in preventing birds being kept in the country and flown to the Continent. At the same time the Post Office, acting under the powers given by the Wireless Telegraphy Acts, dismantled all private wireless stations and later establised a special system of wireless detection.[4]

When war broke out MO5 pulled off a master-stroke that would have deep implications for the German intelligence service and the outcome of the war itself. Back in 1911 the chief of intelligence of the German Admiralty had been part of the Kaiser's entourage visiting London. One evening this officer was followed by New Scotland Yard officers across the capital to a hairdressing establishment very near Pentonville Prison at 402a Caledonian Road, Islington (the building no longer stands), and run by a 42-year-old man called Karl Gustav Ernst. It was most strange for the Admiralty officer to visit such an out-of-the-way establishment, and the stupidity and arrogance of such a visit were shown when enquiries made by the British counter-espionage service found that Ernst was the hub of German spying in the country.

Ernst was of German background; he had been born at 21 Chart Street, Shoreditch, London on 26 December, 1871, and had a German wife.[5, 6] His address was used as a letterbox for the Germans: it was his business, on receiving letters from Berlin, to readdress them with British stamps to various German agents living around Britain. The head of the German secret service at the time was Gustav Steinhauer, who was a personal friend of the Kaiser and had previously been a private detective for the Pinkerton Agency of America. Steinhauer's *nom de guerre* was Madame Reimers, but he was not averse to calling himself 'The Kaiser's Master Spy'. He supervised the working of fixed agents and travelling spies from offices in Berlin and headquarters in Potsdam, and he was in communication with Ernst.

MO5 carried out an extensive investigation into Ernst's activities, and all letters to and from his address were intercepted and the contents examined and photographed before being expertly sealed and forwarded. In this way a complete and extensive genealogical tree of the German espionage system in Britain was built up. The Germans never suspected a thing, and their ignorance helped MO5 to know of their intentions and gather the names and addresses of some 22 agents.

This made it clear that what the Germans wanted was naval information.[7]

Later Steinhauer visited Ernst, as he wanted the post office to extend its role. Ernst was to make a statement outlining the details:

> I am sorry I was introduced into this business. Kronauer introduced me. I thought it was only a private inquiry business. I have only seen Steinhauer once. That was just before Christmas in 1911.
>
> He came to my shop on a Sunday morning. My shop was open and I had several customers there. He said to me, 'Are you Mr. Ernst?' and I said 'Yes.' He said, 'Do you know me?' and I said, 'No.' He said, 'You have heard of me; I am Steinhauer. I see you are busy now. I want to have a quiet chat with you. I will come back after the shop is closed. What time do you close?' I said, 'Twelve o'clock.' He said, 'All right, I will come back then,' and went away. He returned later and came into my parlour, where we sat down and had a long talk.[8]

As soon as war was declared Karl Gustav Ernst was arrested and instructions were sent by wire all round Britain for chief constables to arrest the spies. In all 22 orders were issued and all but one were detained and interned successfully. Otto Weigals escaped via the port of Hull.[9] The others arrested, and their places of arrest, are listed below.

Antonius J. F. Dummenie; London
Karl Stubenwoll; Newcastle
Karl Meyer; Warwick
Johann Kuhr; Newcastle
Oscar Buckwaldt; Brighton
Karl Hemlar; Winchester
Friedrich Apel; Barrow-in-Furness
Max A. Laurens; London
Franz H. Losel; Sittingbourne
Thomas Kegnamer; Southampton
Adolf Schneider; London
Karl von Weller; Padstow
Marie Kronauer; London
Celse Rodrigues; Portsmouth
Friedrich Diederichs; London
August Klunder; London
Lina M. Heine; Portsmouth
Heinrich Schutte, Weymouth
Friedrich Lukowski; Newcastle

Otto Kruger; Mountain Ash
Johann A. Engel; Falmouth.[10]

Ernst was sentenced to seven years' penal servitude. Later he was to
state in his petition against deportation that he had built up his hairdressing business since 1899, he considered it second to none in the
neighbourhood and his clients included officers and the chaplain of
Pentonville Prison. He continued.

> Such treatment is served out to people in Russia but not in England.
> It might have been so also here in the days of the Inquisition. If I
> am sent to Germany they will surely arrest me there as an English
> spy and I shall be out of the frying pan into the fire. Therefore I pray
> you to release me.[11]

These arrests drew a curtain across German intelligence and a form of
paralysis took over. They knew nothing of the British Expeditionary
Force build-up in France. Four British divisions had assembled and
were holding the city of Mons, drawn up along the Mons–Condé
Canal. On 25 August von Moltke was of the opinion that the decisive
battle in the west had been fought and decided in Germany's favour
and that forces could be transferred to East Prussia. Two corps were
sent, with plans to send a further four. These forces arrived some days
after the Battle of Tannenberg. As a result they were wasted, being too
late to do any good and being absent from the Battle of the Marne,
where they might have had a decisive influence. The first that the
German army knew of the British build-up was when they found
British troops facing them. They were aware that a British landing had
taken place at Boulogne, but not in any large numbers.[12] The
Schlieffen Plan, that all-encompassing drive to victory, received a
change of emphasis when the Kaiser issued this order from his Army's
Supreme Headquarters:

> It is my Royal and Imperial Command that you concentrate your
> energies for the immediate present upon one single purpose, and
> that is, that you address all your skill and all the valour of my soldiers
> to exterminate the treacherous little army of the English and walk
> over General French's contemptible little army.[13]

Germany was caught blind and with its pants down. Intelligence would
be and always is a prime requirement for a fighting nation. New ways
of infiltrating the British Isles would have to be employed, and new
ways of countering this threat developed. It would be a fight to the
death, for the stakes were too high to lose. One would have to break

7

the other: Britain was formidable at sea and Germany supreme on land. In this titanic stuggle to outlast the opponent, intelligence and time could make the difference. Lord Kitchener planned for a long war and needed time to recruit and train his proposed 70 British divisions.[14] Germany, meanwhile, would make full use of sending communications via neutral nations such as Holland and Sweden, or via Belgium.

Time was needed to starve Germany of food and imports and isolate it on the Continent. Britain must allow Germany to reach its peak of power and begin to fade gradually as the grip tightened. This economic war in the naval blockade of commercial and financial services was feared by the German military elite: 'Its diabolical efficiency was the most awful thing in the world.'[15]

Not only this, but Britain set up a cable and postal blockade. The destruction of the cable is described as follows:

> In August from the waves slowly rose great snake-like monsters, thick with slime and seaweed growths, responding reluctantly to the grapnels which dragged them to the surface and beyond and laid their bulk athwart the deck of a boat, soon to be returned, severed and useless, to the depths. They were Germany's cables by which she maintained direct communication with the rest of the world.[16]

As far as telegraphs were concerned, Germany was now isolated. This must have been a major blow to the Central Powers, as at the second Hague Conference in 1907 Germany had pointed out that the telegraph gave belligerent nations a more rapid and sure means of communication than the post. If they believed this and followed that policy, they were in trouble from the start of the war![17] Germany responded by developing the U-boat in an attempt to force the islanders into submission, and very nearly succeeded. But, as always, Germany wanted to know what the British fleet were doing and where they were located.

A great benefit to the British war effort was postal censorship. On 3 August, 1914, the day before war was declared, the postal censorship department consisted of just one person. It was to grow so that by the closing years of the war an average of 375,000 letters were examined each day. In 1917 it is estimated that some 180 million postal packets were examined, with around 356,000 detained as likely to be of some value to the enemy. By the end of the war the department employed over 4,000 people.[18]

To relieve the strain on the general post office at Mount Pleasant, London, a large building called Salisbury House, near the Bank of England, was used for censorship. By March, 1915, the expanding department moved to York and Imperial Houses in Kingsway, and after more growth relocated again to an entire block of buildings in Carey Steet, near the Strand. With the staff constantly expanding, a branch office was set up in Liverpool in December of that year, to deal only with mail from North and South America.[19] And the tentacles of Britain's postal censorship reached out to a number of strategic locations in the Empire. Sub-branches were established in such places as Gibraltar, Alexandria, Singapore, Hong Kong, Shanghai, Sierra Leone and Halifax (Nova Scotia).[20] Such a network became a very powerful weapon, and great knowledge was thereby obtained which was as important a weapon in waging the war as the tank, battleship and infantryman. Germany was slowly strangled and isolated by Britain's grip over a great deal of world correspondence.

The Americans and other neutral countries began to complain long and hard at the delay and intervention of mails, resulting in business contracts, cheques, drafts, money orders, securities, and similar property being lost or detained for weeks or months. Any neutral ship found bound for northern Europe was stopped by the British navy and compelled to enter a British port, where the mail was impounded, taken to the nearest censorship offices and only allowed to proceed after careful examination.[21] The USA, France and Britain had adopted Article 1 of the 11th Hague Convention of 1907, which stipulated that henceforth postal correspondence would be 'inviolable' on the high seas from action by belligerents. This referred to letters in any closed envelope. However, the despatch of goods by 'postal parcel' was not covered by this stipulation, and the British and French maintained that parcels not constituting letters, correspondence or dispatches were subject to the rights of policing, examination and seizure which a belligerent nation could properly exercise in the time of war. But the method of applying this principle was the chief cause of difference with neutral governments.

The protection against the seizure of letters on the high seas was overcome by Britain and France by compelling ships to enter their own ports, on the principle that they could detain postal parcels containing goods on the prohibited list which would aid the enemy. Once ships were safely in the Allies' jurisdiction, and not at sea, they were free to examine both letters and postal parcels, and took full advantage of this. At one time the government began to weaken and Colonel George Kynaston Cockerill (Director of Special Intelligence) was asked to attend the Home Office to see Reginald McKenna, the Home Secretary, and the Hon Charles Edward Henry Hobhouse, the Postmaster General. Upon being told the government was coming round to the view that postal censorship ought to be abolished, Cockerill made an overwhelming case to the contrary, showing the type of communications being intercepted, and the ministers agreed that such a course of action would be unthinkable,[22] and to their credit stood firm.

At that time the USA was swinging back and fourth between sympathy for Britain and sympathy for Germany, and continued to do so until a great propaganda disaster for the Germans took place: the sinking of the *Lusitania* on 7 May, 1915, by Kapitänleutnant Walther Schwieger in his U-20. Together with the sinking of other neutral shipping in ever greater numbers by the U-boat fleet (moving the terms of engagement to all-out war was authorized by the Kaiser after much soul-searching and in-fighting between different naval factions as a result of the winter of 1916–17, the 'turnip winter' and the time of Germany's severest food shortages),[23] this moved American public opinion towards the British cause and led to the USA's later entry into the war. The German military commander Ludendorff was later to write, 'We reckoned on a decision in our favour at the latest before America with her new armies could intervene in the war. Without the U-boats we calculated that the Quadruple Alliance must be defeated in 1917.'[24]

The censorship of post took place in a systematic way. Letters were first sorted into private and business sections, as far as was indicated by their outward appearance. After this somewhat general classification, they moved on to another room. Here people – mainly women – worked in separate sections at long tables where letters were opened, read and resealed with a small label on which the official's identity number was printed. Each section dealt with a specific country. At the head of each table sat an officer. On large blackboards hung on the wall, plainly visible to all, were written names of critical importance, or a short sentence in code. For further guidance they had two lists. The 'White List' consisted of the names and addresses of high-ranking statesmen, members of the government and diplomatic corps, and undercover names and addresses used by British intelligence. These were an exempt classification and their post was not opened. The second list, the 'Suspects List', contained the names and addresses of suspects and known enemy agents. Post to these, when found, was to have special treatment and was forwarded to another department. Here experts opened and secured the post without trace, leaving no sign that it had been examined by the censor. Tests could be made for secret writing by a number of experienced chemists.[25] Business letters were examined by groups of 25 to 30 specialists. All had knowledge not only of the language of a particular country, but also its economic position and business practices. Each group was given mail from the same specific districts, firms and branches, so they became thoroughly familiar with the methods of individuals and business houses. This was very useful in tracing connections between seemingly unrelated facts, and by this method much was learned.[26]

Suspicion could be aroused by a letter saying nothing that justified its writing. Such letters often contained much about the welfare of the family, with lots of terms of endearment, love and kisses.[27] Sometimes a stroke under a signature would indicate the direction in which a certain word should be read, for example to give details of the movement of troops. What gave this away was the mathematical precision in which the stroke was drawn, rather than a flourish of the pen. This would attract the trained eye of the experienced examiner.[28]

It is interesting to note that as the war progressed the number of suspect messages detected declined. In the first six months of 1916 they averaged over ten a week. Twelve months later this number was halved, and as censorship expertise developed the Germans appeared to give up the postal method of conveying secret information.

Another important arm in the counter-espionage fight was 40 OB (Room 40, Old Admiralty Building). It was situated in a quiet wing, and even high Admiralty officials and Cabinet ministers were in almost total ignorance of the mysterious department. Referring to this unexplained and confidential department as just '40 OB' helped it to remain incognito. There was a need to decipher codes intercepted by wireless and other means, and 40 OB was the pinnacle of the art, staffed by men of great intelligence and flair.

The Admiralty at the start of the war had a stroke of luck, in that the ideal man to take charge of 40 OB's formation and development was already based at the Admiralty: Sir Alfred Ewing, a scientist who was then Director of Naval Education (and later principal of Edinburgh University). He was well known as a solver of cryptic puzzles, but just as a hobby. Now he was called on to turn this pastime into a profession. He began by researching the code books at the GPO, Lloyds of London and the British Museum. From this small beginning developed a very important department – Ewing described himself as 'nothing more or less than an official eavesdropper.'[29, 30] One of the department's spectacular results was the deciphering of the famous 'Zimmerman' telegram: a wireless intercept of a message to the German ambassador in Mexico, giving instructions to secure Mexico's co-operation during the war in return for Texas and other southern US territorial interests. The communication of this to Washington did more to bring America in on the Allies' side than the sinking of the *Lusitania* itself.[31]

Back in June, 1913, Sir Basil Thomson (son of an Archbishop of York) became head of the Criminal Investigation Department of New Scotland Yard. Under his control Special Branch police were responsible for the arrest and detention of suspects; British

11

counter-espionage had no facilities for this aspect of the investigation. Thomson described the police as finding themselves the general servants to the Admiralty and War office. His room at New Scotland Yard became the meeting ground of the two services.[32] This Herculean task could become very onerous, as throughout the war there were an average of four interrogations a day, and sometimes as many as ten.[33]

Counter-intelligence would have a lot to contend with during the war in telling friend from foe, in view of the numbers of refugees and aliens resident in the country. In the early days of the invasion of Belgium large numbers of refugees began to arrive in England. The first party of 437 persons arrived on 6 September, 1914. They were looked after by the War Refugees Committee, who received them and found hospitality for these unfortunates. They travelled by the Antwerp to Harwich or Tilbury shipping routes, or Ostend to Folkstone. Numbers increased when the position got worse, and the Belgian government found itself obliged to ask if still larger numbers could be received in the UK. The resulting influx became too large for voluntary organizations to handle and local government, on behalf of the government, took on the task. In addition, numbers of Russian and Polish Jews fled Belgium and were placed in the care of the Jews' Temporary Shelter. At the beginning of October, 1914, it was estimated that between 2,000 and 2,500 Jews had settled in England. Others in the early days were housed at Alexandra Palace, Edmonton Refuge, St Giles Home and Hackney Wick Refuge.[34]

However, enemy aliens presented another problem. The government was concerned that London was within range of attack by zeppelins and other airships, and to counter this threat elaborate precautions had been taken. There was concern that these might be defeated by ill-intentioned persons at vulnerable points. It was felt that an airship raid might be timed simultaneously with some other attempted operation, such as a landing on the coast, with which enemy aliens might assist by serving as guides, signallers and spies, or by conveying information with regard to the location of British forces.[35] With this in mind, parts of Britain were marked out as Prohibited Areas for aliens. In England these included the whole of the east coast and the south coast from Dover to Southampton. In Scotland the effect was such that the only areas left unprohibited were the central mountainous regions of the Highlands, parts of Perthshire, Stirlingshire and Glasgow, plus a restricted area round the city, and the agricultural counties on the Solway Firth and the borders.[36]

With this background, on 7 August, 1914, the War Office issued instructions for the internment of all male Germans and Austrians between 17 and 42 years of age, except those who could clearly prove that they were exempt from military service. These instructions gave rise to various difficulties, as accommodation was not available for such large numbers. So the day after the instructions were issued a conference was held at the War Office, at which it was decided to restrict internment for the present to those Germans whom the police regarded as dangerous, either as possible spies or as persons who might in certain circumstances commit offences against the state. Considerable numbers were apprehended and interned under this arrangement.

But by 27 August, 1914, the Commissioner of Police reported that a large number of Germans had now been thrown out of employment; he feared they were rapidly becoming desperate and dangerous, and asked for authority for their internment. But the Home Office stated that internment was to apply only to persons of military age, reservists or those actively dangerous, and that mere destitution should remain a matter to be dealt with by the civil authorities. On 7 September the decision was taken by the Secretary of State for War to intern all German reservists and instructions were issued to the police to carry this out. But owing to lack of accommodation the arrests could only proceed slowly, and when between 8,000 and 9,000 had been interned arrests were brought to an end by the lack of accommodation. Nevertheless, on 20 October, 1914, further instructions were given for the internment of Austrians and Germans of military age, but once again the order was handicapped by lack of places in the camps, so the procedure was not completed. However, in the counties and provincial towns the situation was better. The great majority of Germans and Austrians of military age had been interned successfully. But the policy of general arrest, especially in provincial towns, had led to many cases of hardship, and some steps were taken to release a number, subject to a police report on their character. In November some 1,100 were released in this way. Often they had to sign the following type of parole.

METROPOLITAN POLICE ALIEN'S PAROLE
I hereby give my parole of honour
(1)   That I will not attempt to leave England without first obtaining permission in writing from the Home Office.
(2)   That while in this country I will not either attempt to communicate with the enemy or to commit or incite to the commission of any act inimical to the interests of this country or of the British Empire.
Signed ....
Witness ....
Taken before on .... day of ....
(Signed) LANESBOROUGH
Major, Coldstream Guards,
Commandant.[37]

By December, 1914, it was reported that a few boys under 17 and males over 45 had also been interned, as they were thought to be dangerous. The majority above and below these ages had not been arrested by the police, but taken on ships by the navy and sent to the camps, as there was no other immediate way of dealing with them. In that month authority was given to release all boys under 17 (in the case of Austrians, 18) and send them back to Germany or Austria, as the case may be. But it was still found necessary to retain a small number who were believed to be mine-layers, and whose release was objected to by the Admiralty.

The total number interned under the successive operations amounted to 12,400 by December, 1914. But there remained at liberty 25,000 male Germans and Austrians above the age of 17, of whom 14,500 were between 17 and 45. Of these 12,300 were in London and just 2,200 at liberty in the rest of the UK.[38] The internment camps were inspected by personnel from the American Embassy in London (German Division).[39]

At a cabinet meeting on 5 January, 1915, the Home Secretary stated that he had at a previous meeting proposed that alien enemies should be required to remain indoors at night; this suggestion had been held over as other ministers said they needed more time for deliberation. He was introducing the curfew subject again as a result of recommendations by the Commissioner of the Metropolitan Police. The Commissioner had given information that upwards of 10,000 German and 6,000 Austrian males aged between 17 and 50 years could be at liberty at night in London. It was considered that many were undoubtedly loyal to the country of their adoption, but a large number were German in sympathy and might, not unnaturally, seize any opporunity of committing hostile acts.

Furthermore, the Commissioner was concerned that, in spite of the provision in the Aliens' Restriction Act prohibiting aliens from being in possession of firearms, rigorous house-to-house searches had discovered a number of firearms – some 82 shotguns, 91 pistols, 370 revolvers and 190 rifles. It was also felt that many firearms may have been clandestinely retained.

The Home Secretary had consulted a number of commissioners of city police and chief constables of some of the larger towns, and they had agreed that the proposal was desirable and practical, without great hardship to individuals and without overtaxing the police. Some indeed said it would be a relief from the efforts which the police were making without specific powers to supervise enemy aliens at night. The Manchester police had already tried to obtain some control by requiring individuals to sign an undertaking that they would remain indoors during hours fixed by the police. As a result a curfew for enemy aliens came into force between the hours of 8.30pm and 6am for persons over the age of 16 years. The alien could not be at a place other than his registered place of residence, unless a change was agreed with the Aliens' Officer. There was also a duty for a person housing such an alien to report any failure to comply.[40]

This, then, was the situation in the UK as Germany probed and sent spies to Britain, using neutral countries and defeated nations for their espionage operations – such as their training school in Antwerp, or agents in places like Sweden, Amsterdam, Rotterdam, Switzerland and The Hague.

'Will you walk into my parlour?' said the Kaiser
    to the spy,
'For I've lots of work to give you, and the pay
    is very high,
And you've only got to send me a report from
    day to day,
All about the English people, and the things
    they do and say.

'There is Fritz and Franz and Josef, though
    their names you may not know,
You may write to them and see them, but as
    'Number So-and-So',
And should you meet your brother or your
    mother at the game,
You are not to recognize them; they're
    numbers just the same.

'You will travel through the country in the
    name of Henry Jones,
Or as Donald P McScotty, selling artificial
    stones;
You will rent a modest dwelling in the shadow
    of a base,
And when nobody is looking you will
    photograph the place.

'Then 'Hoch' unto your Kaiser, 'Am Tag' your
    daily cry,
God bless our Krupps and Zeppelins, the
    victory is nigh.

15

God bless our shells! and dum-dums! Kultur
    shall fight her way
God, Emperor, and Fatherland in one
    Almighty sway.'[43]

CHAPTER 2

Carl Hans Lody

In life one's destiny is often shaped by time and place. The truth of this is highlighted by the story of a junior lieutenant in the *Seewehr*, the Second Corps of the German Naval Reserve.[1] Carl Hans Lody was aged 39 years at the outbreak of the First World War. A man of five feet eight and a half inches,[2] he had dark hair parted in the middle, and blue eyes which were described as having a look of keen intelligence in their depths. He was of South German appearance.[3]

A German national, he had been educated in Germany and, after completing his year's service in the German Navy from 1900–01, had joined the First Naval Reserve and then entered the merchant service. As a result he had travelled a great deal and had found employment on English, Norwegian and American ships. In 1912 he married an American lady of German descent, the daughter of Gottlieb Storse, a wealthy brewer of Omaha, and looked forward to making his home in the United States. He was to say, 'I more or less cast off all ties which connected me with Germany, and was looking forward to becoming a naturalized American citizen. This would have been so if my matrimonial relations had lasted, but unfortunately they did not; they broke off and I dissolved my marriage.' It created considerable comment when the wedding, which was almost clandestine, took place. Miss Storse had met Lody while on a tour of Germany and other European countries.[4] After the dissolution of the marriage, Lody was to state that he received the sum of $10,000 from his former father-in-law, as compensation for his financial losses, in the spring of 1914. Because of this marriage Lody had applied for transfer from the First Naval Reserve, which normally kept officers and men up to the age of 39 years, until transfer to the *Seewehr*. 'I did not want to be called on, as I was looking to leave Germany entirely.'

During this time he had been employed as a tourist agent running excursions for the Hamburg-Amerika Line. On the steamer

17

Cleveland he had been round the world four times with about 550 to 600 English, German and American travellers, and had also served on the *Meteor* on its cruises to Norway. As a result he had acquired a large circle of friends in the United States, and was well known in the New York Athletic Club, the Japan Society and the Peace Society. He was spoken of as being versatile, quick-witted, and having many pleasing ways. He was especially attractive to the young women on the liner.

Lody had returned from Norway and was in Berlin in the critical days at the end of July, 1914. He reported to the general office of the Naval Department, but he had in mind to go to New York. He wanted to be released from the Second Naval Reserve on account of being an invalid after an illness in 1904.

> I was operated on after a very serious illness, as the medical man will know. I had an abscess which was located behind the stomach, caused from a very badly cured typhoid attack of fever from which I suffered in Italy on account of the bad water at Genoa. Furthermore, there was a liver abscess in connection with that. The operation took place in Kiel during a drill, and I could not finish the drill, and in those days it had attracted the attention of the medical world. There were two English surgeons present at the operation, and they were much interested. They took out two ribs in my left side in order to get at the actual place, and in consequence my left arm was weakened, and furthermore, which was more important, my eyesight grew weak. I noticed that, a year later, I had to use glasses for reading.
>
> Consequently, my career as a seaman was closed as soon as I discovered that, and my doctor told me that I could not go any further. In consequence of this again, I knew I was no more good for any actual fighting service.

As a result of his application, Lody was called in for an interview in August, 1914, with a superior naval officer, one of three or four interviews he was to have. As Lody described it:

> I am known in Berlin a little, not in any military circles, but more or less I am known, and they knew I had great interests in America. That I had travelled a great deal and somehow or other I am known to be an American, or, at least, they always considered me half an American, and it was put before me by a certain person . . . to choose the way via England on my way to New York and to give notice of my safe arrival in England, and to remain until the first naval encounter had taken place between the two powers and gather information as regards the actual losses of the British fleet, and then I was at liberty to proceed on to New York.[5]

18

Lody stated that he was very unhappy about the suggestion; although there was no pressure placed on him in the strict sense of the word, there was certainly an understanding in the military and naval world that if a suggestion was made one felt obliged to obey. The German military attaché to the USA, Franz von Papen, who dominated the agencies of espionage and sabotage there, in fact had his office at the Hamburg-Amerika Line.[6] And the Kaiser himself had spoken of this shipping firm, and another, as 'Two patriotic companies, whose officials, employees, and agents have throughout the world proven their zeal and devotion to the cause of the Empire, and whose tact and discretion have already helped my government in many an embarrassing position.' It is clear that Lody would therefore be well known in the company and his situation a useful opportunity to exploit.

> I have never been a coward in my life and I certainly would not be a shirker . . . When it was put before me I must admit I felt uneasy; I felt that I was not a fit man for a job of that kind. I am so well known to hundreds of people in the travelling world and on the highway of our international course, and I am so well accustomed to be called by my own name that already I felt that I would make a blunder the first time I had to sail under a different flag and different surroundings. I knew I would be a bad man to disguise . . . I said I could not travel without the necessary documents to protect me going about . . . It was said to me that I was sufficiently an American to travel as an American; and in consequence of that a couple of days later I received an American passport.

Lody was always to maintain that, after being absent from his home for a couple of days, between 6 and 19 August, he received by ordinary mail a plain white envelope containing a passport already signed by a Charles A. Inglis.

Lody then began practising the signature. He said, 'I could not get it, it caused me more trouble than anything else.'[7] This passport was a perfectly genuine document that the Germans told the real Inglis had been lost – by them! – after he had applied to the American Embassy for a visa to enable him to continue his travels in Europe. His passport had been passed by the Embassy to the German Foreign Office so the visa could be arranged.[8, 9] Lody continues:

> My services were considered absolutely as an honour and free, because I happened to go there, and they know I am in so-called well-to-do circumstances. Or I do not think they would ever have dared to have approached me with such a proposition.

19

It was said with regard to expenses I would certainly have been rec-
ompensed later on after the war, or when I returned. But as I had to
remain here in England until the first serious or important naval
encounter was to take place I could not tell you how long I should
be away, but it was understood that I should not wait longer than
the middle of October, so then I should have been at leisure to proceed to New York or so, without waiting for the outcome of the
battle.

As an American tourist Lody arrived by steamer at Newcastle at 6pm
on 27 August, 1914, making his way to Edinburgh,[10] where he booked
into the North British Station Hotel, taking room 318. Whilst there
Lody was busy, and at 3.45pm on 30 August he went to the telegraph
counter at the city's general post office. He wrote out a telegram to
Adolf Burchard at 4 Trottninggatan, Stockholm. 'Must cancel
Johnson very ill last four days shall leave shortly.'[11]

William Mills, a counter clerk, found that the telegram was incor-
rectly written on an ordinary white inland telegram form. Being a
helpful person and seeing the mistake, he gummed the white form on
to the proper yellow form. However, he could not bypass a second
error, as it bore the signature of 'Charles' only. Mills requested Lody
to complete the signature, which he did after moving away from the
counter. This message was then despatched, and would be sent on to
Gothenburg after examination.[12]

It was the task of Malcolm Brodie, a clerk in the secretary's office,
to examine the telegram. The address of Burchard was known to the
British authorities and all communication with it was suspect. A copy
of the telegram was later to be endorsed, 'This is evidently a
prearranged code – meaning that he was being watched and in danger
& would have to leave Edinburgh which he did later on.'[13]

Lody was not aware of the precautionary measures that had been
undertaken in respect of letters and telegrams. An account by a person
engaged in this censorship is as follows:

I was shown into a large hall where about 80 men were sitting at
long tables opening letters, reading them and closing them again
with small labels on which their identity numbers were printed.

An officer was in charge of each table and sat at the head of it. I
was introduced to one of these superintendents, a Major Z. He
showed me where to sit, gave me the necessary materials, taught me
the simple routine which I must follow when dealing with the letters, explaining, however, in great detail what subjects were most
important at the moment in those which would pass through my
hands.

Several names were written on a large blackboard which hung on the wall, plainly visible, and we had to keep a sharp look-out for any mention of these in letters we read. The names were those of persons suspected of sending information to Germany via neutral countries. In addition, a short sentence was scribbled up on this board: 'Johnson is ill'. The Admiralty knew that somewhere in Britain a German officer was travelling about who intended to use this formula to convey the news of certain movements of the British fleet.[14]

At midday on 1 September Lody moved to Bedford House, 12 Drumsheugh Gardens, Edinburgh, a boarding-house kept by Mrs Julia Anna Frances Brown. He gave his name as Charles A. Inglis of New York, USA, and stayed as a weekly boarder.

Then on 4 September the British intercepted a letter posted in Edinburgh addressed to the same Stockholm address. It was sent on to London where continental letters were examined; again, the letter was inspected by Brodie. He opened the envelope, inside which he found a written communication in English and enclosed with it was a further letter addressed to Berlin; this letter was sealed. It was opened and the contents were written in German. All the correspondence was then photographed and forwarded to the proper authorities.[15]

The letter in English read:

> Will you kindly communicate with Berlin at once by wire (Code or whatever system at your disposal) and inform them that on Sept. 3rd great masses of Russian soldiers have passed through Edinburgh on their way to London and France. Although it must be expected that Berlin has knowledge of these movements, which probably took its start at Archangel, it may be well to forward this information. It is estimated here that 60,000 men have passed, number which seem greatly exaggerated. I went to the depot [station] and noticed trains passing through at high speed, blinds down. The landing in Scotland took place at Aberdeen. Yours truly Charles.[16]

Lody later told how he obtained the information concerning the Russian troops.

> In Edinburgh everybody was speaking about it. I heard it in the boarding-house and I heard it in the barber's shop. If I may say so I heard it in the store where I bought my shirt; he was absolutely sure. He said he had got it from a friend and he had got his – well, from his intimate friend at the North British Depot, the station – and he says that he walked up to them that particular Sunday and I said, 'Well now you tell me about those Russians', something like that. Well I took the matter rather serious. I took it for granted one night, and I said in the boarding-house – I am not sure whether Mrs

21

Brown will remember – we were chatting as usual and talking about the war and other matters, and I met Mr Brown. 'Well,' I said. 'It sounds so ridiculous that Russia should pass here and you do not hear anything in the papers: you do not hear in France?' He said, 'It is an absolute fact – there are 102 trains passed through it: I know it is an absolute fact they have passed through Edinburgh. I knew it as rumours.[17]

The rumour had in fact grown to fantastic proportions: huge, bearded men, with the snow of the steppes still clinging to their boots, were landing by the thousands in order to help on the Western Front.[18]

The letter, in German, was addressed to Herr Stammer[19] (Captain Stammer of the Admiralty Intelligence Staff in Berlin), and stated:

In the North Sea as far as I can ascertain 22 small vessels have been sunk. Also that a small cruiser is lying at Leith. And 4 armed cruisers and about 10 torpedo boats and 2 destroyers are lying at Grangemouth.

It ended with information that the Forth Bridge was barricaded.

Lody was to state that he had made up his mind not to go near any place where he could be challenged or where it was forbidden. He went up Carlton Hill, which is an elevation at the end of Prince's Street, and a public area where the National Monument is situated. From there Lody could view the whole bay, seeing with the naked eye as far as the Forth Bridge. He could also look right into Leith, noting every ship at the pier. Being a naval man he could distinguish between a cruiser and a battleship. To view the situation at Grangemouth, Lody simply walked along the bay, just like thousands of other people going about their daily business.

Lody deduced that the Forth Bridge was barricaded in the following way:

We were two hours along the shore with Sprinkles [an American Lody had become friendly with on his travels to England, and who was also staying in Edinburgh]. There was a little steamer with the Government flag passing and our intention was to go a little nearer to it and they said, 'It is no use: they will not allow you to do so,' and I said, 'All right: keep away.' And we asked a man and he said, 'Yes, that is right.' That was sufficient information for me to know the Forth Bridge was barricaded.[20]

Lody's English and German letters containing the false rumour about the Russian troops were allowed by British Intelligence to go through, as the information they contained was either misleading or of no value. It was hoped to lull the sender into a false sense of security, and eventually by this method to trace him. It is understood that Lody's information about the Russians later caused a great deal of worry to the German general staff.[21]

Lody had decided to become more mobile and to this end on 7 September, 1914, he went to 19–31 Haymarket Terrace, the business of a motor and cycle engineer. He called at the shop, speaking to the owner's daughter, Miss Mary Downie, and made enquiries about the hire of a bicycle.

He gave his name as Charles A. Inglis and said he was an American of 130 Pearl Street, New York. His holiday had been spoiled and he was going to have a holiday in Edinburgh while staying at Drumsheugh Gardens. He was going to ride about Edinburgh as he could not get home to America very easily because the boats were so crowded. He said he wanted to go to Rosyth and Queensferry, and several other places.[22]

She agreed to hire him a bicycle and warned him, when out cycling, to stop at once should he be challenged by a sentry, as some parts of the road were well guarded. He appeared surprised at this warning and said, 'Oh, I am only going to be cycling about for pleasure!'[23]

So Lody spent his time in and around Edinburgh on the look-out for information, trying not to place himself in a dangerous situation, and waiting for the first large naval battle. He generally remained in his room until about midday, returning often between 5pm and 7pm, and after dinner he sometimes went out again on his cycle, letting himself in by the latch-key.[24]

On 14 September he sent his next letter to Adolf Burchard. This was also intercepted by the British. The envelope was found to be a mere wrapper, and the real communcication inside it was addressed to The Editor, *Ullstein Verlag*, Berlin C.

> Enclosed cutting from the Edinburgh *The News of the World*. Typical for the English way of causing ill-feeling and at the same time characteristic of the perfect ignorance of journalists in this country regarding the difference between military weapons and military tools. But this does not make any difference, the population here believe everything. Yours truly (sd) Nazi.[25]

On the morning of 15 September Lody told Mrs Brown that he was going to London, saying that he would be away for perhaps two nights. He packed a small despatch box for the visit. She saw that it contained only a shirt, a pair of socks, a collar and some handkerchiefs. As a result she said to him, 'Your wardrobe will not be troublesome to you!'[26] Lody made his way to London and booked into room 603 at the Ivanhoe Hotel, Bloomsbury. He busied himself in examining the measures taken for guarding public buildings in the city. He was to state that he did not observe the buildings himself, but saw reports in newspapers and intended to send cuttings.

Later, reference was found in his notebook regarding a report that he wrote on 16 September. This report was never found by the British, but Lody said that he never sent it, as he felt it silly to write in the way he did.

I wrote the report telling about Hyde Park, and the recruiting of the New Army, and I told him how big the fellows were in comparison to the Scottish, the chaps I saw there, and the Londoners appeared to me to be very big men. I wrote also I was disappointed no naval combat had taken place; I said 'Why do not you come out?', I am waiting for your battle to come. I want to go to New York.[27]

On Thursday, 17 September a Miss Ida McClyment caught the 2.20pm train from King's Cross for Edinburgh, as did Lody. They sat in the same carriage and got into conversation, Lody giving her his card.[28] Lody later left her and went into another carriage to have a smoke:

I overheard a conversation between two men. My attention was drawn to them when they coughed, so I turned round and looked at them, and there was a man in naval uniform. I judged a petty officer, but he had no mark on but distinctly he wore the regular peajacket that seamen wear. They were talking about Harwich, and they said they have laughed about it and I wondered about it, listening to it, and thinking he was talking in a rather free way, considering the present times. He was talking about his number on the submarine and how long he remained on the water, and how foul the air was, and that they could not hear anything because the noise was so much, and that he was saying he was going up north that night to the submarine base in Rosyth. I did not know whether he knew him, the gentleman opposite him. I do not know whether it was the station before Newcastle, but when the gentleman left him I took his place, going into the corner, as I was sure to hear something.

Lody got into conversation with the sailor talking about Harwich and after a few minutes or so the sailor asked, 'What country are you? Are you from the other side?' Lody replied, 'Yes, I am an American.' The sailor replied, 'Well, we have a large number of Americans over here,

24

and I suppose you are in a hurry to get back?' The conversation then turned generally to the war. The sailor told Lody that he had left his boat at Harwich and they spoke about the sinking of the cruiser *Pathfinder* by torpedo.

The talkative sailor then said, 'We are going to put out mines as the Germans have done so.' He continued, 'We have a big surprise in store for the Germans.' Lody states that he did not credit this very much, and left him after shaking hands and going into the dining car. He did not join him again. Lody said that he had no explanation for this, but he did not like it and felt he had had enough. He rejoined Miss McClyment and they had a cup of tea together.[29]

Upon returning to Drumsheugh Gardens, Lody continued to walk and cycle around the area. In Prince's Street he made the acquaintance of two young girls, and they went out on one or two evenings.

On 25 September he returned his cycle to Miss Mary Downie, saying that he was unable to ride it after an accident with another cycle, and he had brought the two bikes in by the railway to Waverley Station.[30] He paid the account and the repair costs. He had been on a trip to Peebles with a friend of Mrs Brown, a Miss McClyment:

When we were coming to some tunnels we collided as an automobile was coming behind us. We had intended to go the whole way from Peebles to Edinburgh. As I say, unfortunately, it caused some little injury to this lady.

Lody was by now getting concerned about his situation:

I was in Edinburgh and I had nothing to do, and simply spent my time. I was terribly nervous. I was unaccustomed to it, and I was frightened walking about Edinburgh. I had this suit made. I was frightened to go about.[31]

However, he wrote another letter to Adolf Burchard in German on Sunday, 27 September, enclosing press cuttings from *The Times* of 25 September relating to the chivalry of British seamen and from the editor of the Edinburgh *Evening News* of the same date relating to the sinking of the cruisers *Aboukir*, *Cressy* and *Hogue*. A transaction is as follows:

Edinburgh
27.9.14.

Situation in Scotland unchanged; fleet up to 18/9 off and on appeared on the Forth, has apparently finally quitted this base and is stationed partly in the outer Firth, Kirkcaldy and on the Tay

25

(Dundee). At the present moment only some Torpedo boats and 2 destroyers are here.

A large passenger steamer is equipped as a hospital ship with a large red cross on the side and anchored in the inner Forth. The bridge is comparatively feebly protected. On the south side (South Queensferry) stands a battery of 2 quickfirers (about 10 c/m); somewhat further toward the sea (about 500 metres) is a second battery of 2 guns.

The coast-place Berwick is well fortified, but unprotected (8 guns of about 10 c/m). On the little island in the middle of the Forth and on the middle pillar stands a small battery of three medium-sized guns. On the North side (North Queensferry) are 2 batteries of 3 guns each, unprotected Kinghorn, in the outer Firth, on the other hand has a battery of about 12 guns of large calibre. I have observed the same at Kirkcaldy. On Wednesday the 24/9 firing practice was held at Kinghorn.

The loss of the 3 large cruisers is taken very calmly here. Due respect is paid to the courage of the German submarines. From my information I learn that the British Admiralty has been told that in Germany a large number of passenger steamers have been equipped for transport and that here sooner or later the landing of German troops is to be expected.

At Harwich all ships lie with torpedo nets out. Hunting for mines is for the present left to a few trawlers who are without escort. In Leith about 15 trawlers are lying which up to three days ago were still outside. There is some nervousness and it is difficult to get crews for trawlers. The connection between Newcastle and Norway (Christiana) by the Wilson line is stopped. The Wilson steamers sail now weekly direct to Liverpool. From Leith Norwegian steamers sail as required to Bergen. All Irish ports except Dublin are closed to foreigners. My enquiries corroborate the fact that a Russian Army Corps (?) was landed at Aberdeen and brought south in 102 trains; although everything about this is denied in the papers, this denial was made in such a way which rather tended to confirm the supposition than the contrary.

The local papers bring out most incredible statements about the cruelties of the Germans in Belgium and the latest is about the Heligoland affair.

Enclosed cuttings for your information. As nothing is to be done here at the moment, I intend to go to Dublin and Belfast via Liverpool, and there to 'take a look round'.

The fear of espionage is very great and every day I see some Germans going to Redford Barracks under the escort of a soldier.

The enterprises of the *Emden* are much commented upon and admired. I am under the impression that the better class people are not quite so confident about the invincibility of the 'Great Fleet'. From my conversations I keep on gathering that the fearlessness and smartness of the German Navy inspire vast respect.

It is advisable for me to vanish for a few days, and to change my place of abode. I can only hope that my telegraphic and letter information have duly arrived. (sd) Nazi.[33]

Lody was now getting very concerned. He had been staying more than three weeks at Mrs Brown's; whenever they asked, 'When are you going to leave, Mr Inglis?, he would say, 'On such-and-such a date'. Lody felt he was misleading them from one day to another and was very uneasy. Finally they became very suspicious and mentioned that Lody's accent was more German than American![34] He therefore made hurried arrangements to leave, going to the Roxburgh Hotel, Edinburgh, on the morning of Sunday, 27 September, where he saw the manageress, Ruth Routledge. He gave her his card, enquired about terms and asked, in the event of his deciding to come, if she could stow some luggage for him, as he expected to be leaving for Ireland on the Monday. This was agreed, Lody saying that he would be away about eight days. The following day, having left Drumsheugh Gardens, he arrived with a box, a rug, a strap and a cardboard box.[35]

Feeling somewhat better, Lody took the train to Liverpool. He arrived between 8.00 and 8.30pm on Monday, 28 September at the London and North Western Hotel, Lime Street, taking room 83.[36] The following day Lody boarded the SS *Munster*, bound for Dublin via Kingstown. The ship made its way to Admiralty Pier at Holyhead, where, upon docking he was challenged by an aliens' officer called Alfred Hussey, whose job was to superintend the embarkation of passengers for Ireland and enquire as to their nationality. Lody said he was an American citizen and produced his papers in the name of Inglis. As well as the passport, Lody had a certificate of registration as American citizen, dated 22 August, 1914, from the American consul in Bergen, Norway (he had obtained this after being told about his mission to England). It all seemed in order to Hussey and Lody was allowed to proceed.[37]

On the ship, when almost approaching Kingstown, Lody spoke to Dr John William Lee, an American physician and surgeon from Minneapolis, who had been studying the diseases of the eye, ear, nose and throat in Vienna. Lody said that his name was Charles Inglis and asked the doctor if he was an American. Upon being told that he was, Lody said he was also. Lee said that he was going to New York on the SS *Baltic*, which was leaving Queenstown on 7 October, and that in the meantime he was going to see a little of the country around Dublin, Killarney, Drogheda, Cork, Blarney and Queenstown. Lody replied he was also going to Killarney and asked what hotel was Lee to stay at. He replied that he was not sure, but it would probably be the Gresham Hotel, as it was recommended to him by one of the officials on the boat. Lody replied, 'All right, let's go there,' and they went to the hotel together. Lee was to explain later that, as he was travelling alone, he went with Lody for the sake of having company, and he presumed Lody felt the same.

Having booked into the Gresham Hotel in separate rooms (Lody was in room 26), they had dinner together on the night of 29 September and after dinner went to the Empire theatre. After the entertainment, arriving back at the hotel, they had a drink and a long talk. Lody told Lee that he represented an adding machine company in America and that he was located in Germany. They discussed the war, but Lee could not recall any statement Lody made in favour of or against either side. They both agreed that the struggle would be a bitter one. Lody said that the German army were a very well-trained body of men, strong-bodied and enduring, and it would be hard to beat them.

They had breakfast together on the first morning at the hotel, then took a tram to Phoenix Park and looked around for about an hour, returning to the hotel for lunch. Lee then left Lody and went to Thomas Cook & Sons to have some money changed. Upon returning to the hotel, Lee could not find Lody, so left him a note saying that he would meet him at 6pm at the hotel.[38]

Lody could not be found as he was busy writing another letter in German to Adolf Burchard in Stockholm, dated 30 September. He had put his short time at Liverpool to very good use:

Dublin 30/9

As I mentioned in my last report, I think it is absolutely necessary to disappear for some time because several people have approached me in a disagreeable manner. That does not happen to me only, but several Americans here have told me that they are sharply watched. Fear of espionage is very great and one smells a spy in every stranger.

I chose the route Liverpool-Holyhead-Dublin on purpose in order to make several observations. On my way through England I had the opportunity to meet various well-known people *viz* Mr B. Cairns MP and W. E. Redmond MP (Irish). Although the opinion of these gentlemen is hopeful, it is nevertheless not free from pessimism. On the whole it is admitted that one has very considerably underestimated Germany's power. Later on in the dining-car I sat in the next compartment to them, that is to say separated from them only by a partition. They could not see me but I could hear everthing. One spoke about the probability of an invasion and of a bombardment of London chiefly by Zeppelins. All important buildings such as Houses of Parliament, Bank of England, Library, etc. are accordingly protected by strong wire nets. I mentioned this already in my report from London of 16/9.

In Liverpool there were comparatively few ships in the docks, but a great number were in the upper Mersey. The *Aquitania* of the Cunard Line is in the Seaford Dock which is the newest and largest one. I took the well-known Elevated Railway right to the Seaford Dock and walked to the Dock Gate. Unfortunately I could not get inside but I saw the *Aquitania* about 30 steps in front of me. Repairs (?) or alterations(!) were being done in the bow. It is interesting to note that the vessel was not in the dry dock but according to my estimation about 28 feet beyond it. All the plates from the top deck downward that is to say starting at the top deck have been re-riveted and 6 plates including the bow have not been repaired yet. People are working at it on scaffolding and ST apparatus. I started a conversation with the dock watchman who told me that the *Aquitania* was to be armed with 12 guns of large calibre and several small ones. The ship is painted greyish black. I did not notice pivots for searchlights or machine guns on deck. She has no rudder protection as the Lloyd Express Steamers have.

The *Lusitania* which will leave on 3/10 for New York is also painted greyish-black, the funnels as well, and as well as I could find out will eventually have guns on board too. Besides them there was a new Allan Liner ready for war in the Mersey.

In the store-houses corn, flour and potatoes are the principal articles stored. I saw enormous quantities of skin and cotton lying in the streets, some of the latter burst open so that the cotton got dirty and wet. One can notice also a certain uneasiness in Liverpool.

At Holyhead I was stopped as an Alien and had to produce my papers, as no Germans, Austrians or Hungarians are allowed to go to Ireland. Even as an American I had to show my passport again which was carefully examined and studied; then my name was put down. Everthing goes smoothly and I hope to be back in three days. Should nothing happen till the end of the month of October I shall have to come back to get my passport altered, because I shall otherwise have difficulties as I shall have been travelling for 3 months. I mentioned already in my last report that the new Naval base for submarines of the Northern Fleet is also at Rosyth/Dumfermline/Fife and that the Firth of Forth is very often empty.

But mines have been laid from Berwick in the direction of Dundee via Kirkcaldy. I shall have difficulties to get out of England again.[39]

Lee did not return until after 7pm, having had his dinner out at a restaurant. Upon meeting Lody again, they went to the pictures near the Gaiety theatre. The next day, Thursday, they toured Glendalough by coach, and after lunch went for a walk to the lake, talking mostly of the country, the scenery and their travels. Back at their hotel, after dinner they went to a show. The next morning the men went their separate ways, Lee to Drogheda and Lody to Killarney, the intention being for Lee to join Lody there on the morning of Saturday, 3 October. Lee suggested that Lody should drop a card in at the post office at Killarney to inform him which hotel he was staying at. But when Lee returned from Drogheda on Friday at about 9pm he found a telegram from Lody awaiting him, saying that he was stopping at a nice hotel, the Great Southern, with moderate rates.[40]

The British also intercepted Lody's letter from Dublin. Concern was mounting as these later letters were of a distinctly more dangerous character. James Cameron, a detective in the Edinburgh City Police, was instructed on the afternoon of Friday, 2 October, to make enquiries at hotels in the city for the name of Inglis. Among other hotels, he went to the Roxburgh and spoke to Miss Routledge. She showed the officer Lody's luggage. Cameron examined a luggage label attached to the straps, finding the crossed-out name of Charles A. Inglis, Bedford House, 12 Drumsheugh Gardens. This information allowed the detective to trace Lody's movements in the city.[41]

As a result, on the same day Deputy Chief Constable D. Moyes sent a report to Lieutenant Colonel V. G. W. Kell of MO5(g) at the War Office in London. Moyes stated that after his telephone call for assistance earlier that day, by the afternoon it had been discovered that a man calling himself Charles A. Inglis had put up at the North British Station Hotel from 27 August, later staying at Drumsheugh Gardens until 29 September. Enquiries at the Roxburgh Hotel found that Inglis had left some luggage there, saying that he would return after going to Ireland. A constant watch was accordingly kept on the Roxburgh Hotel in case the man should return.[42]

Matters now moved into top gear. After more enquiries were made at the ports, a message was sent the same day by the War Office to the Assistant Inspector General of the Royal Irish Constabulary in Dublin:

D.36 Suspected German Agent believed to be passing in name of CHARLES INGLIS as American Subject travelled from Edinburgh after 26 Sept. via Liverpool & Holyhead where his passport noted and name taken. Stop. Stayed last night Gresham Hotel Dublin believed moving on to Belfast. Stop. Should be arrested and all documents seized minutest search necessary probably has code with him.

30

Stop. Important to get specimens of his handwriting if possible.
Kindly wire result
Subsided London.[43]

The Royal Irish Constabulary now showed that, when required, it could move very quickly. By 7.23pm on 2 October they had made enquiries and replied to London as follows:

> Dr John Lea [*sic*] of United States arrived in Dublin on 29th with Charles Inglis and stayed at same hotel Inglis has gone to the Country today Lea will join him there tomorrow should he be arrested also description 35 years five feet eight sallow complexion darkened cropped moustache. Had a letter from Austria with him. Inspector General RIC.[44]

At 9.45pm the same day District Inspector Cheesman went to the Great Southern Hotel, Killarney, and examined the visitors' book. Among the names he found the entry of Charles Inglis, New York, who had arrived by the 3.18pm train that afternoon. The Inspector went up to his room, number 26. Tapping at the door, he got no answer. Upon opening the door he found the room in darkness – there was no one there, but he saw a small bag near the door. As he returned downstairs once more, he immediately saw the suspect coming up the hotel steps and moving on into the lounge. Cheesman had left his head constable and others outside, and they followed Lody in.

The Inspector went up to him and said, 'Mr Inglis, I presume?' Lody replied, 'Yes, what do you want?' Cheesman said, 'I want to speak to you. Come up to your room, please.' Lody appeared upset and frightened. Once in the room the police officer told Lody that he had instructions to detain him as a suspect German agent under the provisions of the Defence of the Realm Act. He was cautioned and Lody asked, 'What is this: me a German agent? Take care now; I am an American citizen.' The police then turned his room upside down and searched it thoroughly. Lody was taken to the police barracks where the Inspector searched him, finding the passport and certificate of registration, £14 in German gold, 705 kroner in Norwegian bank notes, and a small notebook. This notebook contained a list of cruisers that had been sunk in the North Sea, names and addresses of persons in Hamburg and Berlin, and what appeared to be a cipher or key. Lody showed uneasiness only when he saw the Inspector examining the small notebook and fidgeted about, walking up and down. In his bag was found a jacket and, upon examination, a tailor's ticket was found sewn inside the breast pocket. This read 'J. Steinberg, Berlin, R.C.H. Lody 8.5.14.'. The prisoner's identity was known!

Cheesman was to say that Lody was not the usual class of man he was accustomed to dealing with, but that he had never met a man under precisely similar circumstances. Lody had pulled himself together wonderfully well after the first shock, but Cheesman was suspicious of his accent when Lody was off his guard and was convinced that the man was German. The Inspector had been educated in Germany and had a fair knowledge of the language.[45]

While this was taking place, much to his displeasure Dr Lee was arrested. But after extensive enquiries nothing could be found against him and by 4 October he was released. His state of mind, however, can be judged by part of a statement that he made on 3 October:

It seems to me that it is very unfair and unjust to detain me here for two days and perhaps longer, for the simple reason that I received a telegram from a man under suspicion of being an enemy's agent. I can realize that precautions must be taken in time of war, and that if it was deemed necessary to detain me, there doesn't seem to be any excuse for such a delay in making enquiries.

I was thrown into a dirty, stinking cell in the police station with a blanket on a board to sleep on at midnight, Friday, and was left there until 2pm the next day, without anyone consulting me. I asked repeatedly to be allowed to have the American consul call on me, but was refused.

Now I am to be kept for another night in a military barracks. As I belong to a neutral country and having been furnished with a passport a year ago, and having been assured that it would carry me through safely to America, I am not a little surprised to receive such treatment at the hands of the British government, when, with a very little effort on its part, my identity could be established without a doubt.

I shall certainly take the matter up with the State Department when I return to America, and ascertain whether you can detain Americans citizens without cause, when they have proper credentials and identification.[46]

When he was released matters were fully explained to him, and an intelligence officer named R. H. Price gave him every facility, paying his car fare to his hotel. He thought that Lee accepted the situation, reporting,[47] 'I think he was quite soothed and he shook hands with me on parting. However, one wonders how he would have felt if he had known that there was already in being a report stating, "Submitted that Inglis should be dealt with by court martial and shot as a spy, if found guilty, and Lee also"!'[48]

Lody arrived in London and was placed in Wellington Barracks in the charge of the 3rd Battalion Grenadier Guards, with instructions that there must be no means of escape.[49] By 7 October it had been decided that he would be brought before a general court martial,[50] and the treasury solicitor was instructed to take up the matter and appoint counsel to conduct the case.[51] It was highlighted that the preliminary proceedings should take place without delay so the court martial could assemble as early as possible.[52] The case was discussed by the Cabinet, and as result by 21 October it was decided that Lody should be tried by the High Court and not by court martial for a war crime. Arrangements were also made to hand him over to the civil police.[53] However, this alteration was shortlived as Lody made a statement that he was a German subject; thus at the Cabinet meeting of 22 October it was decided to carry on with the original plan.[54]

Lody's court martial took place on Friday, 30 October, Saturday, 31 October and Monday, 2 November, 1914, at the Middlesex Guildhall, a then beautiful new stone building in the Tudor style situated at Westminster Broadway, opposite the side of Westminster Abbey. The *Daily Express* was to write:

> If the finding of the court martial is against the accused man – a German [Lody had in fact been interviewed by a member of the American embassy staff, but had readily admitted that he was a German and would make no effort to solicit aid from the US government][55] – he may be sentenced to be shot within 24 hours. There is thus a grim fascination about the life-and-death struggle which none of the spy trials during the past few years has possessed.[56]

Of the trials of the spies who were to be shot in the Tower of London in the First World War, Lody's court martial was the only one not held in camera. So, with the benefit of the reports of the press who witnessed the proceedings, I set out the scene:

'How say you, Carl Hans Lody, are you guilty or not guilty?' The Judge Advocate was addressing the alleged German spy, Carl Hans Lody, alias Charles A. Inglis, who was called upon to plead to charges of 'war treason' against Great Britain by sending two letters, one from Edinburgh on 27 September and the other from Dublin on 30 September, both signed 'Nazi', to one Herr J. Stammer, 'attempting to convey to a belligerent enemy of Great Britain, namely Germany' information with regard to the defences and/or preparations of war of Great Britain.

Without hesitation the prisoner, with a courteous bow to the court, answered to each charge in a stong voice with a pronounced American accent, 'I beg to plead not guilty'.

There had been a stirring prelude to this dramatic incident – the first of its kind in the modern history of England. The court, an

33

oak-panelled, mellow-lighted room, was given over to the military; at every door stood guardsmen barring entrance and egress with fixed bayonets. Only the privileged few gained admission to the body of the hall after close examination; the public gallery was thrown open and quickly thronged.

Promptly on the stroke of ten the double doors beneath the royal arms at the rear of the magisterial dais were flung wide. A glimpse of soldiers presenting arms, and Major-General Lord Cheylesmore,[57] an elderly man wearing the blue dress uniform of his rank, with gold epaulettes, a double row of gold buttons, and a silver star on his breast, advanced to the president's chair, a kind of choir stall with a little oak canopy. He was followed by the other members of the court, who wore khaki dress and caps. Each saluted the President, and then doffed his cap on sitting to the President's right and left in a quarter-circle.[58]

The President read the orders of Major-General Sir Francis Lloyd, commanding the London District, for the assembling of the court martial. 'And now,' said his Lordship, 'the accused is brought before the court.' A resonant order, 'Quick march!', was heard from below the court and immediately armed guards came up the steps leading from the cells. A sturdily-built civilian stepped after them into the dock, with two powerful Grenadiers beside him. He admitted his real name and raised no objection to any of the officers who were to try him for his life. As stiffly as his guards, he stood at attention, while each member of the court took an oath to give him fair trial. From general to major each officer, all nine of them, solemnly swore:

I will well and truly try the accused person before the court according to the evidence. Further I swear I will duly administer justice without partiality, favour or affection. I will further swear that I will not divulge the sentence of the court until it is duly confirmed, and I further swear that I will not on any account at any time whatsoever disclose or discover the vote or opinion of any particular member of this court martial unless thereunto required in due course of law.[59]

There was not room for many onlookers in the body of the court. Lord Mersey, formerly Mr Justice Bigham, sat at the side, with two or three army officers. A few ladies had seats in front of the clock, and a score more fashionably-dressed persons looked down from the gallery, craning their necks for a peep at the alleged spy. They found if difficult to see him, for a glass canopy covered with wire netting jutting out from beneath the gallery screened him.[60] With the knowledge that the punishment for war treason is death, every other person in the court sought to obtain a view of the unflinching prisoner. They saw a young

34

man in the prime of life, unmoved while people stared at him except for a flushed face. Of medium height, well built, with a small head, deep-set eyes, biggish ears and sharp features, with dark glossy hair,[61] he was dressed in a well-cut blue lounge suit. A typical clerk rather than the traditional dangerous spy.[62]

Mr Bodkin appeared for the prosecuting officer, Colonel Godman of the 3rd Battalion Scots Guards, with his friend Mr Gattie. For the defence appeared Mr George Elliott, KC, with his friend Mr Roland Harker.

The case against Lody was overwhelming. Evidence found on him at the time of his arrest and in his recovered property that he had left with Ruth Routledge at the Roxburgh Hotel was conclusive.

During the three-day hearing Lody generally conducted himself with an air of easy affability.[63] As nonchalant as ever, the prisoner listened to the evidence against him, and even smiled with other people in court when reference was made to one letter, which had been permitted by the authorities to go through the post, making reference to the passage of Russian troops through England.[64] He seemed to be possessed of high spirits and a sense of humour, for when one of the witnesses, an elderly Scottish boarding-house keeper (Mrs Brown of Drumsheugh Gardens) was asked if she could see Charles A. Inglis in court she looked everywhere except at the dock. Lody, who was sitting, stood up and gently waved his hands to attract her attention, while he smiled broadly and almost broke into laughter at the absurdity of the situation.[65] A flutter of excitement also swept through the court when a prepossessing young woman, Miss Ida McClyment, fashionably attired in a smart brown costume, told of her meeting with the prisoner on the train from Kings Cross to Edinburgh.[66]

When it was time for Lody to give his evidence his counsel announced that he would call Lieutenant Lody. 'Lieutenant!' There was a stir: the accused man, if guilty, was no common spy but a commissioned officer of the Kaiser. A show of heads appeared above the ledge of the public galley; women who had been knitting military garments dropped their work and craned forward; every eye in the building was focused on the spruce young prisoner as between his towering guards he stepped quickly to the witness stand. Composedly he took the oath to tell 'the whole truth and nothing but the truth'.[67]

As his interrogation by Mr Bodkin progressed, it got to the point of Lody's first attempt to send information from England (the telegram of 30 August) and the prisoner was asked if a code was used in it. Lody said, 'Yes; that is to say it was not actually a code because it only consisted of two words.'

> Q.   Are you willing to tell the court what those two words were?

A.	Yes, I am willing to say what those words, which words they were. They are 'shall' and 'leave'.
Q.	Now the telegram begins, 'Must cancel Johnson very ill last four days shall leave Scotland shortly'. Now 'Johnson very ill last four days', is there any meaning at all in those words?
A.	No
Q.	None?
A.	No, none at all. To save my life I could not say because I could not choose anything else. I had to send up a telegram and I was told not to make telegrams too short, but, well, I suppose there is a custom in other services – I could say it was said to me – it was said 'Do not make it too short, but something which is not deceiving to communicate to somebody in the third person'.
Q.	What does the word 'shall' mean?
	(After a pause)
The President:	Are you going to answer that question?
	(After a pause)
Mr Bodkin:	He said he was just now.
Mr Hawker:	I quite agree or I should not have put it to him in such a direct way.
A.	I said I was ready to say which was what.
The President:	Are you prepared to answer what the word 'shall' meant or not?
A.	Arrived.
Q.	What?
A.	It means 'arrived'.
The President:	It means what?
Mr Harker:	It means 'arrived'. Would the people in Berlin know by receiving a telegram at that time from you what had arrived?
A.	Yes, they would.
Q.	What was it: if you are willing to tell?
A.	That a portion of the ships stationed at the Firth had arrived.
The President:	A portion at the Firth stationed where?
Mr Harker:	At the Firth of Forth. And 'leave', does that mean a portion of the Fleet has arrived and leaves shortly – is that what it means?
Mr Bodkin:	If so, 'leaves' means something.
A.	It means something else.
Mr Bodkin:	If so, he had better tell us.

Mr Harker:	Does it mean anything else?
A.	No
The President:	It means a portion of the ships has arrived and leaves shortly?
A.	Exactly, sir.[68]

Interest reached its highest pitch when, weighing every word, the prisoner's counsel asked, 'Who sent you to England?' Now for the first time fortitude deserted the accused. For some moments, while the court waited in silence, Lody struggled to retain mastery of himself. The question of whether he should disclose the name of the person whom he represented as primarily responsible seemed to flash through his mind. But he thrust aside any such temptation, and quivering from head to foot, with tears coming from his eyes, he answered in a voice charged with emotion: 'I have pledged my word of honour not to name that name. I cannot do it. Although names are discovered in my documents, I do not feel that I have broken my word. But that name – no, I cannot give it. I have pledged my word of honour.'

Lody was pale and seemed dazed. A hush fell on the court, broken by a sob from a woman in the gallery, and then with an effort the prisoner regained his self-possession. Turning to his judges he bowed, saying, 'I beg your pardon. I have had a month's confinement and my nerve has given way.' A glass of water was handed to him.[69, 70]

On the second day of the hearing, when police inspector John Briggs was giving evidence, it was considered desirable that the court should be cleared of both press and public. During the temporary absence of the prisoner, Mr Bodkin passed information to the judge advocate and president that a person was still in the public area of the court and had not left, as ordered. The man was removed from court under guard, until enquiries could be completed. Mr George Elliott pointed out that some credit was due to the defence because Mr Rowland Harker had called attention to the man's presence.

The Times of Sunday, 1 November, reported the matter as follows:

A dramatic arrest in court took place while the court martial was in progress, a young man of foreign appearance being seized by the police. He appears to have obtained admission to the court both on Friday and yesterday, and at one time was sitting in a prominent position near Lord Mersey, who attended as a visitor. He attempted to shake hands with Lody on being removed from court. As far as can be ascertained, the man obtained entrance to the court by showing some naval papers, but an official of the Admiralty who was present was able to inform the police of the character of these papers. After being questioned and searched, he was removed under an escort of Guards with fixed bayonets and taken in a van to Wellington Barracks.[71]

Lody wrote to a friend in Omaha, America, on 31 October:

My feelings run riot when I can permit myself to review the dramatic events of the last three years and what is to be the probable climax of it all. I am prepared to make a clean breast of all this trouble, but I must protect my friends in the Fatherland and avoid as much as possible humiliation for those who have been near and dear to me.

I am in the Tower. Hourly while I am confined here an unfriendly guard paces the corridor. My counsellor is an attorney of standing, but I ofttimes feel that he is trying to do his duty to his country rather than defend his client. Next week I shall know my fate, although there can be hardly a doubt as to what it is to be. I have attended to such legal matters as were necessary, but whether my wishes will ever be carried out I do not know.

You may have an opportunity to say a word to some of those for whom I feel an interest. Ask them to judge me not harshly. When they hear of me again, doubtless my body shall have been placed in concrete beneath this old tower, or my bones shall have made a pyre. But I shall have served my country. Maybe some historian will record me among the despised class of war victims. A spiritual adviser already has been to visit me. It was his presence, more than anything else, which made me realize that what your own Gen. Sherman said of war is true.

Doubtless my demise shall be heralded as that of a spy, but I have spiritual consolation. Others have suffered and I must accept the reward of fate.

I am your affectionate friend.

Carl Hans Lody[73]

On 2 November the court martial assembled for the third time, to hear the speeches of counsel. The court was more crowded than at previous sittings: scores of people were refused admission; fashionably-dressed women filled seats usually reserved for barristers, and found places even on unoccupied seats of the magisterial dais, where too sat Major-General Sir Francis Lloyd. Mr Elliott, for the defence, intimated that he did not propose to call evidence on behalf of the prisoner. Following on, Mr Bodkin stated that Lody was a skilled and dangerous man; the class of man against which international military law was aimed; and it was for such a tribunal as this to protect the interests of the state.[74]

When his advocate rose to make a plea on his behalf, the prisoner

38

passed his hand across his brow, moistened his lips, and listened with a resolute demeanour. In his speech Elliott said:

> First of all, sir, may I say on behalf of Lieutenant Lody that it is by his own personal wish here, and as his advocate I say, and frankly say before you, and from his point of view I say it fearlessly before you, that he came into this country in the service of his country; that he came into this country as a German actuated by patriotic motives; that he came here, secondly, in obedience to suggestions of his officer superior on command; and, thirdly, that he came here absolutely voluntarily in the sense that he was not personally compelled to come and entirely at his own expense . . . .
>
> I therefore wish to approach this case, if I may, on behalf of this man for whom I plead – as pleading in the sense which I have told you – not as a miserable coward asking for forgiveness for his offence, not as some fear-stricken wretch whom the thought of punishment reduces to a condition in which both his mental and physical faculties are destroyed, but as a man born in a land of which his is proud, whose history and traditions he cherishes. His own grandfather was a great soldier who held a fortress against Napoleon; and it is in that position that he wishes to stand before you here today, as a man who, believing it to be his duty and his noblest mission, took upon himself that which subjects him admittedly to conditions if he were detected from which he would be the last to shrink.[75]

Now came a great silence. A few formalities, then Lord Cheylesmore said the court would retire to consider its findings. After an absence of six minutes, the judges were in their seats again; their findings, though not disclosed, were obvious. For instead of ordering the prisoner's release, the president asked Lody if he had any statement to make. Everybody strained to hear his reply. 'I have nothing to say on my behalf.' The court literally gasped with astonishment. The President ejaculated an incredulous 'What?', which brought these additional words from the prisoner: 'No sir, not on my behalf.' Still the President did not feel satisfied. 'You have nothing to say?' he asked again. Not a sound was heard in all that crowded court as the prisoner bent his head. He seemed to think deeply. All eyes were riveted upon him as he looked up in a voice full of weariness and declared, 'I have nothing more to say'.

Then the stillness became even more intense as people leaned forward listening for the sentence of the court. The President spoke, and once again people caught their breath in astonishment. 'The court will be cleared for the sentence.' Swiftly Lody glanced round the court, and

39

then with head erect followed his guards below. And so the crowd of spectators trooped silently out, breathless and wondering.[76, 77]

On 4 November written instructions were issued to the general officer commanding London district, Horse Guards, marked 'Secret' (these were of the same type that were to be issued prior to each execution). They stated that His Majesty had confirmed the findings of the court, and that promulgation of the sentence should take place the following morning. There must be then at least 18 hours between Lody being told of his fate and the shooting. Every consideration was to be given for religious consolation, and an interview with his legal adviser could be allowed. However, no communication was to be made to the press until a communiqué was issued, and, in order to avoid publicity, the coroner was not to be informed until the evening before execution – leakage was feared by summoning a jury early.[78]

On 5 November a letter was sent to Major-General Pipon, CB, the Major of the Tower of London, at the headquarters of London District in Horse Guards.

I have been directed to carry out the execution of the German Spy who has been convicted by General Court Martial. The time given me has been short, so short that I have only had a few hours to arrange and have been directed to keep it secret. Under the circumstances the Tower is the only possible place and has been approved by the War Office, If I have not communicated with you before it is only because time has pressed.
Major-General Commanding London District.[79]

The night of 5–6 November was wet, with drizzling rain.[80] Lody was delivered by police van to the Tower. He was informed of his forthcoming execution, and he wrote two letters before his death.

London, Nov. 5th 1914.
Tower of London
To the Commanding Officer of the 3rd Battalion Gren. Guards.
Wellington Barracks

Sir
I feel it my duty as a German officer to express my sincere thanks and appreciation towards the staff of officers and men who were in charge of my person during by confinement.
 Their kind and considered treatment has called my highest esteem and admiration as regards good fellowship even towards the enemy and if I maybe permitted, I would thank you for making this known to them.

I am, Sir, with profound respect:
Carl Hans Lody.
Senior Lieutenant, Imperial German Naval Res. II.[81]

The second letter, also written on 5 November, was to his relations in Stuttgart:

My DEAR ONES,
I have trusted in God and He has decided. My hour has come, And I must start on the journey through the Dark Valley like so many of my comrades in this terrible War of Nations. May my life be offered as a humble offering on the alter of the Fatherland.

A hero's death on the battlefield is certainly finer, but such is not to be my lot, and I die here in the Enemy's country silent and unknown, but the consciousness that I die in the service of the Fatherland makes death easy.

The Supreme Court-Martial of London has sentenced me to death for Military Conspiracy. Tomorrow I shall be shot here in the Tower. I have had just Judges, and I shall die as an Officer, not as a spy.
Farewell. God bless you,
Hans.[82]

John Fraser, a yeoman warder of the Tower at the time, writes about the execution:

The following morning, 6 November, 1914, broke cold, foggy, and bleak, and at a very early hour Lody was brought from his cell [29 the Casemates], and the grim procession formed up on the verandah of the Tower Main Guard. [Lody said to the Assistant Provost-Marshal who fetched him from his cell, 'I suppose that you will not care to shake hands with a German spy?' 'No. But I will shake hands with a brave man.'] It was led by the Chaplain, solemnly reading the Burial Service, followed by the prisoner, with an armed escort marching on either side of him, and the firing-party of eight stalwart guardsmen bringing up the rear.

Nobody liked this sort of thing. It was altogether too cold-blooded for an ordinary stomach (particularly that of a soldier, who hates cold-bloodedness) to face with equanimity, and it is not too much to say that, of that sad little procession, the calmest and most composed member was the condemned man himself.

For the Chaplain, in particular, it was a bad time. He had never had a similar experience, and his voice had a shake in it as he intoned the solemn words of the Burial Service over the living form of the

41

man it most concerned. His hands, too, as he held the book, trembled a little, the more honour to him!

The escort and the firing-party, too, were far from comfortable, and one could see that the slow march suitable to the occasion was getting badly on their nerves. They wanted to hurry over it, and get the beastly business finished.

But the prisoner walked steadily, stiffly upright, and yet as easily and unconcernedly as though he was going to a tea-party, instead of to his death. His eyes were upturned to the gloomy skies, and his nostrils eagerly drank in the precious air that was soon to be denied them. But his face was quite calm and composed – almost expressionless.

Then came a queer and pathetic little incident. As they came to the end of the verandah, the Chaplain, in his nervousness, made to turn left, which was the wrong way. Instantly Lody took a quick step forward, caught the Chaplain by the right arm, and, with a polite and kindly smile, gently guided him to the right – the correct way.

A few moments later the procession disappeared through the doorway of the sinister shed [the miniature rifle range; here spies were blindfolded and secured by straps to a chair],[83] and shortly after that came the muffled sound of a single volley [by the 3rd Battalion Grenadier Guards].[84] Carl Hans Lody had paid!

When I think of Carl Lody a phrase always slips into my head – just three little words: 'A gentleman, unafraid!'[85]

The New York Times commented on the execution: 'Many of the retainers and employees of the Tower had been awakened by the eight-man volley',[86] and 'visitors that day were told of it and all spoke in whispers'.[87] An oak tree was planted in his native German village bearing his name.[88]

CHAPTER 3

Carl Frederick Muller

Carl Frederick Muller was aged 58 in 1915, having been born on 21 February, 1857. He could make a claim to be Russian, as he had been born in Libau.[1] He was an expert linguist, speaking Russian, German, Dutch, Flemish and English, with hardly a perceptible accent.[2] His father was Henry Julius Muller, and his mother a native of the same town. His father died when he was 11 and when his mother also died he lived with his uncle, Mr Schneider, who was the mayor of the town.

On reaching 16, Carl Muller went to sea, but by 17 he had entered the service of the American Shipping Company in Hamburg, and up until 1881 he worked on several English and American ships. But in 1879 his work was interrupted when he had to return to Russia. He had received his call-up as a soldier, having passed his examination as a lieutenant, but poor eyesight and cramp of the legs prevented him from passing the medical. By 1881 Carl had married a Norwegian girl and they crossed the ocean to New York, where he worked as a ship's rigger. After staying there for 18 months he returned to Hamburg and started a business as a beer retailer. Things went well, but in 1886 there were difficulties for Russians in Hamburg, due to Bismarck's new law, and Russians were expelled from the city.

Muller took his wife and children to Antwerp where the family opened a boarding-house. In 1892 Muller's wife died, so he sold the boarding-house and took a position for two years in a shipping office in Dunkirk, later moving to Bremen to work in a clothing and outfitter's store. But once again he was ordered to leave Germany, this time moving to Rotterdam where he secured employment checking cargos with an English firm. In 1899 he had a sudden attack and suffered a serious illness.

The following year he moved back to Antwerp, where he entered into business with an Englishman, a Mr le Blanc, as a cargo

43

superintendent,[3] and as such dealt mostly with German steamers.[4] It appears that most people in the city took him for a German.[5] The firm was styled 'le Blanc & Muller'. All went well until 1904 when his partner died, so Muller carried on by himself. His business involved the preparation of ships, painting, dry-docking, repairing engines and selling 8hp, 9hp or 10hp engines to the large Rhine lighters. He obtained agencies from a carpentry factory and afterwards the Kattendyke Works, as well as a firm in Germany[6] called the Herfurther Motor Manufactory Company, which made motor winches.[7]

But on the outbreak of the war on 4 August, 1914, all business stopped. At that time Muller was staying at 4 Rue Osy; his landlord was a Mr Dorst. Not happy with the situation, Dorst moved away, leaving the entire house in the charge of Muller. After a week or two large numbers of Belgian refugees descended on Antwerp. Muller stated that he went to the police commissioner telling him that he had eight rooms and eight beds, where a number could stay; but he wanted respectable people because it was not his property. Until 4 October, when the Belgian military authorities ordered all refugees out of the town, he estimated that he had some 120 people coming and going.

By 8 October there were perhaps only about 5,000 people left in the city. Much looting was taking place, with people breaking into shops. There was little to eat, and Muller said that he lived on rice and barley. The waterworks and gasworks had been blown up. On 7 October the bombardment of Antwerp began. Muller states:

> Yes, at half past 12, dinner time, the bombardment started, and at 4 o'clock the airship came; I was standing at the door, and the airship came and chucked a bomb about 50 yards from my house. Then I got that attack and lay senseless the whole afternoon; that was the time I got this shaky nervousness.

Muller's explanation as to what happened next is as follows. At 12.15pm on 8 October he found that the Germans had entered Antwerp, as he saw them in a large square called the Place la Commune. This was quite close to Muller's address – there was only the university and hospital between. The Germans broke into the Athenaeum, where there were 700 beds which had been filled with Belgian wounded, and took possession of it themselves. Nearby was a public house which the Germans also filled. Later a German officer and two soldiers called at Muller's address asking for water. There was a well there, and Muller informed them that he had supplies which the Germans immediately took over. Muller went to bed with the Germans downstairs, but at 10 pm he was called.

At 8 o'clock they sent me to bed; the officer ordered me upstairs; then at 10 o'clock a soldier came – I must come down to the officer. When I come down to the officer he says I must go along with them people; there was another under-officer outside and that man says: 'Now, you must show me where the big horse stables are in Antwerp'; then I had to go with him till 2 o'clock at night to show him where the stables were.

Muller continued to live in his house with the quartered soldiers until 26 October, when he found that his money was getting very short. As a result he paid a visit to the civil governor. Freiherr (or Baron) von Fleckenberg, telling him that he was an agent for a German factory. The German asked about engines for motors and machines that this firm manufactured. After interviews with the general consul and the civil governor, it was agreed that Muller could go to Germany, as the engines were needed in Antwerp. He claims that he was given a passport for just six days. From Antwerp Muller made his way to Rosendaal through the German frontier at Esschen, and on to Herfurt in Wiesbaden where the Herfurter factory was situated. After negotiations with the factory director he left on 28 November, accompanied by an engineer. Arriving back at the frontier the same evening, at the central railway station called Goch, he claimed that he was arrested, and was put in a dungeon for eight days. Then one night about 1am he was woken and taken by car to a fortification at Wesel. He was to remain there until 28 December, 1914, when he was sent back to Antwerp.[8]

It appears that during these months he was recruited by the German secret service. His background made him an ideal choice for a spy: he was short of money and already helpful to the forces of occupation; he had not run away when Antwerp was under siege, as he was at home with the German race; he was a man who could speak many languages, and had a sound knowledge of shipping.

On 9 January, 1915, Muller boarded at Rotterdam the ship *Whitby Abbey*, of the Hull and Netherland Steamship Company and bound for Hull. It was to arrive on 11 January. During the voyage Muller had a conversation with a steward, Minor Taylor. He told Taylor that he was going to Sunderland, England, to stay with friends.[9] He also told James Dalton, the line's passenger clerk, that his temporary address was 39 Amberley Street, Sunderland, and these details were given to the Aliens' Officer.[10]

At midday on 12 January schoolteacher Miss Jessie Neilson Speir came home to this address for lunch in her normal way. She found Carl Muller there, which was quite unexpected and a great surprise. Miss Speir had met Muller in the summer of 1913, when she was on a ten-day holiday in Antwerp with her friend Miss Campbell, and they had become acquainted with Muller in their hotel. After they left Belgium she sent her new friend a postcard or two, and Muller replied on one occasion. She was to agree that she might have written that Muller would have been safer in England, but she never gave him any invitation to visit her.

Muller told the family that the Germans had imprisoned him, and that he had been fed on rye bread, rice and suchlike fare, and had been generally badly treated. But he had been allowed to leave the fort, having somehow or other got permission to move from Antwerp on condition that he did not return. As a result he was in a very shattered and nervous condition and wished to see a doctor. Jessie formed the opinion that he did not appear to be shaky or ill, but looked much older than when she had last seen him in 1913. Muller was asked what he was going to do. He replied that he would possibly go to America to see his son, or he might go to Switzerland. But in any event he wanted to stay in Sunderland for two weeks. Jessie had not heard of his son before, and she advised Muller to go to the USA.

In the course of that day Muller said he was Russian and Mr Speir suggested that he should register as an alien at the central police station, as Sunderland was a military area. Jessie Speir went with Muller to the police station, where they saw Inspector Pinchin. He examined Muller's passport and explained that because Sunderland was a military area Muller could not be allowed to stay, but he could move to Durham. Muller would not agree to this, and said that he would go to London, with the explanation that he might be able to get money advanced there. So Pinchin looked up the times of the trains, finding that one would leave at 12 noon the next day. Muller was next taken to the doctor. Later Muller asked Jessie Speir about possible lodgings in London, and she recommended him to Guildford Street, where he could stay.[11]

But there was a problem, in that there was not sufficient acommodation for Muller at the Speirs' and he was therefore introduced to a Mr Walter James Dawson, a draper, who lived at 22 Amberley Street and was a friend of the family. He invited the visitor to stay with him overnight, and true to his word Muller turned up at 10.30pm. The two men stayed up talking for an hour. Muller spoke again about his harsh treatment by the Germans during their occupation of Antwerp. He said that his motor cars and other possessions had been commandeered and his bank balance seized, that he himself had been in prison and for a considerable time was very poorly fed, and after that the intolerable behaviour of the Prussians in the city made his life unbearable, so he took the opportunity of leaving. But he appeared to have no definite plan as to what he planned to do in England.[12]

On 13 January, 1915, Muller booked into a boarding-house in London at 38 Guildford Street, off Russell Square, which was run by Mary Elizabeth Tansley.[13] Two days later he sent a postcard to the Speirs in Sunderland.

> Dear Friends,
> Arrived all well, but knowing to express my thanks for the kind reception. I only say, 'God Bless You All' staying at 38 Guildford Street and getting much better, hoping to see you again. I always remember you.
> thankful
> C Muller

Jessie Speir replied the following day, saying that they were glad he had arrived safely, and complaining about the dreadful weather. She told him to be sure to visit the Houses of Parliament, Westminster Abbey, Buckingham Palace, St Paul's and Hyde Park. And 'I hope you manage to have some luck in London, after all the "fire and water" experience of the past few months. This war will leave many "bleeding hearts" in its train.'[15] Walter Dawson also wrote to Muller:

> I am very glad to know that you have got lodgings, and found a resting place at last. It was my hope that you could have stayed in Sunderland long enough to have recovered from the effects of the hardships you had undergone, and that we might have been permitted to offer to a Russian guest that hearty welcome, and sincere sympathy, which he is always so ready to accord the stranger when travelling in his country. But war has altered everything, and even the sacred duty of hospitality is interfered with, and curtailed by these military regulations.[16]

Little did they know that their new friend had his own reasons for being in England, and that his health appears to have been only a cover. Just a few days after booking into his boarding-house he embarked again for the Continent on 16 January. Edward Abraham, the Aliens' Officer, remembered Muller taking the *Princess Juliana* to Flushing. Before he could embark he had to complete a boarding card, on which he gave his destination as Rotterdam.[17] He stayed until 27 January, when he returned to England on the *Orange Nassau*,[18] booking in again at 38 Guildford Street.[19] On 29 January, 1915, Muller wrote two postcards to Jessie Spier in Sunderland, posted on 30 January from London, WC. The writing is very small and the odd word is unreadable:

WC London. 29.1.15
Guildford Street, 38 Russell Square.

My dear little friend

After staying a couple days here I got wire from Rotterdam which forced me to go there. Left 17/1 and returned last night. Got 500 frs. [.......] and some of my clothes, in a few weeks I hope to get the rest and if I am fit for travelling go to America or Switzerland to restore my health.

But now my little sister how will it ever be possible? Don't forget Miss Cambell will write as soon as possible. To repay all this kindness this goodness I received from you. Your kind families and Mr Dawson!

Thinking of this dreadful war, of this frivolous killing of million people, of my suffering, a person should think human beings turned to wild beast. And get to find such friends as you are to me. God bless you all and if prayers is able to strenghthen my wishes. You be aware of God's blessing. Excuse my writing and Postcards. I am leaning in bed. I suffering severe shock of nerves, hope to be better in a couple of days, goodwill is the best medicine.

I would write much more and to Mr Dawson but trembling to much.

C Muller[20]

Miss Spier replied, still in the belief that Muller was a friend:

I was delighted to have your postcards this morning and to know that you have returned safely to England once again. I hope to hear very soon of your complete recovery to good health and spirits, and I sincerely hope that suffering for you is now a thing of the past. Those of us who have been more fortunate and have not been called upon to suffer directly as you have, certainly do sympathize with you deeply. You mention something about our kindness to you, and I reply that we are only sorry that it was not in our power to show you greater kindness, and any little thing which we may have done to please you, gave us also our share of pleasure. I shall never in my life forget your goodness to me while in Belgium last year – goodness which touched me so vitally that I shall never forget, for just at that time I felt as if the world was full of buffets and you, instead of buffeting, treated my kindly. This world will not know itself after this trying war, for mankind the world over will, I hope, be more brotherly and kind – it will be good to be alive when that day comes.[21]

During Muller's time at Guildford Street he got on quite friendly terms with one of the forty residents, a Mr Pratt, who was a member of the Bar. He spoke to Pratt about the siege of Antwerp, saying that he was in business there. Pratt recalled:

And he told me then when the German troops did enter the city he went to them and got into comunication with them; that he gave them certain information as to where they could obtain water. He told me in connection with that that the main water supply was interrupted and that he told them where there were wells from which they could obtain a supply of water and he also gave them information as to where they could stable their horses; and in consequence of that he became on friendly terms with German officers and they visited them at the house where he was staying. That house I understood from him was in the north part of the city.[22]

Muller wrote to Mr Dawson in Sunderland:

38 Guildford Steet
Russell Square
London
1st February 1915

Dear Mr Dawson,
Firstly, please accept my apologies for writing in German. I am well aware how much I embarrass myself by doing so but I wish to express my gratitude to you as sincerely and succinctly as possible. However, I am sure that I have no need to worry as a well-educated man like yourself will of course be familiar with German, and besides which the language I employ is of no importance in comparison to the true reason causing me to write this letter.

On 17 January I received a telegram summoning me to Rosendal and did not recieve your wonderful letter until my return on the 28th. I had an awful trip as I am still suffering with this dreadful stomach illness, which sent me straight to bed on my arrival home. Today has been a lovely day and the first on which I have been able to venture out. I have bought some clothes and been able to get some money. I am temporarily having to content myself with the small sum of 800 Fr. each fortnight as there is no hope of receiving my savings from Antwerp for the moment.

Nothing comes from America but I will receive more in a fortnight and be able to go to S[....]erland where I found so much warmth and kindness with the [....], yourself and the doctor. I can honestly say that you renewed the enthusiasm and strength I lost in this dreadful war which had robbed me of all belief in mankind and humanity. How distressing it is to observe the speed at which men fall to the level of wild animals, and distance themselves from all things humane.

But more importantly, esteemed Mr Dawson, how can I possibly find the words to express and repay even a small part of my immense gratitude to you? Please do not hesitate to notify me of any desires or requests you or any of your family may have. It would always be the greatest pleasure to do absolutely anything within my power for you or your family. Please allow me this greatest pleasure. Sincerely, a thousand thankyous for all the joy and happiness you gave me. I had been desperately lonely before my stay with your family where I experienced such warm friendship. I now know that the world is simply not large enough for a man ever to be alone. I promise you, and indeed myself, that if my health holds one day we shall meet again and assure you without exaggeration that day will be by far the happiest of my life.

Finally, dearest Mr Dawson, please pass on my most heartfelt and sincere greetings to your dear wife and son (the others) and of course to you. I desperately hope that you will understand my poor English handwriting but please at least convey to Miss Speir and her family all the love that my pen can only so pathetically express.

I must finish for today in the hope of a swift reply, as I remain, Sir, now and forever your faithful and thankful servant.
Muller[23]

But Muller had not let the grass grow under his feet and had been busy. The following letter in English, written in black ink, was intercepted:

London 3rd Febry. 1915.
Walden Street, 5,
Whitechapel.

Dear Sir,
Hearing you are not at home I postponed to send the goods via Folkestone awaiting your further orders. Would you be kind now and send me some of the Rotterdam *Courant* papers for everybody here is anxious to hear about the latest carrying on of the Germans in Belgium and I fancy this paper writes and brings the particulars of this the best of all other papers.
With best compliments to your family and all friends.
I remain,
Yours truly,
(sgd) C. Lempret.

Tests were made between the lines for invisible ink and words were found written in German, translated as follows:

> According to exact information from the last 14 days 15,000 English troops have left for France via Southampton and a small place which I cannot yet learn the name of for Boulogne and Dieppe. Recruiting is going very slowly. Troops are coming and going via Folkestone. At Newcastle and Sunderland there are many sailors. It is impossible to get near the docks without a special pass. I have visited the Horse Guards barracks which is the headquarters for recruiting yesterday 34 and today 22 [men] were brought over from the War Office with bands.
> (sgd) A.E. 111.[24]

Ada and Henry Perdaux, a car man, had lived at 5 Walden Street, Whitechapel for some 13 years and had never had anything to do with or heard the name C. Lempret.[25] Muller had chosen an address at random, as he was to do with his next letter, also written in black ink and intercepted by the postal authorities. This time he used 22 Deptford High Street, the home of a house furnisher, Josiah Edward Mitchell, for the past ten years.[26]

> London 4th Feby. 1915.
> Deptford High Street, 22.
> Mr. Fr. Laybaker,
> Rotterdam.
>
> Dear Sir,
>   I received your letter 1/2 ult., and haste to answer for your offer I thank you very much and will consider so soon my partner returns hoping to come to the conclusion to accept, although your price is rather high we will asking the market prices here and then let you know what we are able to pay will understand free to our magazines. Hoping to do good business together.
> I remain,
> Yours truly,
> (sgd) L. Cohen.

Tests once more were very revealing, but greatly worried the British security services. It was clear that a major spy was at loose in England and had to be caught as soon as possible, but where to start? The hidden German text was translated:

Visited today Hampstead Gardens, the quarters of the Australian troops. Saw 600 to 800 men, new recruits who will require training. Yesterday evening about 4 o'c many soldiers were on their way to Waterloo Station, about 4,000 in full dress. In St James's Park about 1,000 were exercising. In Epsom 10,000 men were drilling daily. Troops depart from Folkestone, Newhaven and Southampton. (sgd) A.E. 111.[27]

During Muller's time in London an incident occurred when Arthur Francis Brys, a businessman in Antwerp before the war who knew Muller well, came out of his office block at 101 Leadenhall Street in the City of London. As he reached the pavement he saw Carl Muller on the other side of the street. Brys said that he stood looking, as he was very surprised to see him. He had always looked on Muller as being German during the ten or twelve years they had known each other. Brys stated that he got something like a chill in seeing him there. Brys asked Muller what he was doing in London and Muller talked round the subject, asking whether Brys knew that he was a Russian. Brys said that he did not believe it as he was sure that he was a German, telling Muller so. No reason was given as to why he was in Britain, but Muller did tell Brys that he had been in prison.[28]

On 5 February Muller once more booked out of 38 Guildford Street and embarked for the Continent. That night he was allowed to board his ship for his passage the next day to Rotterdam.[29] Mary Tansley did not see him again until 13 February, when he turned up at her door.[30] But there was already unease about his activities. On 16 February Inspector Buckley of the Criminal Investigation Department at New Scotland Yard paid a visit to 38 Guildford Street; he had a search warrant. Information had been received that the foreign gentleman was a spy, although at that time the authorities did not know that he was responsible for the intercepted letters. Nothing was found, and the matter was filed.[31] But this visit did not deter Muller, as on 20 February he sent another letter, which was intercepted like the others:

To Mr F. R. Lybecq
PO 447 Rotterdam,
Holland.

London. 20 Febry. 1915.
54 Howard Street, [no such number could be found]
Strand.

Dear Sir,
Received your letter confirming my orders only today and hope you shipped goods by this time as the Zeeland is running their boats

52

. The miniature Rifle Range at the Tower of London on the east side of the inner wall between the Martin and Constable towers (*Royal Armouries*).

. Interior of the Rifle Range (*Royal Armouries*).

3. The Casemates, where the spies spent their last night

4. The execution chair.

regularly to Tilbury as I learn the prices raisened considerably in Holland on eggs and cream there. We must find out first of all what the markets said here to give any orders for this. Hope to be soon in receipt of your futher orders.

We remain.

Yours truly,

(sgd) W Dorst & Co.

Written in invisible ink on the back of the letter in German was found:

In Woolwich for ammunition and guns also armoured car and airships as well as shells with petrol and Naphtha filling. All the principal trains to the coast are stopped on account of military transports as by Harwich, Folkestone and Southampton cavalry very small shortage of horses, artillery also by Tilbury and also 13 guns, 13 inch for sea use and 6 and 10 inches for land. Hendon 20 airships stand always ready constantly practising. Cannot leave London. I will get permission from authorities to go to Newcastle and Sunderland. Great movement of troops here and inland. (sgd) A.E. 111.[32]

While in London one Monday morning, Muller went south of the river, making a call at 111 High Street, Deptford. He had met the owner of this bakehouse, John Hahn, a short, rather stout, clean-shaven man,[33] on 12 May, 1912, in Antwerp at the wedding of the daughter of his landlord Mr Dorst. Meeting again the following year, when the Hahns paid a visit to Mrs Hahn's parents, Muller had some conversation with Hahn but there was no great familiarity between the two – it was more a passing acquaintance.[34] Mrs Christine Emily Hahn was therefore surprised by this visit, telling her husband that Muller had arrived from Antwerp and wanted to see him. Hahn, anxious about the condition of his dough, came out to the front of the shop, spent hardly a minute in conversation, and treated Muller in a rather offhand manner. Thinking about the visit later, Hahn was sorry about the way he had behaved, and told his wife to write inviting Muller to call and see them again. Muller did not answer, but on the following Sunday turned up unexpectedly again and stayed for tea. Muller invited Hahn to visit him at Guildford Street, and on another occasion they went to the Hippodrome together.[35] Muller was getting ready to implicate the unsuspecting Hahn in his activities!

Hahn was British-born and a British subject, though his parentage was German; his father had been naturalized in 1896. At the age of 14 years Hahn was sent to Breslau in Germany to learn the German system of bakery and confectionery. He remained in Germany for a number of years before returning to Britain. It appears that he lived an honest life and was a respectable tradesman. But just before the war circumstances were not good for Hahn. He went bankrupt, and only held his head above water by borrowing money from his wife's father. When war broke out the anti-German feelings of the local population became very strong. There was a riot in Deptford and his shop was attacked by a mob and wrecked. This left Hahn with a sense of grievance, and his position was so poor that he had to rely on the help of his wife's uncle for the supply of flour. It was with this background that Hahn would be tempted by Muller, a man of persuasion with a powerful mind.[36]

On 21 February Muller called at Hahn's address again, arriving between 3pm and 4pm and staying until about 7 pm. Mrs Hahn laid some paper and envelopes on a table in the shop parlour at Muller's request.[37] Muller asked Hahn to write a letter in English to a contact of Muller's on the Continent who could help Hahn with a position. Hahn had been complaining that he could no longer exist on just his baker's shop, so he was tempted to help. After gaining Hahn's agreement, Muller wrote a secret letter in German using lemon juice. He later said that he showed Hahn how this was done:

> I said, 'I will show you the way to write to him, to write in lemon.' Mrs Hahn went away and me and Hahn was there upstairs and he got the lemon up from below from the baker's shop and I wrote a couple of pieces of paper and showed him how to put it on the fire, and I said 'You write a letter to Lybecq and you can see nothing of that'.[38]

Mrs Hahn heard her husband say, 'I will post it for you; there is a box just by my door.' She then saw him post the letter in the post box on the corner; again, the letter was intercepted by the post office.[39] The letter was written in Hahn's handwriting on paper watermarked 'Chariot' with a picture of Minerva driving a chariot; written in English in black ink.

Letter addressed to Mr Fr. Libecq,
Post Box 447,
Rotterdam, Holland.

London 21sr Febry, 1915.
154 Lewisham High Road.

Dear Francis,
Just a few lines to let you know I am still well and healthy and I trust this will find you the same. We have not felt much of the war here. John Wassal has also joined Kitchener's Army. How is Louis and

Carlos? I hope they are well, I will now close hoping you are well. I will now close hoping to hear from you soon.
I remain,
Your friend,
Charles Van Dyck.

The Lewisham address was that of Authur Norris Pring, a tea merchant and insurance broker who had never heard of Charles Van Dyck. Written on the back in invisible ink in German, in the same handwriting as the other letters found using this method, was the following message:

> The Dreadnoughts *Lion* and *Tiger* are lying at Chatham for repairs. Amongst the sailors a sickness has broken out which has claimed many victims some sort of inflammation in the nose. The total of men sick must run into some thousands. Provisions are being shipped to France via Newhaven. Many soldiers are being sent to the coast harbours, many are coming back from France, some wounded and some because they are on [leave]. I hope this week to receive from the Police my identity card and I shall then be able to go about freely. About 400,000 men will probably be sent over. (sgd) A.E. 111.[40]

But Muller was still hoping to return to Sunderland, and with this in mind he went to Bow Street police station's Alien Registration Office, where he saw Constable Edward Mugridge. Muller told him that he was a Russian subject and wanted to go to Sunderland, producing his Russian passport. The document appeared to be in order, and as there was no restriction against alien friends travelling to and from a prohibited area the officer stamped his card, but told him that on arrival he must report to the local police.[41] Muller must have been very pleased that Jessie Speir still considered him to be a true friend as she wrote in her letters of 8 and 18 February, 1915:

> We are all glad to hear that you are feeling so much better. In a couple of months time you will be quite as sprightly as ever you were, and I hope that you may be as happy. This war has been the means of knitting together many friendships, and ours is one of them is it not? What a glorious day that will be when mankind will be brothers all the world over? But that time is not yet.[42]
>
> * * *
>
> We shall be very pleased for you to come and see us again if you can arrange to do so with the military authorities. We have no desire to restrict you in any way, and shall be pleased to have you with us once again, but we strongly advise you to gain permission and then

there will be nothing to fear . . . I wonder if we shall be subjected to famine, now that the blockade has commenced. I was pleased to read your reassuring remarks about the inability of the Germans to do much.[43]

★　　★　　★

24.2.15.
Guildford Street

My dear little friend,
I am happy to inform you that I have got the permission from the Police authorities here to travel all over Great Britain as a good Alien. Now as I find London a grand city and plenty to be seen, still it is for me very dull, always alone! So you can hardly imagine how pleased I am to be able to travel about, visit my dear friend and have a good time all the way around. I am thinking to leave here on Saturday 10 o'clock and arrive in Sunderland about 4.10 afternoon so I am able to stay there till Monday. You being free of your hard working hours. I hope will have a jolly good promenade and pleasant hours and enjoyment for I think we all need some other attraction to lead our mind from this dreadful war.

My sincerely greeting to your dear family to Mr Dawson, Miss Cambell. I always remain.
Your true and sincere friend
C Muller.[44]

But Muller was now going to make a fatal mistake. He had involved Hahn, so that the handwriting on the letters changed, but this was to be his downfall, as Hahn was not a spy by nature and was out of his depth. He was unsettled and a simple man who had been told that Muller's contact might be able to get him a livelihood elsewhere. So he took it upon himself to write one more letter, which he signed in his own name! The main letter was written in black ink in English; the hidden information that he sent in German was described by the British as trash. It was just pure rumour that Hahn had picked up when overhearing sailors talking in a nearby public house.[45]

Mr Fr. Libecq,
Post Box 447,
Rotterdam, Holland.

235 Queen's Road,
Peckham, London.

Dear Francis,
I received your letter for which many thanks. I was glad to hear from

you after such a long time. I thought something had happened to you as I had not heard from you for such a long time but you have nothing to fear in Holland as your Country is neutral. We do not feel much of the war here, old England will show these Germans something. I must close now as I have an appointment to keep so trusting to hear from you soon.
I remain,
Your old friend,
Charlie Thompson

The Peckham address was that of Robert Tilbury, a registered medical practitioner who had lived at the address for 13 or 14 years and knew nothing of a Charlie Thompson.[46]
Written on the back in German using invisible ink:

In the absence of A.E. 111 I do myself the honour of informing you that on Thursday 25th about 4,000 to 5,000 men were collected in the Manchester canal and will be sent thence to Boulogne. In Deptford spotted fever has broken out amongst the troops; 550 men are already attacked. Eczema has got a strong hold of the Canadian horses; 50 cases per week succumb to this misery.
(sgd) Hahn[47]

On 24 February John Barr Fetherston, a clerk in the secretary's office of the GPO, examined this letter, postmarked Deptford SE at 12.15am that day, and found the secret writing.[48] It was sent on to Sir Basil Thomson at New Scotland Yard,[49] and after enquiries with Deptford police station it was not hard to trace Hahn, as he had a somewhat unusual name for the location. By a strange coincidence his shop was only a few yards from the reputed site of the tavern where Kit Marlowe, a British secret agent of centuries before, was stabbed to death.[50]
    That day Inspector George Riley of Special Branch at New Scotland Yard pulled up outside 111 High Street, Deptford. On entering the shop he saw Mrs Hahn and spoke to her while other officers searched the premises. Her husband was not at home. After the conversation the Inspector began to search the shop parlour. In this room was a chiffonier on which he found a green pen-holder, and on an inside shelf was a piece of lemon. It was still juicy and had the appearance of having been pierced at the top. In the top drawer he found a writing pad containing a number of sheets, one of which was blotting paper. By holding the blotting paper up to a looking glass he was able to read marks on it: M Muller, 38, Guildford St., Russell Square, WC! He could also decipher 'Dear Friend, I shall come to see you . . .' But Hahn's fate was sealed when the officer saw these words: 'Char[...]s

57

Thompson, 235, Queen's Road, Peckham, SE, London.' He also found that the paper had the watermark of Chariot Fine Wove brand. Searching further, a nib was found hidden behind a small clock.

The officer was now in for a long wait. He remained by the door from 2 until 10.30pm, when Hahn came in. He did not see Riley, who followed Hahn into the living quarters, saying, 'I am a police officer, and I have searched your house and found certain articles. Who are your friends and associates here?' Hahn wrote two names down on a piece of paper and said, 'Mr Muller is a friend of mine who I have visited today at Russell Square.' The inspector then showed Hahn the lemon, which was a shock to him as he exclaimed 'The lemon!' in a tone of surprise. The arrest was made and Hahn was searched, but nothing was found. Transport had been standing by to take the prisoner to Cannon Row police station for questioning.[51]

The next day, 25 February, at about 12.30pm Inspector Edward Parker of the Special Branch at New Scotland Yard went to Norfolk House, 38 Guildford Street. His enquiries revealed that Muller was a resident of room 42 and that he was not at home. He waited with his sergeant in the smoke room, which adjoined room 42, leaving other officers outside. After only 30 minutes Muller approached the front door and two young police officers followed him.[52] Muller was a tall, worried-looking man with a perpetual frown.[53] One of the officers said, 'Are you Mr Muller?' Muller replied, 'Yes.' 'Somebody wants to see you.' Muller said, 'All right', opened the door, and they all went in. Parker then made himself known to the suspect. 'Are you Mr Muller?' 'I am.' Parker said, 'I am a police officer. I am going to arrest you on suspician of espionage.' Muller replied, 'You are mistaken. I am a Russian subject and you will find all my papers in order.'[54]

He was then conducted to his room and a search was made. There was correspondence from Hahn, Miss Spier and Mr Dawson, and an envelope addressed to F.R.Libecq. In a small memorandum book was a list of addresses, including Post Box 447, Rotterdam and 111 High Street, Deptford. A dressing-table drawer revealed three pieces of lemon and some cotton wool, together with Manos and Swan fountain pens.[55] Muller said to one of the policemen, a Sergeant MacDonald, 'What is the meaning of this? I have done nothing out of the way. Look at the state of my nerves.' He held out his hands, saying, 'I have only recently come out of the German fortress at Westende where I have been interned four weeks by the Germans, and my health has been in a very bad state since.' MacDonald formed the opinion that he was nervous and shaky. The sergeant searched Muller, finding a lemon in his overcoat pocket.[56] Muller said that he had just gone out to buy some cigarettes and tobacco, and upon seeing a wagon in Guildford Street bought the lemon there.[57] When Parker asked what if was for, Muller pointed to his mouth and said 'My teeth.'[58] In a cardigan pocket was a list of seaports such as Portsmouth, Southampton, Hull, Dover and Plymouth. There was also a guide to the Tower of London. Little did Muller know when he bought it that he would soon be part of its rich history![59]

Some days later, Charles Ainsworth Mitchell, an expert in the chemistry of inks and writing fluids, was busy in the examination of the items found at both addresses. Upon looking at Hahn's green pen-holder he discovered that the nib had been lacquered, which would help to prevent corrosive action. Upon examination microscopically he saw on the surface cellular matter that corresponded to that of a lemon. The acid juice of a lemon would tend to corrode a nib gradually, eating out a slight amount of iron. If corrosion had taken place when the pen was returned to the lemon there would be a trace of iron left behind in the fruit. There is an absolute test for the presence of iron, known as the 'Prussian blue'. When he applied this test to the lemon found at Deptford, Mitchell obtained a result showing a very faint trace of the metal. He followed the same procedure with the black Manos pen from Muller's address. This was strongly corroded and contained iron, having the cellular matter of lemon on the nib. When he tested pieces of lemon from the room he got very pronounced reactions, suggesting that the nib had been pushed in and out of the lemon on many occasions. The ink-filler in the pen box was unused.[60,61]

The prisoners had been held at Cannon Row and were ignorant of each other's arrest. On 2 March instructions were given that they be taken to the Tower of London instead of Wellington Barracks. The orders stated that it was essential that they should be carefully guarded and not allowed to see or communicate with each other or any unauthorized person.[62] A report continued that it was equally desirable that no knowledge of their arrest should leak out until after 18 March, for reasons which were of the highest importance from the Admiralty point of view.[63] Much of the information obtained by Muller was correct, and as Sir George Aston was to write later, Muller was a most dangerous spy.[64] From 8 March to 19 March summaries of evidence were taken from witnesses in the Tower. And on 17 March an identification parade took place in the police hall in the Tower. Inspector Goatley reported that Muller was placed among nine other men of similar age and appearance, but the gatekeeper at Hendon aerodrome failed to identify the prisoner.[65]

As Hahn was a British subject they could not appear before a court martial so the trial took place at the Old Bailey the Central Criminal Court, on 2, 3 and 4 June, before the Lord Chief Justice of England. Muller pleaded not guilty of the charges, unlike Hahn. The case against him was solid and clear. Muller put forward a defence that he was collecting facts merely for the purpose of sending them over to a journalist who wanted information about the war.[66] He stated that he met this journalist, previously unknown to him, at a railway station in Flushing, Holland, when obliged to wait two-and-a-half hours in a waiting room. On the journey they got into conversation, and as a result Muller agreed to send on information, after being taught to write in lemon! He stated that all he sent was trash and imagination, anything but the truth, saying:

> At first I had confidence in the man, but when I come over here now I says to myself 'Muller, do not be a fool, it is dangerous ground you are working on. Write to him a lot of trash to keep a friend in case the war is over and you are ruined, then you can always fall back on him for this place as Interpreter.' In all my letters I wrote it is all trash. The Misses will tell you in the house where I live I never go out of the door, never, nobody come to me, only the representative Mr Wilson that is the only man comes to visit me once.[67]

He did under examination say, 'Naturally I knew I would get into trouble when I come and spy in a country.'[68] Muller also confirmed that his signal was 'A.E. 111.', details of which he had given to Hahn.[69] He also confirmed that he had shown Hahn how to write with lemon.[70]

Muller was found guilty of all charges after the jury had retired for only 20 minutes.[71]

Clerk of the Court: Prisoner at the Bar. You stand convicted of felony, Have you anything to say for yourself why the Court should not give you judgment according to law?

Muller: I only got to say that I am innocent. I never in my life had any intention to help the enemies. I cannot say no more; if you do not believe me all the chances is taken from me away. To give my proof is in Antwerp; I cannot get any things here; I am starving here helpless in a strange country. The jury convict me – what will I do; I am helpless; do with me what you like; yours is the power, and I am an individual alone before you. Keep me in gaol. Give me a chance after the war is over to obtain my proofs – that I have not got to die in my old age as a spy – give me a chance – keep me prisoner – give me another try to give me a chance to get my proofs over. That will prove my innocence. Give me a chance, I beg you, my lord – give me a chance, so I save my honour in my old days for my children. I can say no more.

The Lord Chief Justice: Prisoner at the Bar. The Jury have found you guilty, upon evidence which in the opinion of this court left them no possible alternative – they have found you guilty, not only of the offence with which you were charged, an offence against the security of the Realm, but they have also found, upon evidence which was clear, that you committed the offence with the intention of assisting the enemy. The court is of opinion that that finding, both regards the offence and the answer to the question as to whether you committed the offences with the intention of assisting the enemy, is absolutely correct, and the court is of opinion that that finding was one which the court itself arrived at if it is for the Court to come to that conclusion. Having found that the offence was committed with the intention of assisting the enemy, the sentence of the Court upon you is that you suffer the penalty of death; such sentence to be executed by shooting; the Court directs that you be handed over to the competent Military Authority for the execution of such sentence, as if it had been passed by a court martial. This sentence will not be carried into execution until after such time as is allowed by the Criminal Appeal Act for giving notice of appeal or notice of application for leave to appeal under that Act; and in the meantime, you will be imprisoned in His Majesty's Prison at Brixton, and the Sheriff of the County of London is hereby charged with your safe custody, and with the duty of handing you over at the expiration of such time to the competent Military Authority.

Muller was taken down and Hahn was brought up.

Clerk of the Court: Prisoner at the Bar. You stand convicted of felony. Have you anything to say why the Court should not give you judgment according to law?
The Lord Chief Justice: Prisoner at the Bar. You have pleaded guilty to offences under the Defence of the Realm Act, of a very serious nature. They are offences against the security of the State. The Court has taken into consideration in your case all the facts that have been placed before it by the Attorney General and by your counsel, and has come to the conclusion that it is impossible, even in view of the circumstances that have been submitted to our consideration, to pass a lighter sentence upon you than that you go to penal servitude for the term of seven years.
Hahn: Thank you, my Lord.[72]

On 9 June Field Marshal Sir Evelyn Wood received a letter from the headquarters of London district at Horse Guards.

You are no doubt aware that a German spy of the name of Muller was sentenced in the Central Criminal Court last week to be shot. I understand that he will in due course be handed over to me for execution.
    I write to ask you if you will allow me to carry it out in the Tower

61

of London as in the case of Lody. It is practically the only place in London convenient for the purpose, besides which it will have more effect on the country at large and possibly in Germany than an ordinary prison would have.

If you agree to this will you empower me to carry out all similar executions on my demand without further reference to you? If you prefer it I will of course refer to you on instructions for future executions.[73]

This was agreed, and from then on the Tower would be at the disposal of the military authorities for all future executions. Muller was to be put to death on 23 June, 1915.[74] On 21 June his appeal was turned down,[75] and the next day a report stated that Muller's solicitors were of the opinion that nothing more could be done for the prisoner and that as far as they were concerned the sentence could be carried out without delay.[76]

The Assistant Commissioner of Police at New Scotland Yard, Sir Basil Thomson, writes of Muller's end:

On 22 June, 1915, Muller was removed from Brixton Prison to the Tower in a taxi-cab, and by a curious fatality the cab broke down in Upper Thames Street. It was the luncheon hour, and a crowd formed immediately. A foreigner seated between two military policemen and going up the street towards the Tower was not lost on the crowd, which raised a cry of 'German spy'. Another taxi was quickly found, and the journey was resumed without further accident. The condemned man was highly strung, and he broke down on the night before his execution. On the following morning he pulled himself together, and insisted on passing gravely down the firing-party and shaking hands with each man.[7]

Prepared bullets were to be used at the execution, and orders were issued that the medical officer at the Tower of London should submit a confidential report as to their effects on the body, as information was required for future guidance as to the extent to which the top of the bullet should be filed and how else they should be prepared.[78] The report states:

On Wednesday, 23 June at 6am in the Miniature Rifle Range at the Tower, the prisoner was calm, shook hands with me and thanked me. I led him to the chair which was tied to short stakes driven into the ground, he sat on it quietly and the sergeant buckled a leather strap round his body and the back of the chair and then blindfolded him with a cloth. The firing-party consisted of eight guardsmen. I watched as closely as possible and went to him immediately after he was shot. I saw no expression of pain. I found no pulse and no sign of life. Death appeared to be instantaneous, and the body retained the same position. The bullets probably in fragments had passed through the thorax and out of the back. Some blood, mixed with what appeared to be pulverized bone, had escaped through the clothing and seven or eight drops had fallen to the ground. The body was carried on a stretcher into the isolation ward.

The body was then fully examined, but it is not the task or wish of the author to reproduce such gory detail for the reader. Suffice it to conclude with the final comments of the doctor:

From a humanitarian point of view I am of opinion that the execution was satisfactory. Death, due to shock, appeared to be instantaneous and therefore painless.[79]

The Germans did not hear of his death for some time, for letters containing remittances continued to be received.[80] The British secret service, unknown to the Germans, continued to use the cipher used by Muller to give false information, as a result of which they obtained considerable sums of money from the spy chiefs in Belgium. Out of the money the service bought a car, which, with grisly British humour, its officers called 'The Muller'![81]

CHAPTER 4

Haicke Petrus Marinus Janssen and Willem Johannes Roos

On 12 May, 1915, the SS *Estrom* docked at Hull, carrying on board Haicke Petrus Marinus Janssen.[1] He made his way to Percy's York Hotel, where he was seen by the proprietor, Alfred Percy. Janssen told him that he had come from Rotterdam and was a Dutchman. He was a traveller in cigars, being employed by his father. He was to stay until 20 May. Mr Percy got into conversation with his guest, who told him that he had been to sea as a mate, and had been presented with a watch for lifesaving.[2] The following day Janssen called at the central police station to register as an alien, where he was seen by PC Richard Cleveland. He told the officer that he was a Dutchman from Amsterdam and a traveller in cigars.[3] On 20 May he moved to London, staying at Cory's Hotel, 7 Spring Street, Paddington, but saying nothing to them about being a cigar merchant.[4]

By 22 May he had made his way to the Crown Hotel in Southampton, where he told the bookkeeper that he was a traveller in cigars. She remembered that for the first two days he did not go out much, and in fact was suffering from a very bad cold and had to spend some time in bed.[5] Nevertheless, Janssen had been busy, and the security services had reason to believe towards the end of May that the enemy was receiving information from Southampton. Suspicious telegrams were discovered, sent by a Janssen, purporting to deal with cigars. From their knowledge of codes used by enemy agents it was clear that these telegrams were capable of another interpretation.[6] For three days, on 26, 27 and 28 May, the telegrams were sent to Dierks & Co, Loosduinschekad Den Haag, a suspect address thought to be used by German intelligence.

26 May, 1915: 'Send immediately 4,000 Sumatra mark A.G.K. 4,000 Sumatra Havana B.Z. and samples Brasiel U.'

Interpretation: Four pattern large cruisers, four destroyers and some submarines were in the port of Southampton.

27 May, 1915: 'Further immediately 800 Sumatra Havana Tip-Top for own account.'
Interpretation:Eight troop transports were then lying in or about to leave the port of Southampton.

28 May, 1915: 'If to less give within lowest price for same quality by raise of 600.'
Interpretation: Six troop transports in addition to eight troop transports (mentioned in the previous telegram) were lying in or about to leave Southampton.

28 May, 1915: 'Send also samples mark Kara Mia Mexico Brasiel cigars Cigars Department.'
Interpretation: Ships carrying war materials were then in or about to leave the port of Southampton.[7]

As a result, on Saturday, 30 May, instructions were sent by telephone to the Southampton police to arrest Janssen at the address shown on the first telegram! So at 6.20pm Inspector John Thomas McCormack of the Southampton borough police made his way to the Crown Hotel. 'I arrested the prisoner on a landing outside this particular room; after I told him that I was going to take him to the police station he said, "Can I get my hat?" I said, "Where is it?" and he said, "In my bedroom." I said, "Yes, you can go into the bedroom but I am going with you" and he went to this particular room and got his hat off the bed in the room.

The Inspector found in the room three or four bags and several cardboard boxes; the boxes contained samples of cigars. Janssen was told he would be taken to the local Bargate police station. Janssen asked, 'What for?' and was told, 'As a suspected person.' He said, 'Who suspects me?' The Inspector said, 'I do among others.' 'What am I suspected of?' McCormack replied, 'Espionage.' Janssen said, 'I am a traveller in cigars.' However, he was later to tell the Inspector that he had not called on anyone in Southampton.[8]

On 30 May Bertram Sumpton, a detective sergeant from New Scotland Yard, travelled to Southampton to collect his prisoner and the property found in his possession.[9] Upon his return Inspector Edmond Buckly of Special Branch examined the items. There was a small attaché case containing some documents, a brown canvas portmanteau, and a brown paper bag in which was clothing and a Dutch passport showing that Janssen was a subject of the Netherlands, being a merchant born at Kampen in 1885. There was a military certificate, dated 20 November, 1910, showing that he had served in the national militia of the province of North Holland. There was also a draft telegram to Dierks & Co, and another from Dierks dated 19 May saying that Dierks were sending him £10. Another telegram from them dated 28 May to Janssen in Southampton stated that £20 was on its way. There were in total five receipts for telegrams sent from Southampton, plus a certificate from Dierks & Co stating that he was in their employ. There was also a duplicate order book, but it contained no orders.[10] In short, Janssen would have a lot of explaining to do!

However, Janssen was just the first of a two-man team that German intelligence had sent to Britain. On 30 April, 1915, Willem Johannes Roos informed the British vice-consul in Amsterdam that he intended to proceed to the UK with the intention of selling cigars.[11] Arriving at Tilbury on 13 May, he stayed in Aldgate, London, at the Three Nuns Hotel.[12] On 15 May he made his way to Newcastle and booked in the Turk's Head Hotel, where he remained until 18 May.

He then moved on to Edinburgh, staying until 27 May at the Rosebery Hotel, 99 Leith Street.[13] This was not very far from the port of Leith, where British naval vessels could be seen. Here Roos visited the aliens' department in the police detective office, where he saw James Sutherland, a sergeant in the Edinburgh city police. Roos told the officer that he was a cigar traveller for the firm of L. Dobbelman of Rotterdam. Asked on whom he was to call, Roos replied that he only came on chance and that he had not been in Edinburgh for 15 years. Upon further questioning he stated that he had seen service in the Dutch navy 1902–3.[14]

On 18 May Roos sent a telegram to Dierks at the Hague: 'Please send money soon as possible, Roos'. This was followed on 21 May by another: 'Have you received letters and dispatch? Roos.' These were intercepted by the GPO, as the name and address were very suspect with British intelligence, but they were allowed to go through. The authorities had to wait only until 24 May, when a picture postcard of His Majesty's Ship *Indefatigable* was intercepted, again addressed to Dierks: 'Wire lowest rate 10,000 Sumatra, S.S.; 2,000 Sumatra A.K.; 22,000 mixture C.I.F., Edinburgh.' by 26 May a telegraphic postal money order for £25 arrived for Roos at the Rosebery Hotel from Dierks & Co. There was a description of the firm as 'General Export Agents – Export and Commission Agents'.[15] At the same time other wires were collected and examined, and it was discovered that each one was sent from a naval port.

Moving on to Aberdeen, Roos booked in at Sutties Hotel on Union Street, where he stayed just two days. On 27 May he went to the aliens' department at the central police station of Aberdeen city police, where he saw John Wightman, a police inspector. He again said that he was a cigar traveller, but this time told the officer that he was employed by Dierks & Co of The Hague.[16] His next journey was to Inverness, where he booked in at Neish's Temperance Hotel on 29 May and reported to PC Donald Mann of Inverness borough police to be registered there as an alien. He said that he was a cigarette merchant.[17] At dinner Roos got into conversation with a chartered accountant by the name of William Gunn. Roos told Gunn that he was a Hollander, and that he was on a commercial visit to see what prospects there were in selling cigars. On friendly terms, they later took a car drive along the Dingwall Road which skirts the Beauly Firth. During the journey Roos said to his new-found friend 'that he understood that Kitchener's army was not out of Britain yet'.[18] During the journey no British navy ships were seen – Gunn could remember that there might have been just a passing coal-boat. Roos returned to London on 1 June, and once again put up at the Three Nuns Hotel.

Vernon Kell was by now hotly on the trail of Ross. He, like Janssen, was using an ingenious code to transmit information about British ships. It appeared that naval ports suddenly craved cigars. But what the Germans failed to understand was that the seamen and others who lived in seaports were hardly ever smokers of cigars, favouring pipes and cigarettes!

On 2 June, 1915, Albert Fitch, an Inspector in the Criminal Investigation Department at New Scotland Yard, went to the Three Nuns Hotel in Aldgate to take Roos into custody. Fitch said to him, 'I am a police officer, and shall arrest you on a charge of espionage.' Roos made no reply. They then went to his room, number 33, where the officer searched his prisoner but found nothing of importance. The room was searched; two locked kitbags were confiscated and conveyed with Roos to New Scotland Yard, where they were handed over to Inspector Buckley for examination. On the way Roos said to Fitch, 'I cannot understand this. I am a traveller in cigars, but I have smoked all my samples, as there is no business in Dutch cigars in this country.'[19]

The bags were then examined by Inspector Edmond Buckley. In them he found a passport; a cigar list in the name of Louis Dobbelman, Rotterdam; a document written in pencil, which appeared to be details of expenses, beginning on 9 April; a pocket book containing a number of notes in pencil, with details of hotels; and a note, 'Mr Mitchell, Glasgow, 28.000, Sumatra S.S., 8,000 Sumatra, M.G.K., 8,000 Sumatra, M.K.K., 16,000 Sumatra, H.B.T., 8,000 Sumatra, H.B.U., 23,000 Sumatra, H.H.D.'

There were also blank memoranda forms with the heading Dierks &

Co, and a Pearson's Magazine for May, 1915, which contained an article entitled 'Plain facts about the Naval War', and some pictures of warships. Written in pencil on page 471 were the names of various ships – *Ajax, Defence, Colossus, New Zealand, Dreadnought, Bat, Iron Duke, Cyclops, Neda, Hiberina, Legion* and *Collingwood*.[20]

In the meantime Charles Ainsworth Mitchell of Amersham, the chemist who had examined Muller's and Hahn's pens and a man who had devoted years of study to the chemistry of inks, examined the documents found on Roos. He first tested to see if there were any sections which were written in any way differently from the rest of the writing. When he checked the note of personal expenses, which was written in pencil, he found two lines on the back which were written in ink, and these attracted his attention at once. The writing was in ordinary ink, so he tested in between the lines for invisible writing. There was nothing to be seen with the naked eye. Ainsworth then tested for scent writing or for a substance that behaved like scent. He obtained figures which appeared in exactly the same way as scent writing does; that is to say, it flashed up through the developer, gradually obtained its maximum intensity, and then faded. He made a note of the figures obtained. He found in the middle of the line a '4' and then in large letters 'K.S.M.'; to the right of that was a letter 'B' and above that in microscopic letters 'S d'; and above that and to its left the figures '34'.

When he saw this, Mitchell decided that it was time to get another witness of these results. He went to the censor's office and asked for the assistance of a trained eye, one accustomed to reading and looking at documents: a Miss Kate Knight was put at his disposal. In her presence Mitchell developed other areas with her, handing the brush and reagent to her to develop these parts. More numbers and figures were found recorded, and the record was signed by Miss Knight. Mitchell was of the opinion that the Roos document was similar to a document developed into a map. The inference was that the figures and numbers referred to places.[21, 22]

On 3 June at New Scotland Yard both Janssen and Roos were interrogated by the Assistant Commissioner of Police, Sir Basil Thomson, together with Captain Hall, Major Drake and Lord Herschell.[23] Sir Basil Thomson writes as follows:

Janssen was questioned first. He was a self-possessed person of about 30 years of age, and he claimed to be a sailor. He knew no German, in fact he had never been in Germany, and being a Dutchman, he had a dislike for Germans. Why, he was asked, did his employers, Dierks & Co, engage a sailor to travel in cigars? To that he had no answer except that he had been unsuccessful in obtaining a berth as officer on a steamer. A friend had introduced him to Mr Dierks because he could speak English and was looking for work. He said that he was the traveller that Dierks had in England. We asked him whether he knew a man named Roos. 'No,' he said, he had never heard of him. He was then sent to another room while Roos was brought in.[24]

Algernon Sprackling, a police constable in the Criminal Investigation Department, took shorthand notes which he later transcribed into narrative form.

I am 32 years of age, and I am in the employ of a Dutch firm of cigar and provision merchants named Dierks. I went to them about 15 April last. I saw an advertisement in the paper, I answered it, and I was directed to go to the Hague, where I saw Mr Dierks. His premises consisted of three or four rooms upstairs. I only saw one clerk, a typist, a boy and Mr Dierks himself. It was two houses. I saw samples of cigars etc. there. It is quite a big shop. He was going to pay me ten per cent commission on what I sold, and travelling expenses. He gave me £25 to come to England. I have been a steward on board a ship, and a long time ago was a seaman. I have been to Liverpool before. I brought 125 cigars with me. I landed in London three weeks ago today. I stayed here four days, but could not do any business, as they only wanted Havana cigars. I went to two shops in Whitechapel, but forget the names. I then went to Edinburgh. I have a friend there named Murass, a Dutchman who became naturalized.

I did not go to Hull. I received a letter from a friend of mine who was living at the York Hotel, Anlaby Road, Hull. His name is Janssen, but he has no connection with my firm. I know him quite well. I did not see him, although I knew he was in England. I went to Aberdeen. My firm sent me there, and it was the first time I had been there. I have been to Inverness, but did not go to Dingwall. I did not go to Glasgow. I ordered some cigars in Edinburgh, between 24,000 and 26,000 I think. I got there about 14 days ago. I have been in Tain. I went there to see the Scottish islands. I arrived at Tain at about 10 o'clock, and left again at 10.30. I was there last Monday. I sent one or two telegrams from Edinburgh. One order for cigars and another for money. I had about £11 left. I was about seven days in Edinburgh. I had about £25 sent to me last Tuesday. It was in the form of a postal telegraph money order.

I met a gentleman in Edinburgh, named Mitchell, who told me that he was a Glasgow tobacco merchant, and that he wanted 24,000 cigars. He promised to meet me at an Aberdeen hotel. I left

69

a letter for him at the Sutties Hotel, Aberdeen, but I have not heard from him since. I met him first in a theatre. He spoke to me and I told him I was a stranger and was trying to sell cigars. He said he would take some if I supplied a price list. I wired to Holland for the price list, and next day he ordered 24,000 cigars. I sent postcards from Edinburgh, and also two letters. I did not post any newspapers or magazines. They were short letters saying there was nothing to do in Edinburgh. They were of no importance.

I have never been to Bristol but I intended going there. My firm did not tell me to go to Bristol to sell cigars. I have not yet received the cigars I ordered. I know the ordinary price of these cigars, but I wanted a special price list for a quantity. The magazine does not belong to me. I wrote the words in the margin. I served in the Dutch navy 12 years ago. I have never served in the German navy. When I came to London I was going to apply for a permit to go home. I have done my work. I wanted to go home because I had spent a lot of money and had done no business.

I know Janssen very well, and I saw him just now. [The paper with figures and initials thereon was produced and Roos said it was a price list and the initials in the margin mean the districts where the tobacco is grown.] The last time I met Janssen was in a restaurant in Amsterdam, and I did not know that he was coming to England. I gave him my address in Newcastle. I got the address I was going to from a hotel book. Janssen wrote me a letter that he had arrived in England, that he was in Hull, and intended going to London. I have not got that letter. I am not a German, but am a real Dutchman born in Holland.[25]

Sir Basil Thomson continues:

Janssen was brought again into the room. He made a faint sign with his eyes and lips to Roos, but of course it was too late. 'Is this the man you say you know?' he was asked. He nodded, and Janssen was silent. On the way over to Cannon Row Roos suddenly dashed at a glass door which opened into the yard, smashed the panes, and jabbed his naked wrists on the jagged fragments of glass in the hope of cutting an artery. He was taken to Westminster Hospital to be bandaged, and later was removed to Brixton Prison, where he was put under observation as a potential suicide.[26]

On Saturday, 5 June secret and urgent orders were sent by command of the Army Council that Janssen and Roos, who were detained on a serious charge of espionage, were to be detained in the Tower of London, and that the prisoners should be carefully guarded with a view

70

to preventing any attempt to commit suicide, especially Roos as he was shamming insanity.[27] The same day Colonel Lionel Boyle of the 2nd Honourable Artillery Company took over custody of the prisoners, one being confined in the cell of the main guard, and the other in married quarters. The Tower then had three prisoners, the third being Robert Rosenthal,[28] who was to be the only First World War spy to be executed outside the Tower of London, in his case by hanging. By 9 June instructions were given that the three prisoners were to be moved from the Tower by Major Lord Athlumney, Assistant Provost Marshal, London District, to the military detention barracks at Wandsworth.[29]

Janssen faced his court martial on Friday, 16 July, 1915, at the Guildhall, Westminster, before Lord Cheylesmore. It lasted just one day.[30] He faced four charges of attempting to communicate information calculated to be useful to the enemy. The evidence was clear and experts stated that cigars would never be kept and transported in cardboard boxes, as they would spoil.[31] What is more, the names of the cigars used by the defendant were unknown-[32] The defence counsel, Mr Eustace Fulton, called no witnesses in Janssen's defence and he gave no evidence himself, saying, 'I am sure I need not remind the court that in this country it is not upon any accused person to prove anything at all; it is no part of an accused person's duty to prove that he is not guilty; it lies upon those who are the accusers to prove that he is guilty.'[33]

After retiring to consider their verdict they returned at 4.55pm.

The President: Has the accused any statement to make or anything to say on his behalf

Janssen: All I say is this I am honoured for saving life at sea and that speaks to my favour. All I want to say is whether it is in English language or German language it is impossible; it is not for me it is for Mr Roos; he sent it to me. I have my price list and I do not understand any of those letters and told him at the same time. I know that I have got a reply from Mr Dierks to send those letters and so I have done. I had notice by the ship in Southampton and then I had a letter from Dierks. He told me to get a seller of 10 million cigars and you will find out that all the telegrams together represent 10 million and 200 cigars ordered by letter and telegrams has nothing whatever to do with ships of war altogether. I was selling cigars in England.

The President: Is that all you have to say?

Janssen: Yes, sir.

71

	Lieutenant George Charles Peevor [see p.88] was sworn.
The President:	Have you any evidence to give as to the character of the accused?
Peevor:	I have no evidence either for or against him with the exception of his own statement that he received a medal for saving lives. I have made some enquiries and find his statement is true. He received a medal for saving lives from the *Volteria*, which was burning in the Atlantic last October. The statement as to that is correct.
The President:	Was that a British ship?
Peevor	A British ship; he received it from the British government.[34]

With that Janssen was taken away to learn his fate at a later date.

The following day, Saturday, 17 July, 1915, Willem Johannes Roos appeared before his general court martial. This was also held at the Guildhall, Westminster, and once more the president was Lord Cheylesmore. He faced one charge of attempting to communicate information calculated to be useful to the enemy with respect to the disposition and movement of certain ships and troops. He pleaded not guilty.

The evidence against him was summarized:

At Edinburgh on the 25th May 1915 [you] sent a telegram addressed to Dierks, Loosduinschekade, 166 Den Haag in the following terms, that is to say 'Wire lowest rate 10,000 Sumatra, S.S., 2,000 Sumatra A.K., 22,000 mixture C.I.F. Edinburgh' meaning thereby that ten battleships and two old cruisers being ships of His Majesty were then in or about to leave the neighbourhood of Edinburgh, and that there were then in Edingburgh 22,000 troops of His Majesty being partly cavalry and partly infantry.[35]

Evidence was given as to his movements since his arrival in Britain. Two experts in the cigar trade, with between them 30 or 40 years' experience, were called to give evidence, as a result of which it became clear that Roos's knowledge of the subject was very limited.[36,37]

As in the case of Janssen, Major Reginald John Drake was sworn in and examined by Mr Muir.

Q.	Are you a Major on the General Staff of the War Office?
A.	Yes.

Q. Have you experience in decoding telegrams?
A. Yes.
Q. Will you look at exhibit No 32. [Handed.] Have you endeavoured to decode it?
A. Yes; it was decoded in the prisoner's presence.
Q. Do you produce that decoding, which shows the German words and the English equivalent of the decoding?
A. Yes.
Q. Does it read in this way: 'Sumatra S.S.' means 'Battleships'?
A. Yes, in German.
Q. The German words?
A. '*Schlaht Schiffe.*'
Q. 'AL'?
A. '*Alte Linienschiffe*' – 'Old ships of the line'.
Q. 'A.G.K.'?
A. '*Alte grosse kreuzer*' – 'Old large cruisers'.
Q. 'K.K.'?
A. '*Kleiner kreuzer* – 'Small cruiser'
Q. 'M.K.K.?'
A. '*Moderner kleiner kreuzer*' – 'Modern small cruiser'.
Q. 'Sumatra Havana'?
A. 'B.U.' – '*Unterseeboot*' – 'submarine'; 'B.T.' – 'Torpedo Boat'; 'B.Z.' – '*Zerstörer*' – 'Destroyer'; 'T.T.' – '*Truppen Transport*' – Troop transport'; 'H.D.' – '*Handels Dampfer*' – 'Merchant steamer'.
Q. Under the heading 'Mexico'?
A. I interpret those as reading: 'S.D.' – 'Sunderland'; 'N.S.S.' – 'North Shields'; 'S.S.H.' – 'South Shields'; 'N.C.' – 'Newcastle'; 'E.D.' – 'Edinburgh'; 'A.D.' – 'Aberdeen'; 'C.R.Y.' – 'Cromarty'; 'I.V.' – 'Inverness'; 'O.W.' might mean 'Orwell', on which Harwich stands; 'C.H.' – 'Chatham'; 'S.R.' – 'Sheerness'.
Q. Under the heading 'Mexico Brasiel'?
A. I take the words, 'p.f. – '*Pferde*' – 'Horse'; 'M.T.' – '*Munition*' – 'Munitions'; 'G.S.' – '*Geschütze*' – 'Guns'; 'K.M.' – '*Kriegs-Material*' – 'War material'; 'L.E.' – '*Lebensmittel*' – 'Supplies in the way of eatables'.
Q. 'Brasiel'?
A. 'C.L.' – 'Calais'; 'H.A.' – 'Havre'; 'D.P.' – 'Dieppe'; 'B.X.' – 'Bordeaux'; 'U.B.' – '*Unbekannt*' –

'Unknown'; 'A.E.' – the German way of spelling 'Egypt'.

Q.   *'Vorstenlanden?'*

A.   'A.T.' – 'Artillery', the same as the English, with a slight variation of the spelling; 'I.F.' – 'Infantry'; 'K.V.' – *'Kavallerie'*; it is spelt with a 'K' in German; 'G.E.' – 'Genie' – 'Engineers'. 'Mixture' I took to mean 'Troops of all arms'.

Q.   Was a telegram, exhibit No 18, submitted to you for decoding?

A.   Yes; that was produced to me on my instructions for search for all telegrams sent to the name of Dierks.

Q.   And how did you decode it?

A.   I took that to refer to ten battleships, two old cruisers, and 22,000 mixed troops cavalry and infantry, which were, on the date the telegram was sent, at or near Edinburgh, or, in the case of ships, about to leave it.

Q.   At the War Office, where you are employed, do they keep records of the situation of His Majesty's ships at given dates?

A.   Yes.

Q.   Are those records open to your inspection when you require them?

A.   Yes.

Q.   Have you inspected them for this particular date, 25 May, with regard to Edinburgh?

A.   Yes; a special return was called for with regard to the Forces in Edinburgh on that date.

Q.   What did you find with regard to the Forces in and around Edinburgh on that date?

A.   That there was in Edinburgh a depot of the Lothian and Border Horse, which is a mounted unit to the strength of 65 men; that there were in the immediate neighbourhood, and in Edinburgh, that is to say, in the Edinburgh and Forth Defences, a total of 18,128 officers and men, exclusive of men on furlough who might be there. I am afraid the figures are different from that given at the preliminary enquiry, as, owing to the form in which the return was rendered, an addition was made of a figure which was included in this total. The exact total is 18,128 on that date.

Q.   Were they all of one kind, or how would you describe them?

A. Well, the Lothian and Border Horse are of course a mounted unit.

Q. What other kinds of troops were there?

A. The others are infantry, included in that return. There would be also gunners, who are not included in that return; it was not asked for.

Q. Would it be correct to describe them as mixed troops?

A. Yes.

Q. And 18,000 odd is only 4,000 off 22,000.

A. Yes.[38]

Again, as in Janssen's case, Captain William Reginald Hall, the Director of the Intelligence Department at the Admiralty, Whitehall, was called to give evidence and be examined by Mr Muir.

Q. Will you look please at the postcard. Is that a photograph of His Majesty's ship *Indefatigable*?

A. Yes.

Q. Where was that ship on 24 May, 1915?

A. At Rosyth.

Q. Where is Rosyth with regard to Leith?

A. Close to Edinburgh.

Q. It is on the opposite side, is it?

A. On the opposite side to Leith.

Q. On the opposite side of the Forth. How long is the journey from Edinburgh to Rosyth?

A. You can do it in a taxi in about 12 minutes.

Q. Is there a train runs across?

A. A train runs across the bridge.

Q. And that postcard bearing that picture was posted in Edinburgh on 24 May?

A. Yes.

Q. I want to ask you with reference to battleships in the neighbourhood of Edinburgh on 25 May. Were there any battleships there on that day?

A. Yes.

Q. About how many?

A. About ten.

Q. Any old cruisers?

A. Yes.

Q. About how many?

A. Well, there were a good number of old cruisers.

Q. More than two?

A. More than two, yes.

<table>
<tr><td>Q.</td><td>Would an observer on the Leith side have an opportunity of seing any of those vessels?</td></tr>
<tr><td>A.</td><td>He would not be able to count them if he were below the bridge.</td></tr>
<tr><td>Q.</td><td>And, in a train going across the bridge, would they be able to see them?</td></tr>
<tr><td>A.</td><td>Yes.</td></tr>
<tr><td>Q.</td><td>I do not know, but do they keep the blinds down?</td></tr>
<tr><td>A.</td><td>Only at night.</td></tr>
<tr><td>Q.</td><td>On the Rosyth side would they have a better view?</td></tr>
<tr><td>A.</td><td>They have a better view on the Queensferry side.</td></tr>
<tr><td>Q.</td><td>Do any of His Majesty's ships visit the Beauly Firth?</td></tr>
<tr><td>A.</td><td>Cromarty Firth, yes.</td></tr>
<tr><td>Mr Eustace
Fulton:</td><td>Is that the same as Beauly Firth – Cromarty?</td></tr>
<tr><td>A.</td><td>It is the same.</td></tr>
<tr><td>The President:</td><td>Your question was Beauly.</td></tr>
<tr><td>Mr Muir:</td><td>Yes; the road which runs from Inverness along the Firth; is that a place you would see ships if they were there?</td></tr>
<tr><td>A.</td><td>The road from Inverness, yes, going up to Tain, you would see ships.</td></tr>
<tr><td>Q.</td><td>Is Tain a place where one would have an opportunity of seeing His Majesty's ships?</td></tr>
<tr><td>A.</td><td>Yes.</td></tr>
<tr><td>Q.</td><td>Would the information as to the numbers and classes of ships to be seen about Edinburgh be of use to the enemy?</td></tr>
<tr><td>A.</td><td>Of the utmost use.</td></tr>
<tr><td>Q.</td><td>Would the fact that ships are absent from the neighbourhood of Tain be of use to the enemy?</td></tr>
<tr><td>A.</td><td>Yes.[39]</td></tr>
</table>

Mr Eustace Fulton would call no witnesses for the defence; indeed, Roos himself was not to be called. After the defence barrister's summing up the Judge Advocate decided that there was no need for him to add anything, so the court adjourned to consider its decision at 1.15pm.[40] Upon returning just ten minutes later, Mr Eustace Fulton stated:

The prisoner has handed to me a list of places where he says he was confined as a lunatic, between the years 1909 and 1913. I propose to hand the list to the court, in case they should desire to have any enquiry made with regard to it.

The defence further stated that they had had no opportunity of making any enquiries into the matter. Major Drake said that he had no knowledge of this before; and they could get it verified through the Foreign Office by the Legation at the Hague, and that he would get a cable off that afternoon.

The document read:

Asylum Medemblik. From 14th. February 1909 to 26th. August 1909; sickness paranoia. From 29th. August to 26th. September 1909, sickness, hysteric excess. From 5th. October to January 1910, hysteric excess. From May 1910 to September 1910, sickness, hysteric excess. On October 10th. through High Court, not responsible. Declared and sended to an asylum at Castricum; remained there till 15th. January, 1913.[41]

The President asked Roos if he had anything to say, and Roos replied:

No, sir; I have only to say that I was not sent out for spying. I have been in Newcastle, and I have been in Edinburgh and Aberdeen and Inverness, and it must be very strange from all the ports from England and all the places – do you understand me? Then about the price list. Mr Dierks engaged me, and he said 'You are a traveller,' and I said 'I am not,' and he said 'I will let you know in a few days,' and after a few days he wrote me a letter at Amsterdam, and he said to me: 'You will have to travel in England, and I will give you commission. We will help you soon. If you arrive in England you will meet one of our agents', and he told me his name; he was living in a hotel in Bristol. I have his name in my pocket book, but if I arrive in London I write a letter to Messrs Dierks that there was nobody and no letters.

And the I went to Newcastle and stopped two or three days at the Hotel Turks's Head; and then I went to Edinburgh; and then I went to see my sister's previous employer; he wanted a teacher for his children last year, and he wrote to my sister. On Saturday afternoon I am in Edinburgh, and I meet a gentleman; his name was Mitchell, belonging to Glasgow, tobacconist, and he says to me 'I believe you are a stranger;' I says, 'I am a traveller for a house which only require for Havana cigars and Manila tobacco, and nothing for Borneo.' Then he said, 'Can I see you tomorrow morning?' I said, 'Yes.' He said, 'Outside the Post Office.' I said, 'Come up to my hotel,' and he said, 'If you be so kind, meet me at the Post Office,' and I met him at the Post Office, and he said to me, 'Do you carry a price list?' and I said, 'Yes.' I showed him the price list, and he wrote on a small piece of paper, and he said, 'Send this to Mr Dierks,' and I send the

77

telegram away. 'He promised to travel with me to Edinburgh, and he talked about an order – he wanted to know the price of 12,000 Havana cigars in Edinburgh, and I said, 'I will let you know at the Hotel,' and I never seen him back.

Then I went to Inverness. My firm say, 'You have to go to Inverness,' and I have been to Inverness, and I first thought if I have come I have been here, and then the message came from the land-lady on Sunday: 'This is a nice day; I have a stranger here from Glasgow; you get a fine road to Beauly.' Mr Gunn had an automo-bile, and Mr Gunn invited me to go to Beauly; on the Tuesday morning I leave Inverness to London, and goes to your Home Office and ask for a permit to go across, and the same afternoon I was detained by some officers, detectives from New Scotland Yard. My price list; I am certain selling in Holland cigars with letters and tobacco, and I ask Mr Dierks what was the meaning, and he said, 'Oh, they are different prices of cigars, and I ask Mr Mitchell, 'Do you know our firm?' He said, 'No, I know Mr Dierks well. I knew he was in the Grays Inn Road, London years ago.' That is all.

On being asked if that was all he had to say, Roos continued:

Yes, that is all I have to say. I told them at New Scotland Yard. I am a very nervous man, you know. I was sent out by somebody. I was sent out and told, 'You must have been to look after warships, and you have to look after troop transports.' No, I never have been a spy. I know I am a Dutch subject, and never would be a spy, never in my life. If you declare me guilty or not – there is much against me – there is much against me. My health; I give you there my state-ment about my sickness, and behind me is the High Court in The Hague, which declared me no trust responsible. I am a man, but you can do with me what you like, and I have never been in England for spying. I married a Belgian woman.[42]

With that the prisoner was removed and the President thanked learned counsel for the way in which they had conducted the case in the some-what unpleasant duty they had to perform.

Roos, like Janssen, was sentenced to death by shooting.[43] An inves-tigation with regard to Roos's mental history produced nothing calling for a modification of this sentence.[44] Janssen expressed a desire to make a disclosure regarding the German secret service system,[45] no doubt to save his life, and two officers were sent to Wandsworth prison to inter-view him. But, as they expected, he was unable to supply any information of value.[46] The King, on a submission dated 26 July, 1915, thereupon confirmed the findings and sentences of the court, and commanded that they be carried into effect.[47] Orders were issued that the prisoners be removed under escort from Wandsworth detention barracks to the Tower of London early in the morning of 29 July.[48] Roos and Janssen were then told of their fate, and subsequently visited by the consulate general for the Netherlands with his vice consul and a clergyman of the Dutch Church from the local Austin Friars. They were to assist as witnesses in case the men wanted to make their wills, which they did. Roos received spiritual comfort, but Janssen, being a Roman Catholic, had already seen a priest. The consul wrote later that both confessed to him that they were guilty of the charges; they wished him to convey their thanks to the commandant of Wandsworth military prison for the kindness shown to them, and to express their regret to the British government that they had allowed themselves to be used by Dierks.[49]

They were to be shot at 6am and 6.10am by a detachment of the Scots Guards; not in the miniature rifle range this time but in the Tower ditch.[50, 51] An account of the double execution is as follows:

On 30 July there was a scene in the Tower of London which for grimness was never surpassed during the war. In the early dawn Janssen was led forth to face the firing-party. His iron nerve, which had not deserted him throughout, held good to the finish and he died as he had lived, a brave man.

[Ten minutes later Roos was brought forward.] His alleged insanity had by this time departed. He had regained his normal self and eyed the fatal chair, from which the bleeding body of his accomplice had just been removed, with a fair show of indifference, begging leave to finish the cigarette he had requested as a last favour. That ended, he took one last look at it, then threw it away with a gesture which represented utter contempt for all the frailties of this world. With apparently no more interest in the proceedings, he seated himself in the chair. There was a momentary twingeing of the face as they fastened the bandage around his face, but that was all. He too died bravely, and met his fate with a courage which could evoke nothing but admiration.[52, 53]

CHAPTER 5

Ernst Waldemar Melin

Ernst Waldemar Melin, a Swede, was 49 in 1915. He was the son of Olaf Melin, who had been a member of the Swedish Parliament for 30 years and owned a shipping company business in Gothenburg, trading with England. Ernst Melin was always to maintain that his brother was a colonel in the Swedish army.

In June, 1887, Melin came over to London for just over a year, returning to enter his father's business, the Angfartugs Aktiebolaget, Thule Steamship Company. There he remained, working as an active and energetic member of the firm; eventually he became a partner, resulting in the firm being renamed Olaf Melin & Son. Unfortunately he acquired the habits of drink and drugs, and as a result his health gave way in 1906. He could no longer be associated with his father's business, being regarded as an impossible person to employ. This led to him taking the cure at various health resorts. His father helped him financially, and he made his way to Paris, where he stayed for one year from 1908–9, before returning to London in 1910.[1] Later, through the influence of a friend (an important ship-owner in Sweden who was later to become Minister of the Navy), he obtained an appointment in a shipbroker's office at Nikolaieff in Russia. But when war was declared in August, 1914, his employment in the export of grain from Russia stopped. All the offices closed and the clerks were dimissed. Melin returned to Gothenburg, going on to visit his parents in Stockholm, where they had retired. His father was by then 81 years of age. He stayed just two days. Ernst told his father that he might go to Hamburg, Germany, in an attempt to find work, as he had friends there of many years' standing. He had lived in the city as a young man in 1886.

But his connections in Hamburg were of little help in finding employment, for his friends had left. He still had a small salary from Russia, but it was not enough for him to live on, and his father wrote that he should not look forward to further help. No doubt having been sorely tried in the past, in declining to give Ernst further money he had acted as many fathers would do under the circumstances; his patience was exhausted. But he still had one friend in Hamburg, a Swedish commission agent named Gerdes who was very well known in the city. Melin had lived with a relation of Gerdes who knew, as Melin put it, 'I was looking out for a berth.'

One day Gerdes sent a note to Melin asking if he would lunch with him, as he had something to propose. At the lunch Melin was introduced to five or six Germans. After the meal it was suggested that Melin and one of the Germans should talk business in Gerde's private room. Melin agreed, and the German suggested that he should go to London in order to try and find out naval and military secrets. Melin said that he was rather perplexed and that he could not decide there and then, but would let him know the answer the next day, when the German again called on him. Melin was concerned that, as help from his father had stopped, he would have to stand on his own feet, which would not be easy without employment. The next day he accepted the German's offer.

Melin then made his way to Antwerp, where he saw Dierks, who told the Germans that Melin had arrived. A meeting was arranged with a Captain Lieutenant Larsson, who concerned himself with naval matters, and a man called Schnitzer, an officer not on active service who spoke of army interests.

Melin was to say:

> Then they say to me they were pleased to see me, and asked if I would go to London to act for them. As far as I could understand what most appealed to them was the navy. They spoke more about the navy than about the army. Then they said to me that I should try to go to the ports round England and Scotland and try to find out what I can.

According to Melin, he told the Germans that he did not want to go round the ports, and eventually they said, 'Never mind, you go over to London and do what you can for us. Have a try.' It was agreed that he should return in a fortnight. He was provided with a code, a Baedeker guide book and about £30. After his training in naval ship identification, he left Rotterdam for London on the Batavier Line, arriving at Tilbury.

Melin made his way to the Charing Cross Hotel, intending to stay the next day at the Strand Palace, but it was full. In a copy of the *Daily Telegraph* he found an advert for a boarding-house at 23 Upper Park Road, Hampstead:[2]

HAMPSTEAD. Belsize Tube – Comfortable English Home offered. Young society. Conversation, music. Single or double rooms. Inclusive. Moderate terms.[3]

This was a convenient location, being not far from Belsize Park tube station on the Northern Line. He made his way there on 12 January, 1915, and asked the boarding-house keeper, Flora Milligan (who had kept house with her sister Eliza for 14 years), if she would let him have a room. He said that he was Swedish, had been in the shipping trade and was in London to seek a position as he was not employed at that time. A room was available and Melin settled in. He did not get up as early as some: it was often as late as 10am before he had his breakfast. Flora Milligan was told that he had to go into the city to obtain his correspondence. Sometimes he would be back after lunch, but on occasions not until after dinner had been served. Melin paid in advance for bed, breakfast and evening meals, lunches being extra. He became very good at bringing in treats for all, in the way of cigarettes, cigars, sweets and fruit.

Flora formed the opinion that Melin was not what she would call strong or a very energetic person of the type who was always rushing here, there and everywhere; rather, he was one who took things very easy. However, he was friendly to all and was very open in conversation with the other boarders.[4]

During his stay at Upper Park Road Melin often spoke to them about the benefit of using lemon juice on his face after shaving. He had tender skin and found it very soothing.[5] However, the strange thing was he went out to be shaved. Flora Milligan was to say that he never shaved in the house, but went to Cranfield's opposite Belsize Park tube station, where there was a paper shop and tobacconist, behind which could be found the barber.[6]

Melin was to maintain that during the fortnight following his arrival at Upper Park Road he went to the City nearly every day to see friends. He was later to agree that he reported what he had seen to Rotterdam, such as the names and insignia on soldiers, and the names on sailor's caps, but he did not leave London. He also sent over details of searchlights and the fact that zeppelins had been flying over London. After these two weeks Melin went back to Rotterdam, going on to Antwerp where he saw his German contacts and Dierks once more.

Then they say to me I think it is not what we want; they say to me. 'We are not satisfied' because I had not gone to the ports which seemed to them the most valuable thing to have. Then they say, 'We do not want you to live in London; we want you to travel round the coast and try to find out things useful to us.' Then I say to them,

82

'No, I do not want to do that.' I said, 'I will stop in London.' Then they said, 'All right, think it over the night and come back tomorrow and let us know.' When I came up the following morning I say to them that I thought it all over, I knew already yesterday what I had decided but I am not going to accept it and goodbye.

Then they said, 'All right; we think it is the best thing too.' Then they gave me money to go back to London to fetch my luggage, the things I had left, and go back to Hamburg. They gave me so little money that I had hardly money to go back. I came to London one night and left the following night by the same steamer.

Melin made his way to Rotterdam, where he saw the German consul, Neist, in company with Dierks. The consul and Dierks had a private interview which Melin could not hear, but he was received very kindly by the consul. He said to Melin that he had heard from Dierks that Melin was leaving them. 'But Mr Melin, you must not leave us; and I hear that the Antwerp people require you to travel about the ports all round England and Scotland, and you have refused it, but we accept you and allow you to stop in London.'[7]

After more conversation with Dierks, the consul said that Melin would be paid £50 a month. Melin states that he said he could not decide the matter there and then but wanted to go back to Hamburg to consider it. Melin still hoped to obtain assistance from his father, but this was once more refused. He explained his visit to London to his father by saying he had received a commission from an old friend in Hamburg to go over and try to arrange business for him because he could not go himself during the present war.

After seeing his father Melin wrote to the German consul, accepting his offer and requesting money. It was agreed that he should now work from the Wesel office. After some days he obtained £50, returning to England on 26 February. Melin wired from Newcastle to Flora Milligan at Upper Park Road asking her to reserve a room for him. She happened to have one free, so reserved it, and he arrived later the same day.

Melin was to state that from that date he sent newspapers to his German agents, with reports of bluejackets (a common term for sailors). He maintained that he never set foot out of London and did not go to the ports.

The British were suspicious of Melin and thought that he was an agent, but there was no evidence against him. Dierks was well known to them as one of the principal organizing espionage agents; he also used the name of Saunderson. Special Branch had detectives working undercover in Holland keeping observation on 166 Loosduin-schekade, The Hague, which was used as a cover as an export office, but business was never seen to be done there.[8] The British found that Melin received by a very roundabout route cheques for £50 on 15 March, 17 April and 25 May, which together with the original sum made a total income of £200.

Then on 14 June John Fetherston, intercepted two postal packets, both addressed to Melin at 23 Upper Park Road, one posted in Tilbury, Essex, and the other Gravesend, Kent. Upon opening one of these he found inside two sealed envelopes bearing unused penny stamps. These were also addressed to Melin. He opened one of them, finding a letter in English, in black ink.

Dear Uncle,

Many thanks for your welcome letter but I am so sorry to hear that you yourself are an invalid and suffering with your old complaint. Dear Mother is a trifle better now and the attacks do not occur quite so frequently than they used to do. We never told her that we had asked you to come over so she will not feel disappointed now. We all wish you speedy recovery and shall be glad to see you here as soon as you are quite well again. If mother keeps on improving we intend taking her to Brighton or do you think the place is crowded out with soldiers? What do you think of Skegness? Would you advise mother to go there, or do you think the air there will be too strong for her?

With love from all your affectionate Niece.

Kate[9]

Fetherston then applied a detection process to the letter, which resulted in the appearance between the lines of writing of a yellow colour: according to *The Times* of 7 April, page 5, 'German Submarine 29'.

The second letter was addressed to Melin in a similar way.

Dear Uncle,

Many thanks for your ever welcome letter in which you tell us that you have taken a small bungalow at Skegness for the season. It is awfully good of you to invite me to spend my holidays there and I thank you very much for your kindness. For the present it is however impossible for me to give you any idea as to when I may be able to come, for you will understand that I cannot leave mother until she is quite well again. When do you intend to move to Skegness? You will surely come and see us before you go, when we can talk matters over together. Trusting that we may soon have the pleasure of seeing you here I remain with love from all your affectionate Niece.

Kate[10]

5. (*above left*) Vernon Kell
   (see p.2). (*Mrs Susan Simpson*)

6. (*above*) 'Sir Basil Thomson
   became head of the Criminal
   Investigation Department of
   New Scotland Yard'. (p.11).

7. (*left*) Captain (later Rear
   Admiral Sir) William Reginald
   Hall. Director of Naval
   Intelligence (see p.75).

8. Carl Hans Lody, shot 6 November, 1914 (see Chapter 2).

9. The memorial to Lody on the wall of the Burgtor, Lübeck (*Gisela Remke*).

10. The North British Station Hotel where Lody stayed in August, 1914 (*Alan Gur*

Upon examination, more writing, in German, was found hidden between the lines:

> In addition to the announcement of the torpedoing of the *Goliath*, the *Daily Mail* raises the question whether this vessel was torpedoed by her own destroyers in the same way as three English ships are said to have been destroyed three months ago. Is this true, and which ships have been destroyed?[11]

When the second postal packet was opened, which appeared to have been posted in Gravesend, a third letter was found.

> Dear Uncle,
>   I trust you have safely received my last letter in which I told you that dear mother was progressing favourably. Unfortunately the improvement has not lasted very long. The pains have returned and seem to be more violent than ever. And to make matters worse there are these restless nights. If the doctor could only let her have a sleeping draught, but he says he must be most careful and give her as few drugs as possible since these might dangerously affect her weak heart. Couldn't you make it possible, dear uncle, and come over for a day and see her? I feel sure it would cheer up dear mother immensely. Dorothy thinks with me that Jack's enlisting has upset her very much although mother has never said so. I only hope he will never have to go out and that the war will be over before his training is finished. If he were compelled to go out to fight these German huns the excitement would surely be too much for her and kill her. Trusting that these lines may reach you in good health I remain with love from all your affectionate Niece, Kate.[12]

For the third time, after examination, writing was found between the lines, this time in English.

> The following Men o' War said to have sunk: *Royal Oak, Marlborough, Majestic, Odeon, Clio.* Also *Revenge* to have been put aground off Selsea [*sic*], east of Portsmouth. Please try to ascertain. Especially men of the First Fleet could give information about the men of the *Marlborough*. Also try to ascertain if German Submarine U12, or any other, has fallen into the hands of the English.[13]

Matters were now urgent: this was serious. Major Drake, on the general staff at the War Office, received the information and as a result gave instructions to the police.[14] It was decided that now was the time to arrest Melin. At 10.15pm on 14 June Divisional Detective Inspector

85

Thomas Duggan of 'S' Division, Metropolitan Police, in company with a Sergeant Askew, went to 23 Upper Park Road. Melin came in while they were there. The Inspector told him why they were there and asked to be shown to his room on the ground floor at the back of the house. Duggan asked Melin to empty his pockets, but he became very abusive and threw his arms about. Upon being told that if he did not submit to a search, force would be used, he became quiet. After the search the police began an inspection of the room. On the mantelpiece was found a little bottle of lemon juice. In the top right-hand drawer of the dressing-table they found a small notebook, in which were a number of names, one being Schedersky.[15] There was also a box of nibs, some dictionaries in German, Swedish, French and English, and a Baedeker's guide to Great Britain.

Examining the Baedeker's guide, the inspector found a dot placed against the names of a number of places, such as Glasgow, Harwich, Portsmouth, Leith, Plymouth and Grimsby among others. In the body of the book the names of various hotels had been underlined at places such as Portsmouth, Plymouth and Hull.

Going through the pages of the dictionary he found a scrap of paper that appeared to have been torn from the notebook. In Melin's handwriting appeared the following:[16]

Edw F. Dartmouth Vernon	Most of Soldiers S. E. E.
F. Surrey	
Manchester, Yorkshire	
B	
H.A.C.	Cyclists
K.R.R.	Y.L.
Buffs, R.O.F.	
28 F	Ammunition
City of L.	
Australians & Canadians[17]	

Melin was then taken to Hampstead police station and the Inspector asked what the lemon juice was for. Melin replied, 'My face'. He was shown the scrap of paper and muttered something that the Inspector did not understand. On being asked to repeat it, he again muttered something that sounded like 'Friend politician.'[18]

Charles Mitchell used his many years' experience in writing fluids to confirm that the bottle contained lemon juice that was not clarified in any way nor filtered. Upon turning his attention to the little box of nibs, on examining one nib under a microscope he found that it had been in contact with some substance which resembled the cellular matter of a lemon.[19]

The following day, 15 June, 1915, the Inspector took Melin to New Scotland Yard, where he was to be interviewed. Melin made a statement:

New Scotland Yard, S.W.
15th June 1915

Mr Ernst Waldemar Melin was seen today by Assistant Commissioner Thompson, Captain Hall, RN, Major Drake, MO5g, and Lord Herschell and stated:
(produced Passport dated 20th February 1915 issued at Gothenburg) 'I landed at Newcastle on 26th February, and I come over from Gothenburg to find a situation. I intended to do some shipping business. I have not taken an office but I am trying to do so. I went down to the City as a rule every day searching for an office. I am paying 25 shillings a week board and lodging which does not include luncheon. I get my money from home through Holland. My people said it was best to send it through a bank in Holland. The money comes from my father and passes through the Rotterdam Bank. My father is 81 years of age. My father instructed his bank to have the money forwarded to me, and the money comes to me through Messrs Schedersky & Co, Rotterdam. I have been to Rotterdam. I came from Russia and then to Hamburg and stayed there some weeks as I thought I might be able to find some business. I could not do so and so I came to London, from Rotterdam. I really do not know the Bank that receives the money here. It is a Bank near the Mansion House. The money comes to me in a letter from Schedersky. They always typewrite their envelopes.'
Asked what was in a small bottle (produced) he replied that it contained lemon juice, and he uses it for his complexion after shaving. 'I have done this for years.' (A.C.C. read the portion of a leaf found in the English-Swedish Dictionary with names of regiments thereon). Continuing, Melin said, 'A part of it I remember very well. I wrote it down out of pure interest. We always talk about these things. *Dartmouth* is the name of a ship which I saw written on a cap. I have not been to Dartmouth. I have not been out of London.' When informed that the *Dartmouth* had not been in English waters for the past 12 months, he said 'I can assure you I saw it on the cap of a sailor when I was in the City.
'I use the benzine (produced) for taking stains out of my clothes. I have a relation called Kate Smith in Holland. I have no relatives in Skegness. Kate Smith is not married and she lives with her mother. I think she is Dutch. She is not a relative of mine. She is not very old and I saw her first in Rotterdam, at the Hotel Weimer.

She is not very tall, rather fair and just ordinary looking. I talked to her in German. I speak German very well having learnt German at School. I am a Swede. I also speak French and Russian. I have not got my birth certificate with me. I have not done any business since I have been here. I have been staying in the same house as the Chancellor of the Swedish Legation. The notes in my pocket book were made when I sent papers away. I have written to Schedersky. I sent a telegram to him a long time ago. He always telegraphs to me when a remittance is being sent. I did not post papers as often as four days a week. I have written to my parents at 23 Englebrekts Gatan, Stockholm. As a rule I wrote my papers at home, sometimes in the post office and once or twice in a cafe. I did not transmit news through Schedersky and I only wrote to him about the remittances. I generally received sums of £50 and when I spent that I used to write for more.'

A.C.C. informed him that the particular business of Schedersky was well known, and that he (Melin) would be charged with Espionage and handed over to Military custody.

He was removed in custody.[20]

On 26 July George Charles Peevor, a second lieutenant in the 10th Battalion Essex Regiment, temporarily attached to the War Office, who before the war had a great deal of experience in preparing and dealing with cases for the Director of Public Prosecutions, visited Melin at Wandsworth prison. Melin then made a second statement:[21]

Saunderson is a relation of an old friend of mine who used to live in Hamburg. Saunderson is now at Rotterdam but he has been in the Army. He has been at the front, and is now in Rotterdam. I have never seen him in uniform. Saunderson is working under instructions from Antwerp and also in connection with the people at Wesel, but the German Consul looks after the money affairs and probably he caused these cheques to be sent. In March I was told to send picture postcards of London to Miss Kate Smith and Saunderson told me I was to visit the English ports and report on what was going on, but I absolutely refused. However, I sent papers with invisible ink reporting the names of bluejackets and soldiers.[22]

Lieutenant Peevor asked him what he used in the invisible writing, and he said, 'I used lemon juice which I have for my complexion.'

Peevor then read to Melin the letters addressed to him from Kate. This had a dramatic effect on the prisoner, who said, 'I would like to see a shorthand writer tomorrow.' The next day, 27 July, Melin made another statement,[23] which this time appeared to be a very full and more truthful account of his actions. He began by giving an outline of his history and circumstances and how he was recruited into the service of Germany, then continued:

Then I accepted the second offer. I had to wait one or two days before a reply came. At last I telegraphed to Dierks and said I accepted the work. He wrote, your letter just received, come to Wesel and I will have the money there. After that telegram I had no money. I had been spending for ten or 12 days. I borrowed money from Mr Gniest, but I would not tell him what for, and went to Wesel. Then people say I hear you have been working for the Antwerp people, it is better to work with us. You will go to London and live in London only if you wish. They gave me money for the trip and for the first month. The Lieutenant at Wesel is Freier, but I do not remember the name of the officer at Wesel, 7 Morgetstrasse. I have forgotten the name of the Officer in the Army. Then he said to me, it may be that you will change your mind, and if you go find out where the ships are lying. You must wire, and they gave me the address Katie Smith, Huize St Joseph, Lent near Nijmegen. Then he said you must have a code if you need to telegraph. The code only contains how many ships in the harbour or going to leave harbour. So they gave me a code. I had to learn it by heart. Already I said if I must have it I take it. Then I left Rotterdam and came to London. I do not remember the date.

Peevor told him it was 26 February, and Melin contiuned:

Oh, yes, of course. I went to Rotterdam and over to Hamburg. I had left things there and had to warehouse – music, etc. Then I went to Gothenburg, thence to Newcastle and from there to London, since which I have been here.

I want to tell you I understand that this Mr Dierks does not go under the name of Dierks. His name is Saunderson – Richard Saunderson. Before the war he was in London. Everything this side for Antwerp goes to his address, and his address is – I may be a little wrong in the number – 71 or 72 (I think it is 72A) Provininerenstraat and he has a Post Box too – No 417. People sending news to him have to send double communications to both his private address and his post box.

I have not seen him since January. He said to me I may be called into service to go to the front, and if I am called I have a substitute. I was writing in March or April, but I was waiting several days for the latest thing to arrive and I did not know what to do. I telegraphed to his private address and had a reply that the money was sent by

bank. I had wired anxiously awaiting remittance, when sent and how
– in my own name and sent off the telegram in the City. That is the
only thing I did with my own name on. The lady there asked for my
address and I gave my address at Hampstead. I had a reply to that.
Then all news for Wesel goes via Kate Smith.

I think I said at New Scotland Yard that I had seen Kate Smith
but I really haven't.

They told me if you do not send any notes we are thankful if you
send us a paper. I had a note in my almanac when I sent my papers
without any writing on. The ticks are when I sent off papers to Kate
Smith. The only thing I had to say was that I had seen searchlights
and Zeppelin bombs had been dropped.

The interrogation went on with further questioning.

Q.	How many newspapers were sent?
Melin:	I think there are about 30.
Q.	How many do you think contained interesting information?
Melin:	I could not say, perhaps half of them.
Q.	Where used you to report information?
Melin:	On the fifth page, that is, by arrangement with the Wesel people.

When asked if he wrote in the margin, Melin responded with details
of his code system:

Yes. I have in my Baedeker a small note. I had intended to tick off
all of them, because I wanted to make them believe that I was
working hard – those things that happened to me in the streets of
London. I did not look around.

About this code. They say to me, I shall buy a Baedeker, which I
bought. If you have seen the Baedeker have you noticed about it?
You have noticed marks on the index, spots, etc. If you refer in the
Baedeker about different ports and places hotels are mentioned.
You notice that there are two spots to five ports, because they said
to me these five ports were of special interest.

The code is made up – did you see the small notebook, did you
notice something about bankers A and R? A = Amsterdam and R =
Rotterdam, four bankers under each of them.

Those in the first row mean Dreadnoughts.
Those in the second row mean Pre-Dreadnoughts.
Those in the third row mean Cruisers.
Those in the fourth row mean Transports.

And if I, for instance, telegraphed to them – Please pay at your convenience, for example, £50 to X Rotterdamsche first row, £100 to Y Amsterdamsche fourth row, payment £40 Rotterdamsche and £60 Rotterdamsche must be effectuated latest (date) all correspondence to x hotel.

The name of the hotel refers to the port; 'at your convenience' means lies; £50 = ten Dreadnoughts; £100 = Ten transports; 'payment must be effectuated', etc, means '4 Dreadnoughts and 6 Cruisers leaving the harbour' on the date given.

More questions followed.

Q.   The bankers' firms are in your book?
Melin: Yes, in the small black notebook. I have no knowledge of the Navy.
Q.   Have you sent any telegrams?
Melin: No, not one. I will tell you that the Antwerp people for Saunderson have the same code as this, but the hotels differ, because they gave me the same code. I had to give them back everything when I went over the second time. We had everything left there, and Mr Saunderson put up the thing to me. Hotels may differ and the bankers differ too, but the code is the same.
Q.   They gave you no prescription for invisible ink, except lemon juice?
Melin: No. I have always shaved with lemon juice, but now I do not use it. I have never had any single communication from them. I only had in March, the end of March or beginning of April a small card from Kate. That is the only thing I had. She said to me that she enclosed an envelope, I am staying with a friend and enclose an envelope addressed to her and asked if I will send a nice picture card of London. You have not to write anything.

Melin was asked if he had been told how to bring out lemon juice writing.

Put it over a candle and heat it. They said, if we write you hold our letters over the candle, but I never had anything, but a small stiff card, and they must, of course, have written.

I asked Mr Saunderson how many people they had working for them, and he said that they have about 150 in England. Of course, I don't know the name of any. I heard Consul Gneist say to

91

Saunderson that is getting much more and he never writes anything hardly. They have never sent anything. I expected the whole time for them to say, we have finished with you, and I was waiting for the first of those cheques just before I was arrested, and I should have decided to go home. My father telegraphed to me that I was welcome home.

I do not know anything else to tell you. I can't understand. I know nothing about Naval things. I haven't the slightest idea. Of course, they had expected that as I knew London for more than 20 years I have had connections in the City, but I have never paid a single visit. I have always been alone. When my father telegraphed I decided to go home.

Asked what his father's address was, Melin replied:

Engelbrektsgatan 23, Stockholm. I have heard for more than two months that he has gone to the north of Sweden for the summer.

I hope you will consider and not make it too difficult to me. I went into the whole thing to make a living and to send harmless things. I cannot understand why they did not send those letters to me, send them through someone else.

My brother is a Colonel in the Swedish Army. Although he is an officer I know nothing about military things, I could not tell you the difference between a Dreadnought and a Cruiser – I haven't the slightest idea.[24]

The general court martial of Ernst Waldemar Melin was held on Friday, 20 August and Saturday, 21 August, 1915; once again it was at the Guildhall, Westminster, under the presidency of Major-General Lord Cheylesmore. Mr Bodkin was to appear for the prosecution, with Captain Wedderburn, the prosecuting officer; and Mr George Elliott for the defence, with his friend Mr H.D. Roome.

Melin faced five charges, summarized as follows. Two charges were of undertaking an act preparatory to the commission of an act prohibited by the regulations; that he came from Rotterdam to Newcastle and London for the purpose of collecting information useful to the enemy, and was in possession of a bottle of lemon juice to further this purpose. The other charges were of sending newspapers containing certain information; possessing a code adapted for secretly communicating naval and military information; and collecting names of regiments and a ship, the *Vernon*. Melin pleaded not guilty on all counts.[25]

The case for the prosecution was watertight, and the prisoner could put forward little defence. Before the prisoner gave evidence, Mr Elliott said:

92

So with the assistance of my learned friend I am going to call him here. I do not want at this stage to take up the time of the Court. I would rather you hear from his own lips – I am afraid you will find him a somewhat difficult witness, but I will do my best to elicit from him in the briefest possible time his story to you, and you will see for yourself – and I must leave it with you of course entirely to judge – you will see for yourselves the sort of man that he is; you will judge for yourselves whether he is the sort of man who would be likely to be, or is a person whom you would judge if you had to select a person for that kind of mission – whether he is the kind of person who has been giving them valuable information, so far as any conjecture on your part can assist you, or whether he is, what I suggest to you he is, unfortunately a degenerate person who by reason of the habits that he previously acquired has reached a stage of degeneration both mental and physical which enables him simply to carry on this kind of desultory correspondence for them, which required no energy or vigilance or foresight on his part – that in using the term 'Espionage' he was the last person in the world to whom it can be applied, because he was hardly capable of making any observations that could be of any value.[26]

Mr Bodkin cross-examined the prisoner; a part of this questioning went as follows.

> Q. And yet you tell us that the first time you went to London all you sent was absolute nonsense?
>
> A. Yes.
>
> Q. And then the second interview came with Lieutenant Freier, and they were pressing you to remain in their service?
>
> A. Yes.
>
> Q. Do you say that they pressed to remain in their service a man who had no knowledge of Navy matters, and who had sent them all nonsense?
>
> A. Yes, they did press me.
>
> Q. What use were you to them?
>
> A. What did I say to them?
>
> Q. What use were you to them?
>
> A. I do not understand.
>
> Q. Of what assistance were you to them; how were you of any advantage to them, if you knew nothing of Navy matters and had only sent them nonsense?
>
> A. For the Army things.
>
> Q. But you said you only sent them nonsense?

A. Yes, certainly.

Q. Did you send them any important Army things, then?

A. No, I did not.

Q. Then why do you say, 'For the Army things'?

A. They say to me that I should try to supply the Army things.

Q. Lieutenant Freier having seen you, you are sent back and permanently engaged?

A. Yes.

Q. And you continued to act for five months – at least four months – 26 February to 14 June?

A. Yes.

Q. And during those four months you got something to come over with, I suppose, in February, did you not?

A. Yes.

Q. How much – £50?

A. I got £50, and then I got. . .

Q. Something extra?

A. Several extras for the voyage.

Q. So that that £50 and the extras plus the three cheques of 15 March, 17 April and 25 May made it up to £200; that is what you got, you know.

A. I had £50 and then had three cheques.

Q. That is £200, is it not?

A. Yes.

Q. And all for nonsense?

A. Yes, I consider so.

Q. Did you think, 'Well, of all the simple people I ever met those German secret service people are the simplest'?

A. If they are – I cannot understand.

Q. Did you think, 'Well, of all the simple people I ever met those German secret service men are the very simplest'? Is that what you thought about them?

A. I had not the slightest idea that they were satisfied with it.

Q. They were satisfied with what you sent them?

A. No, not at all; they were satisfied to engage me; they thought with my connection I should be able to find out.

Q. They are not only satisfied to engage you, but they are satisfied to pay you money?

A. I cannot understand how they thought.

Q. But they paid it?

94

A.   Yes, they did.
Q.   Like simple people?
A.   Yes, it is absolutely marvellous.
Q.   Then you must have hoodwinked them?
A.   I beg pardon?
Q.   You must have deceived them?
A.   Yes, I think I have.
Q.   Did you ever have a letter or any communication from anybody to say 'The stuff you are sending is rubbish – find out something worth having'?
A.   Not a word.[27]

Melin was found guilty, and on 8 September, 1915, Major-General H. Popon, CB, the Major of the Tower of London, received a letter from the Major-General commanding London District, based at Horse Guards. This stated that he had received directions from the Army Council to carry into effect the sentence of death passed upon the prisoner Melin, who had been found guilty of espionage. He accordingly ordered that Melin be shot within the precincts of the Tower of London on 10 September at 6am, under the directions of his assistant provost-marshall.[28]

In the three weeks between sentence and his date of execution Melin was a model prisoner and gave no trouble. When his time came he shook hands with his guards, thanking them for the many kindnesses they had shown him. He was to be shot by a detachment of Scots Guards,[29] again in the miniature rifle range. Melin died with the greatest resignation, without any attempt at heroics, but like the gentleman he once was.[30, 31]

CHAPTER 6

Augusto Alfredo Roggen

Augusto Alfredo Roggen was described as a neat, dapper, dark little man, not at all like a German, born in Montevideo in 1881. However, he did say that his father was German who was naturalized in Uruguay in 1885, and that he himself was married to a German woman.[1] He said that in South America he was in business as a farmer, but without a farm of his own.[2]

He spoke English quite well and in March, 1914, stated that he had arrived in Hamburg, from Montevideo. He spent some time travelling around the country, going to Switzerland shortly before the outbreak of war. However, in May, 1914, he returned to Germany, making his way to Frankfurt. It was the opinion of the British that it was then that he joined the German secret service, moving on to Amsterdam and Rotterdam, and the German spy school.[3]

Arriving from Rotterdam on 30 May, 1915, he docked at Tilbury on the ship *Batavia 4*. Here he was interviewed by the Aliens' Officer, Walter Richard Perks, who examined his passengers' arrival form. This gave Roggen's address as 'Ruston Proctor & Co, Lincoln', although Roggen had no authority from the firm.[4] Roggen told Perks that he was going to Scotland. The officer was not suspicious, and Roggen was allowed to enter the country.[5] Making his way to London, he booked in at the Bonnington Hotel in Southampton Row.

At 4pm on 2 June, Roggen went to Messrs Thornton & Company of 7 Princes Street, Hanover Square, who were well-known buyers and shippers of horses. They had many agencies in foreign countries, including one in Montevideo. There he saw Henry Beeton Brown, the auctioneers' clerk. He said that he wanted to buy three good-class hackney mares at about 500 guineas each and seven at 300 guineas each, for shipping to Montevideo. This was a very large order worth about £3,900 and a surprise to Brown, as Roggen was a complete stranger and had no letter of advice or introduction. All he had was a copy of the *Livestock Journal* in which Thorntons advertised, but there was nothing in it about hackney mares. Asked for the name of his agent, Roggen gave Mr H. Flores of Binneweg 127, Rotterdam, saying that the money could be paid through 'The London and River Plate'. It was apparent that Roggen did not know much about horses and Brown was not happy about the business, referring him to the senior partner.[6] After his visit Thorntons heard no more of this stranger, and no order was received. It was a mere pretence visit, to give colour to his story that he had business in Britain.[7]

On 4 June Roggen took a train from King's Cross, setting out on his quest to obtain naval information. He was very talkative on the journey and asked a great many questions of fellow passengers – so much so that they took a strong dislike to the foreign-looking stranger, and one rudely asked to know where he came from and what he wanted in England. Roggen then gave a very full cover story. He was told that unless he kept away from the coast he would find himself under arrest. The hostility frightened him. He got out at Lincoln, where he stayed at the Great Northern Hotel.[8]

The next day Roggen paid another unexpected visit, this time to Ruston Proctor & Co Ltd, the large firm of agricultural implement makers whose name and address he had used on his passengers' arrival form. He saw Edmund William Spalding, a colonial traveller for the business. He said he wished to enquire on behalf of himself and a friend about agricultural machinery, mentioning traction engines and threshing machines, but Spalding soon found that Roggen knew absolutely nothing about the subject. The firm, like Thorntons, had an agent in Montevideo, and a store there. The machinery was on display, so anyone wanting to buy could view the product without needing to travel to Britain. When Roggen was told this he asked no questions, but told Spalding that he intended to return to Uruguay very shortly, although being afraid of German submarines he proposed to return to Holland and take passage in a neutral ship.[9] This visit was also a cover for his future activities, and MO5 later suggested that he went to Lincoln to ascertain the number of troops in the city.[10]

After 10pm on Saturday, 5 June Roggen booked in at the Carlton Hotel in Edinburgh, where he saw the manager's wife, Mabel Irene Livingstone. Filling in his form at reception, he gave his business as farmer. He was to stay until after lunch on Tuesday, 8 June. On the Sunday he had all his meals in the hotel,[11] and during the day he went to the local police office for registration, seeing a detective called Robert Mackenzie. He said he was a farmer who was interested in automobiles for agricultural purposes, and readily gave details of the firm he had visited in London, but after saying that he had come from Lincoln he denied any business visit there. Roggen told the officer that he had been in Switzerland at the outbreak of war, and had travelled through Germany to Rotterdam and on to London. He said that while passing through Germany he had been taken for a spy and been closely followed.[12]

Later that day Roggen got into conversation with Mrs Livingstone, telling her that he was travelling partly on business and partly for his health. He spoke of coming from Lincoln, and the conversation moved to his time in Switzerland and Germany. Roggen told her that he had found it best to get out of Germany as quickly as possible. Talking of sighseeing, he wished to see the country. He was advised that he might go round the Trossachs, which he did the next Monday, being away from the hotel from 8.30am until after 10.30pm. Before leaving on the Tuesday he asked Mrs Livingstone for details of a suitable hotel where he could stay, and she suggested the Trossachs Hotel. He evidently thought he would prefer to go to the Tarbet, saying that he wanted to know if you could get fishing there. Roggen seemed very keen on fishing, but he had no fishing tackle.[13]

Before he left the city at 5.15pm, Roggen sent off two postcards to Holland. One address, that of H. Flores, was already familiar to MO5 from the cases of Janssen and Roos, and Breeckow and Wertheim (see Chapter 8). The cards were intercepted and photographed and the originals sent on, in the hope that, having signalled his safe arrival, he would receive a communication from his employers which would indicate the real nature of his business. The despatching of a postcard was the usual method adopted by German agents to announce their arrival at the scene of their activities.[14]

H. Flores, Esq.,
Rotterdam,
Binnenweg 127.

Edinburgh, Carlton Hotel.

Dear friend,
I can tell you that I found a most pretty place to stay and where I can have fishing and walking about in the mountains. In three weeks I will be back again and then I will take a Dutch ship to go back to Montevideo. Please do everything you can to get a ticket for me on a ship leaving at end of June. My address is Tarbet Hotel, Loch Lomond.
Yours very affectionate friend,
Augusto Roggen
Don't forget my girl.[15]

★   ★   ★

A. Grund, Esq.,
Ivers and van Staa
Rotterdam

Edinburgh, Carlton Hotel.

Dear friend,
   Now I have found a very pretty place to stay a fortnight and where
I can go fishing and walking about in the mountains. Then I will
come back and take a Dutch ship back to Montevideo. Don't say
anything about that to my girl. My address is Tarbet Hotel, Loch
Lomond.
Your very affectionate friend.
Augusto Roggen.[16]

Between 12 noon and 1pm on 9 June Roggen booked into the Tarbet
at Loch Lomond. He saw the bookkeeper, Jane Walker, saying that he
had come from Balloch and proposed to stay between eight and ten
days. After taking lunch he purchased a map showing the freshwater
Loch Lomond and the head of Loch Long,[17] which is a seawater loch
and part of the Firth of Clyde. It was two miles from the Tarbet Hotel
to the head of Loch Long. The significance of Loch Long was that for
the previous two or three years it had been used as an Admiralty
torpedo testing range; there were then eight targets fixed in the loch
for the torpedo to run under. It was a prohibited area, in that no enemy
alien or unregistered alien should visit it and fishing was banned. The
range was situated down the centre of the loch, being partly in
Dumbartonshire and partly in Argyllshire. The torpedo works were in
Argyllshire on the western side of the loch. Here repairs and alterations
were carried out during the testing programme, although the torpe-
does were made in Greenock.
   By this time the British security services were very concerned about
Roggen's movements and were hot on his trail. He was only at the hotel
for about five hours before he was arrested by Superintendent John
Wright of Helensburgh police. Roggen was told that he was being
arrested on orders from the War Office; he was searched and his property retained.[18] He was taken to London, where the Superintendent
handed over the property to a Special Branch inspector, Edmund
Buckley. Among the prisoner's property was a loaded Browning
revolver, with six cartridges in the magazine and an additional 50
rounds of ammunition.
   In a small ordinary dressing-case was a bottle of liquid.[19] This was
later examined by, yet again, Charles Aynesworth Mitchell, who found
that it was a solution containing the essential oil of peppermint in spirit,

with another fatty oil floating about in the liquid. He had never met such a mixture before. He made enquiries with scent experts and those making hairwash substances, but no one could suggest a use for it in their industry. Tests found that it could be used for invisible writing which could subsequently be developed. One had to be careful, as it tended to leave an oily mark, and you would need a fine nib to prevent the oil running off.[20] On a piece of blotting paper attached to a writing pad was found an initial 'G' with a full stop after it, and practically all of a name: a capital 'B', and a small r-e-c-k, then a blank followed by a ' . . .w'. Filling in the blank with the letter 'o', one would obtain 'Breeckow', the name of another spy in custody at that time. It was thought significant that Roggen was at the Bonnington Hotel, London, at the same time as Breeckow was at the Ivanhoe Hotel, which is not far off. As both had been in contact with Flores, it was possible that they were also in contact with each other.[21]

In a small pocket book, under the address of the Amsterdam consul for Uruguay, appeared the half-obliterated address 'Binnenweg 127' (the address of H. Flores). On another page was the address 'Manson Brewery, Heaton Street, Gainsborough'; under it very faintly was written 'Ivers and van Staa' (the address on Roggen's second post-card). This was clever, as unless the addresses were known to the person examining the papers it would not be thought suspicious, but would be a useful reminder to Roggen of his contact's correct address.[22]

Under interrogation he was very talkative, but did not admit that he was a German spy. However, he could offer no explanation for sending postcards to suspect addresses. But, unlike others, he did not pretend that his sympathies were for Britain.[23] He made a written statement in the presence of Major Drake and Captain Hall, RN, which included the following strange remark: 'When I went to Loch Lomond I stayed at the Tarbet Hotel. I was very glad when I got there as I wanted to go to a quiet place where there was nothing to see.'[24]

He was tried at the Guildhall, Westminster, on Friday, 20 August, 1915, before the president, Major General Lord Cheylesmore. He faced four charges under Sections 48 of the Defence of the Realm (Consolidation) Regulations 1914: doing acts preparatory to the commission of an act prohibited by the regulations. These acts were, briefly, coming to England and going to Scotland to obtain information for the enemy, and sending the two postcards to known spies. He gave no evidence himself, and did not go into the witness box or address the court. He was found guilty and sentenced to be shot.[25]

The day after the court martial Roggen wrote a four-page letter from Wandsworth detention barracks outlining the facts of the case as he saw them. It began:

Referring to my yesterday trial I must tell you that only yesterday morning my solicitor told me after speaking to the counsel, that there were no evidences against me, and that I just as well not go to the witness box. I was prepared to go there and did not prepare myself to speak to the court from my place. It was a mistake that I did not speak, because I thought my solicitor was still going to speak.[26]

Consideration was given as to whether the letter contained anything which would justify the alteration of the findings or the sentence of the court, but there was nothing and the sentence was confirmed.[27] To avoid publicity Roggen was removed from Wandsworth detention barracks early on the morning of 9 September. At the Tower of London he was told of the sentence and given access to any religious consolation that he might require.[28] He was to be shot at dawn the next day.[29] However, at 9.15pm on 9 September a letter from the Uruguayan Minister was received by the resident clerk at the War Office.[30] It stated that he had only just heard of the sentence of death, which was unexpected – it had upset him. The letter ended: 'Please do your best in the interest of humanity, if humanly possible. Roggen is a young man, and his family is a very respectable one. There must be something wrong but it appears a cruel sentence.'[31] Matters were urgent, and, unable to contact the DPS, the clerk telephoned the Adjutant General directly. It was decided that, to avoid any cause of complaint from Uruguay, the execution should be postponed for a few days to allow consideration of any representation that the Minister might make.[32] The representation was received the next day.

The life of a man is at stake; I do not permit myself to doubt for one instant the legality or the correctness of the sentence that has been passed; on the other hand, from the reading, which only now I have been able to make, of the proceedings, it appears beyond doubt that Roggen has been sentenced to the capital punishment merely on suspicions. Indeed if your Excellency takes the trouble to read the 16 short declarations made by the witnesses for the prosecution, your Excellency will see that there is not a single one of them, not one, which formulates a concrete charge, and your Excellency will also see that they are all of absolute vacuity. Neither detectives nor the witnesses say aught that is not either vulgarity or a suspicion without the support of any proof whatsoever. Your Excellency may verify this by a simple reading of the documents.

As there is no proof whatever, and only conjectures, is it not a cruel and excessive punishment to apply the death penalty merely on suspicion? I have the highest idea of the rectitude of

English judges and I would never venture to question their opinions.

Only the impression of the present moment, of the cruelty that is in the atmosphere in which we live today, can have brought about the irrevocable penalty for mere suspicions.

Where is the proof to be found? It does not appear from anything in the proceedings. No neutral foreigner who may happen to come from Holland, from Spain or from other nation, can have failed to come in contact, in any of these nations, with enemies of the Allies, who swarm everywhere, be they Germans or Dutch or Spaniards. But, if such meetings may lend themselves to suspicion, they do not in themselves constitute crime if they are not accompanied by acts which prove that spying is being carried on or prohibited information being transmitted.

I do not frame any reclamation; I limit myself to begging for a new reading of the proceedings, and to ask that a search should be made not for a suspicion, but for proofs, before it should come to happen that a man still young, born in a country friendly to England, should be subjected to the last penalty. He was born in Uruguay, a hospitable and friendly land to British sailors, where they are always received affectionately as has been shown in the case of Admiral Sturdee, on his return from his glorious expedition to the Falkland Island, and as has been seen in the case of the sailors of HMS *Glasgow*, who were welcomed and fêted enthusiastically. Sir, an honourable family would suffer the shame of seeing one of its number condemned to death, to a debasing penalty, without a single proof to justify such a terrible sentence. The last penalty should only be applied, according to Spanish legislation, when the proofs are 'as clear as the light of day'; and I, speaking from my conscience, can say that I only find suspicion and nothing beyond. A penalty of military prison would be sufficient for a case of suspicion and that is what I ask as a special mercy from the undeniable rectitude and high-minded criterion of the judges of His Britannic Majesty in these cruel circumstances.[33]

The letter was acknowledged on behalf of Field Marshal Earl Kitchener.[34] It was found that there was nothing in the petition to justify commutation of the sentence. But a minute stated that 'whether for reasons of international politics if it would be desirable to do a favour to the Government of Uruguay, was not a matter for us, but for the Foreign Office'.[35] As a result the papers were sent to the Secretary of State. It was felt that explanations of the relationship subsisting between Roggen and known agents was inadequate, highly improbable, and sometimes contradictory, and was unsupported by evidence

either documentary or oral. It was the opinion of the military authorities that the facts were sufficient, if unexplained, to justify the sentence
of the court martial; and that if the prisoner had been able to furnish
an explanation it is certain that he would have done so. But the experienced counsel who appeared for the defence did not tender Roggen's
evidence and thereby expose his client to cross-examination. He took
this responsibility well knowing that the facts if unexplained were most
damaging, and possibly fatal to the prisoner. He knew also that as a
result inferences of a grave character would be drawn, as the only
person who could offer explanations had omitted to do so.[36] The
Foreign Office wanted nothing whatever to do with the case and were
anxious that the military should reply directly,[37] which was done on 15
September.[38] The British were to lose no time and the same day Major-
General Lloyd wrote to the Major of the Tower that Roggen was now
to be shot at 6am on 17 September.[39]

On 15 September Roggen's solicitors, Robinson & Co, had an
urgent request from him that they attend the Tower to discuss the position and arrange to send on a rough statement that he had prepared
for the War Office,[40] which consisted of eight pages of handwritten
notes, reproduced here with their original spelling.[41]

From 18 July and I have been arrested beginning of June. Have not
even been charged as spy, only suspician in which very easily get.
Even Judge was pleading for me. Before and after trail everybody
chiefly solicitor and council told me that I was alright and of course
never could be shot. And that such law would make the suspician
guilty, and then send the prisoner to a camps.

It is very hard luck on me to have been in connection with Holland
but you know my hole correspondence from which also the jury said
it was harmless and the judge was pleading for me. That I am not a
spy proofs my hole life here in England and everything.

I have not been trying all that spies have done, not collected
communications to enemy. I registered myself properly every
where. Not had secret writing and code on me. Not been to any
military and navy place.

Tarbet Hotel has been recommended to me by Landlady at
Carlton Hotel, Edinburgh. There were only two guests except me
and I don't think somebody goes to such a quiet place to live when
he has the intention to spy. His going and coming would always be
noticed. And he could easily be looked after. Is it worth spying on
the torpedo trying place? and is information about that of use to the
enemy? I think spying might be done at Dundee and Inverness that
would be useful to the enemy. And then at a big place a spy can hide
himself better. But the chief thing is that I have only been about four

hours at Tarbet and had dinner and tea there after dinner. I lay down to sleep on the lawn. I have at hotels always been together with officers and did not once sit down with them and tried to get conversation with them what could not have been difficult for me, if I wanted to get informations.

My Legation knows that I have my own money to live and that I never had been in desperate position. I like the English character and the soldiers specially. Ask at the Wandsworth where it seems that they liked me and have therefore been splendidly treated. They have always made an exception with me as they say, and knew that I was alright. I have always been good [...] there and don't think that somebody who has done something wrong and has a bad conscience can always have good spirits and get heaver. I way one-and-a-half stone more than before I went there, and than I did all my life. Ask please the medical officer, the surgeon and the three solders who where on guard with me.

My solicitor told me that he was to see me the day before the trial but he did not come, because as he and the council told me five minutes before the trial I was alright and need not go in the witness box and say nothing, that there were no real evidence against me. I knew then that I would never get out absolutely free and that I would be sent to a camps. I did not know that I could speak to the court without going to the witness box. If I had known that all witnesses would go again to the trial I would have had more to ask them, it would have made a little difference.

I have always been asked about my ideas about the war and have answered them. Perhaps it is not right but always have my heart in my mouth, as you say and every body has the feeling that he can trust me. That has been always told to me all my life.

The sympathy of the Uruguay and Argentine are absolutely for England, France and Belgium and have Germans clerics been sent out of nearly all chief business houses. It would even be [...] to have been arrested in that suspician.

I have been over here for business but of course it was curiosity too, to see what England was like during the war. To my life and everything here has been so correct that even the suspician of being over here in purpose to help the enemy will be taken from me.

I understand of course quite well that you take up the slightest suspician against everybody because you have to be careful.

Augusto Ruggen[42]

There was now no hope for Roggen, and on 16 September his solicitor took a last trip by taxi to confer with his client. They discussed the matter, but Roggen's legal adviser pointed out that he was afraid there

104

was nothing further that could be done for him.[43] He faced death as a brave man, marching to the chair with a defiant air, refusing to have his eyes bandaged. In the last moments he gained the admiration of all those present for his courage and self-control.[44]

From O.C. Troops Tower of London.
September 17th, 1915.
To Resident Governor and Major of H.M. Tower of London

Sir,
I have the honour to inform you that the prisoner Augusto Alfredo Roggen was this morning, by sentence of General Martial, shot by a Detachment of the 3rd Battalion Scots Guards at 6am.
  All the officers required by law were present, and a coroner's inquest was afterwards held.
I have the honour to be, Sir,
Your obedient Servant,
Walter Hurley Colonel
O.C. Troops, Tower of London.[45]

Not long after the execution a request was received from his widow, directed through the Dutch government. She asked that his body be sent to Holland, but after due consideration the Foreign Office refused the request. About a year later a ship was stopped en route from Holland to South America. The boarding officer found on the passenger list one Dr Emilio Roggen, the brother of the dead spy. He did not know of his brother's fate and was greatly disturbed. He was likewise interrogated, but found to be a respectable straightforward person. His story was that upon the declaration of war he was forcibly detained in Germany and required to serve as a medical officer in the field. After two years he had at last gained his freedom and was returning now to his native Uruguay. Finding nothing against him, he was allowed on his way.[46, 47]

CHAPTER 7

Fernando Buschman

Fernando Buschman was born on 16 August, 1890, in Paris. His father, Francisco Buschman, born in Hamburg, Germany, was a naturalized Brazilian who had a music and instrument business in that country. Fernando's mother was Brazilian, but of Danish extraction. When Fernando was six years old he was sent to Austria to be educated in Vienna. He returned to Brazil for a few months' holiday when he was about ten, but returned to Austria when his family found him a place in a convent about four hours' ride from Vienna. At the age of 15 he left, going to a mechanical engineering school at Karlstein in the Austrian Alps, and later at Zurich. His father died in 1907, so Fernando moved to live with his mother in Vienna. She would not leave the city as her husband was buried there, but Fernando later returned to Brazil to work with his brother in Rio de Janeiro. This did not last long, so he entered a firm of mechanical engineers, Messrs Ahrends & Co, where he worked for about two years. He then returned to Vienna to see his mother, but stayed for only a few months before moving to Paris.

Buschman was at the time very enthusiastic about the aviators Santos Dumont and Blériot. He had some savings, and intended to manufacture aeroplanes. With the help of a Mr Pevier, he produced two aeroplanes at Issy and obtained a permit for trials. But the business was not a success, because flash floods swamped his aircraft completely. So he returned to Brazil and a change of direction, starting a business in partnership with his cousin in about 1912. But after a disagreement he left, and set up with a Mr Bello in a firm called Buschman & Bello. It was a general business importing food from Germany and England, and exporting bananas and potatoes, but it was not very well funded. However, Buschman continued his travels, and in 1912 went on business to Norway and Sweden. On the way there he met a lady called Valerie, and love blossomed between them.

Although her parents came from Dresden, the couple were married in London.

After his marriage he continued his business in Brazil, visiting Dresden occasionally to see his wife's parents. Business improved and, with his German connection, in September, 1913, Buschman & Bello opened an office in Hamburg. Buschman remained in Germany until April, 1914, returning to Brazil with his wife and her parents. He subsequently commuted between his Brazilian and German offices.

In September, 1914, he returned to Hamburg to close his German branch, as, in his words, 'war was raging'. He made his way through Madrid, Barcelona and Genoa, doing business en route. Upon tidying up his affairs in Hamburg he moved on to Dresden, staying with his wife and her family until February, 1915. But Buschman was later to say that he did not get on well with his in-laws and quarrelled with them and his wife. He left, and in Genoa met a lady whom he had known for eight years, a society woman who employed a very old gentleman, a professor, as a kind of secretary. Buschman stayed with her for three or four weeks on very friendly terms, being with her all the time. But the lady (he never named her) planned to go to Holland in May. He states:

We had long conversations together, and we made arrangements. I have known her for such a long time, and we were on such confidential terms, and as owing to the war my business was not progressing at all, and I had to wait, I endeavoured to do some new business; and she offered me quite confidentially to lend me money when ever I wanted any . . . It was not possible to write to her direct, owing to her position in the world, in society . . . It was the secretary, or attaché, as I have called him, who gave me the address of Flores [a name well known to the British; that of a German schoolmaster who had been wounded in action and was now active in espionage][1] as being somebody who he knows in Holland, and who would undertake to hand over any communication.[2]

Buschman stated that he went to Barcelona and then on to Madrid, arranging business with a man called Lerroux in respect of boots and mules. He decided to come to London, and received from Brazil lists of companies in London. He was also informed that several British firms had written to Bushman & Bello saying that they did not want to do any more business with them owing to their German name. His partner had therefore changed the style of the firm to Marcelino Bello, and wanted confirmation that this was all right.

On 14 April, 1915, he arrived in London and booked in at the Piccadilly Hotel. But he was short of money, a condition that was to

107

trouble him throughout his time in the metropolis. On 17 April he sent a telegram to Flores: 'Rotterdam. Please wire Piccadilly Hotel £12. Fernando Buschman.'[3] He received a reply by 21 April and obtained the money.

In the meantime, on 20 April he visited a general shipping company called Messrs Bolus & Co, at 487–9, Salisbury House, London Wall, in the City. There he met Emil Samuel Franco; a director brought Buschman to Franco's office and asked him to see what he wanted, as Buschman was speaking in French. Buschman told Franco that he was concerned as to why they had stopped sending orders to his firm; the last order, for dried fruits, was about 18 months before. He suspected that it was because his name was German, and he wanted to prove that he was not. He produced a Brazilian passport and a certificate issued by the French consulate stating that he was of Brazilian nationality. The meeting went well and the two men became friendly. That same day they went to the British Bank of West Africa where Buschman sent a wire to his partner, asking for another £12. He also sent another telegram to Flores: 'H. Flores, Rotterdam. Lozano Madrid will buy last price to-day 2d each Fernando Buschman. A. Yes.'[4]

Buschman had a somewhat fantastic explanation for sending this communication.

> A former maid of the lady whom I know is married in Madrid. The lady in question had told me she had taken an interest in her maid during the time of the war; because the husband of the maid had to leave his business to rejoin the Swiss Army, the husband had left a large collection of fans; I do not know whether it was in Madrid or in Seville, but she had given me some notes . . . in order that I could see whether I could sell the collection.[5]

The friendship between Buschman and Franco flourished, so much so that the two men spent much time in each other's company, spending the greater part of the day together and practically every evening. Franco was an accomplished linguist and could speak Spanish, but conversed with his friend in French. Buschman said that he felt very lonely in London and found it difficult to get on with the British people. It was explained that Buschman intended to go all over England in order to visit merchants.

At 9am on 23 April, Franco went with Buschman to Waterloo station and waved him off, believing that he was going to see dried fruit merchants in Southampton. Upon his return, Buschman told his friend that he had come back via Portsmouth. The next day, at Franco's suggestion, Buschman left the Piccadilly Hotel and transferred to the Strand Palace, as it was cheaper. Whilst there he received a telegram: 'Fernando Buschman, Strand Palace Hotel, London; send you today by wire £10 account Flores, Dierks & Co'.

On 4 May Buschman went to Holland, telling his friend of his destination. They both took the train from Fenchurch Street to Tilbury, where Franco saw him off. Buschman returned to England two weeks later, on 16 May.[6] Unfortunately money was still a problem, so Franco suggested they both move into rooms at 36a Harrington Road, South Kensington. The rent was paid in advance on monthly terms. On 18 May Buschman sent a telegram to Flores: 'Please wire funds through Embassy, must pay rent monthly in advance. Fernando Buschman, Savoy Hotel.'

Having got no reply he followed up with another to 'Madame de Klimm, 24 Plats, The Hague' – the address of the German military attaché, Colonel Osterdat! 'Have wired tutor for funds but no reply, please do necessary; am entirely without; Fernando Buschman, 36a Harrington Road, South Kensington.' This time he received a reply, obtaining £25: 'Fernando Buschman, London, Kensington, 36a Harrington Road. Funds sent today by Legations, Flores.'

The last telegram that was sent by Buschman reads: 'H. Flores, 127a Binnenweg, Rotterdam. Surprised have submitted many offers please wire immediately funds through bank; Buschman, 36a Harrington Road, South Kensington.'

The British had intercepted these telegrams[7] and were fully aware of the danger of Buschman at loose in the country.[8] They had a New Scotland Yard officer working undercover in Holland to investigate the places where the telegrams were received. Dierks had an address of 166 Loosduinschekade, The Hague. It consisted of two floors, first and second. The first floor was fitted out as an export office, while the upper floor was for residential use. Flores' premises at 127a Binnenweg, Rotterdam, were a kind of tenement consisting of two floors over a cafe, and were kept for boarders by a German woman called Selbach. Flores was known to still be employed as a schoolmaster at 18 Gedempte Vest, and had been followed to the offices of the German consul at 131 Nieuwhaven.[9]

On 4 June it was decided that now was the time to arrest Buschman. Inspector George Riley of New Scotland Yard went to 36a Harrington Road at 12.10am, but Buschman was not at home. The Inspector waited at the lodgings, where Buschman had his own bedroom and shared a sitting room with Franco. At 1.45am the suspect came home. Riley said in French, 'Are you Mr Buschman?' Upon this being confirmed, Riley replied, 'I am going to search your rooms.' Buschman said, 'What is it you have against me? I will show you everything you wish to see.' Riley searched his prisoner's bedroom and the common sitting room.

Among Buschman's possessions was a 'literary' composition entitled *Impressions of London*,[10] which contained some interesting comments.

General impressions of London

Comparing London with Paris, at a grave and important time like this, there is a great difference such as I did not expect to find. Paris still has life – that is why the meritorious city of the world is great – but we do not see many carriages, and at times there is hardly any life in the great boulevards. Further, the scarcity of young people in the streets does not tend to brighten matters. The wounded soldiers, walking about the streets, also go to indicate at every moment, to the passer-by, that we are at real war and that the war is horrible.

In London one does not see many wounded soldiers, on the contrary, the many soldiers that are to be seen at all times appear healthy and courageous. Their faces are not the faces of soldiers we are accustomed to see but the faces of 'sports men' in all respects. They have a way of walking with their little sticks – the salute is given in a half-hearted way and not very frequently. All this does not alter the impression that they are good soldiers and that they ought to be able to fight well. Life everywhere is the same – great – from morning up to 8pm. There is a tremendous number of carriages and motor cars and I can always say it compels me to stop. Here, which I think very good, is that they do not speak of the war but of current events; and this is very good because in Paris they only speak of the war and each Frenchman is well versed on military topics. Therefore it seems easy for one interested to know something more [...] of military things and to know them and also that the Frenchman believe that they have no spies in their country. I am not of the same opinion because I do not believe that in a country, with so many elements, they are going to be devoid of someone who will work in the interests of the enemy for money or other reasons.

To remain silent is the best system – like the English do and we could learn much from them, they do it like this: Yesterday I saw the route march of the reserve guard and I liked the spirit of the people, who were in great numbers watching them. It appears that every Saturday about 3pm this march takes place by the Bank of England. The Military bands play very well but I find it strange that in the middle of the column 12 or 14 [...] with [...] different and different costumes playing the trumpets and drums. It is true in the city there does not exist the sentiment which we call 'militarism' and very far from it, this then is the marked manner of [...] contented pleasure and peace.

110

How is [...] very few sailors and more officers from time to time [..]
marines [...] are not seen. They must be in the war area and it is not
known [...] is the most potent in the world.

As, at 8pm when the night sends the sun to rest it is an impression
[...] little light [...] below and the houses [...].

Now searchlights begin their work over the city and watch for two-
and-a-half hours, if a Zepplin is not seen in the sky or something
similar to it at 10.30pm they discontinue the search as they know
they dare not come later.

It is very strange to see eight to 12 recruits with a military band of
about 20 men, moreover I think it is a good idea as it makes one feel
as though you wish to follow the band.

Yesterday there was a rumour that the German Squadron had
bombarded Dunkirk but today it appears to be a false rumour as no
ships were seen and it is evidently noises from cannon of great
calibre.

Tomorrow it is Sunday and I hope that the day is fine to spend a
little time in Hyde Park.[11]

On 5 June Buschman was interviewed at New Scotland Yard by Sir
Basil Thomson, Major Drake of the War Office and Lord Herschell.
He made the following statement:

I am a Brazilian. I have been to Holland on business for my firm. I
met a member of the firm of Dierks & Co at The Hague. I spoke
to him about doing business but never really concluded any business with him. He is a very curious fellow and it is difficult to know
what he is at. I have not got a camera or typewriter, I was introduced to Mr Dierks by a Mr Flores at Rotterdam. He asked me if
I could furnish him with goods, and I told him I could not supply
any goods for Germany. I promised to supply him with coffee and
rubber. I was doing other business for Mr Flores. We are supplying guns for the French Government. I only saw Mr Dierks once.
He has a very small office on the first floor, quite a small room. I
saw some samples on the floor, but I do not know what kind. I did
not see any clerks. I did not take his office as meaning serious business. I came to no arrangement and undertook no business for him.
I did very little business with Mr Flores, and had no contract with
him.

After my arrival on 14 April I stayed for about a fortnight at the Piccadilly Hotel. I then changed to the Strand Palace Hotel at the suggestion of Mr Franco, and stayed there about three weeks. I then went back to Rotterdam and Amsterdam and stayed in Holland about a week. I came back about 17 or 18 May and went to Savoy Hotel. My business in England was to sell picric acid, rifles and cloth. Formerly I sold Flour and potatoes, but no cigars. I wanted some money so I sent a telegram to Mr Flores to send me some. My mother is in Vienna. She is a Dane.

He was asked whether he would be surprised to hear that Mr Dierks had telegraphed to him.

I received a telegram from him. It probably arose in this way. My mother was anxious because she had not heard from me, and she wrote to Mr Flores. Flores probably went to Dierks, and you must understand that Dierks is a very embarrassing man, and bores me very much. [The telegram was read: 'Flores desires news of you'.] I cannot explain why he should have telegraphed in his own name. I have also received telegrams from Mr Flores. I am afraid these telegrams have disappeared. I have my suspicion of Mr Dierks. The offices that he occupies does not suggest genuine business. Mr Dierks has never sent me money.

Pressed as to why Mr Dierks should take such interest in a comparative stranger, he replied:

I had certain suspicions that Mr Dierks wanted me to do something for him. It was possibly for me to get certain information. I have my suspicion of Mr Dierks. I am not a person who would furnish information. I admit that if Mr Dierks really sent the telegram, it is very strange. I give you my word of honour that I did not go to Southampton or Portsmouth. If you tell me that I am suspected of being a spy, it is a mistake.[12]

It was not until 24 June that the prisoner made another statement, again at New Scotland Yard in the presence of Sir Basil Thomson and Major Drake. Very little documentation about the investigation into Buschman's activities is available today, and thus details of much of the evidence against him can only be surmised from the questions put to him in this interview and his answers. After being cautioned in both French and English he was told that figures written in invisible ink were found on his papers. He replied:

It is impossible that 3137 should have been found on the card. I play the violin. The writing 'British Expeditionary Force' found on the blotting paper is not mine. I have never used blotting paper in Mr Franco's house. This blotting paper was in the drawer.

He was told that in a magazine above the words 'Nuevo Mundo' the characters 'K 1283' had been developed, and that there were also pinpricks.

It is impossible. I had no shares in the company with Dierks and Flores, and I can only account for their sending me telegrams inviting me to a meeting because Dierks had some wild scheme in which he wanted me to take a part, but I refused to have anything to do with it. Dierks was quite in the air. He said he wanted people who could speak Spanish, and all sorts of languages.

He was asked who put him on his guard against Mr Dierks.

It was a man named van Staa, who has a business in Rotterdam. He is a Transport Commission Agent and the name of the firm is Ivers & Van Staa, Glashaven, Rotterdam. I am not sure of his nationality. I think he is Dutch.

Buschman was asked why, on the card given to him on the ship, he filled in the address to which he was going as 4 Great Tower Street, whereas in fact he went to the Savoy Hotel. He replied, 'I understand from the consul that I had to give the address of a place of business.' He was told that in completing the register at the Strand Palace Hotel on 25 April he stated he had come direct from Paris, and that his last address was Rue St Augustine 26, whereas in fact he had come from the Piccadilly Hotel, to which he responded, 'I did not wish to tell the management of the Strand Palace Hotel that I had just come from the Piccadilly Hotel.' He was then shown a picture of a group of four men, but said he did not know any of them. The list of the developed characters was read to him, but he said he had no knowledge of them. He was shown some figures in the newspaper *Heraldo de Madrid*. 'I cannot see them. The bottle of scent which has been found in my luggage was given to me by a lady in Madrid and I can give you her name if necessary.' Buschman was finally told that he had seen the nature of the evidence to be produced against him.

I am much obliged but do not know anything about it. If any kind of paper is developed this kind of figure will appear. I have no doubt that you know all about Flores and Dierks, and I can only assure you that I have done no business with them. I only want to do business in Spain, and I have neither the time nor the inclination to do anything for Dierks. I was never a soldier or a sailor, and I am absolutely ignorant of all military matters. I am not a good business man as I am more wrapped up in my music than business. I have never done any business with these two men. I was always with Mr Franco or one of his friends when I was in London. I never went to Southampton.[13]

The court martial of Fernando Buschman took place at the Westminster Guildhall on Wednesday, 29 and Thursday, 30 September 1915. Once more the president was Lord Cheylesmore. The prosecution was by Mr A.H. Bodkin for the prosecutor, Lieutenant Peevor. Appearing for the defence, Mr Curtis Bennett was instructed by Tyrrell, Lewis & Co.[14]

The prisoner faced four charges, all under Section 48 of the Defence of the Realm (Consolidation) Regulations 1914. The first was that he came, on or about 14 April, 1915, to the UK to obtain information useful to the enemy. Second, he was in possession of the address of H. Flores, a person concerned in the communication to the enemy of information about naval and military matters. Third, he came from Rotterdam on 16 May, 1915, for the purpose of collecting information useful to the enemy. And fourth, between 26 and 27 April, 1915, he visited Southampton and Portsmouth for the purpose of collecting information for the enemy. To all these charges Buschman pleaded not guilty.[15]

It was found during the trial that Franco was not involved in any actions against Britain, being just a friend of the prisoner who was at one time intending to go into partnership with him. But this came to nothing, like his other so-called business leads. At the time of his arrest Buschman could not prove that one single piece of business had been conducted; all he could say was, 'I was working towards it. In three or four weeks, it was not possible.'

Found upon the prisoner had been a small notebook containing a reference to a trip to Southampton. This was no doubt the reason why he changed his mind and admitted to visiting the city.

> Q. Having addresses at Southampton which had been entered in your book, did you go one day to Southampton?
> A. Yes.
> Q. When you got to Southampton where did you go to?
> A. I go to see this address what I have in my book.

Q.	Do you remember the address or not?
A.	Not.
Q.	You went to some business firm was it?
A.	Yes.
Q.	Did you do any business or not?
A.	No.
Q.	Why not?
A.	Because this business was not a business what I wanted to do, it was not a concern that inspired me with much confidence.

Buschman stated that he had eaten lunch at a hotel, but he could not name it. He had asked a waiter for the times of the trains back to London, and was told that he had plenty of time and could go through Portsmouth, getting a direct train from Portsmouth to London about 5pm. He said that he followed this advice, staying in Portmouth just half an hour when he left the station to buy cigarettes.

During proceedings Buschman would not name his mystery lady friend, and could give no reasonable explanation of his contact with known German agents.

Q.	Were you surprised to see the name of Dierks?
A.	I was not surprised; I did not know what they were; I thought they were bankers.
Q.	You have told us when you went over to Holland you saw Dierks. Did you say to him: 'Well, Mr Dierks, it is extraordinarily kind of you to send me £12; where did you get it from?'?
A.	I did not speak to Dierks about the money which he had sent me.
Q.	There is this lady who is so kind to you, and you have an arrangement to write to Flores, and somebody whose name you had never heard of sends you £12 on account of Flores; did not you ask Dierks what he had got to do with Flores and the lady?
A.	I had no reason to ask Dierks why he sent me the money. It is sufficient that he has the order.
Q.	But you found he was not a banker when you went over there. Did not you ask him: 'How do you, a business man, send me £12?'?
A.	I had no reason to ask him.[16]

In his summing up Mr Bodkin outlined the case:

The evidence of Mr Franco is, as indeed it is the evidence of the accused, that from first to last he never did one piece of business in this country at all. Nothing is easier than to call on persons whose names you may have in the course of a previous business life come across when you are in the country in which they carry on business. Secondly, if that was not a real business enterprise on the part of the accused, what was it? One test is, how does he get the necessary moneys to pay the expenses whilst he is in this country? It is for the Court to say whether, recollecting the time at which this long story is told for the first time, whether there is one word of truth in it; this mysterious lady with the chambermaid and the thousands of fans, and somebody in Madrid who is to sell them for 2d apiece which is to be immediately wired out to a German schoolmaster in Holland; the lady who is unnamed; not one single fact disclosed about her which could give us the opportunity of testing whether any such person exists or not – in my submission that story is incredible. He may have had a female acquaintance – not unlikely he had Madame de Klimm, and he says this one; a curious sort of lady who puts him on to the address at 127a Binneweg, Dierks & Co of that unpronounceable name and unpronounceable address, Grund and Ivers & van Staa of Glashaven, and Madame de Klimm of 24 Plaats, every one of them the addresses of persons known for varying periods to the Secret Service in this country, and in respect of which names and addresses – every one – in the defence of this country, to carry out the objects of these regulations, a warning has been given to the post office and telegraphic authorities in order that communications should not go from this country to them, and as an explanation of the connection with those addresses is this story of the Attaché Flores, and Dierks who is connected with Flores and sends money when the necessary woman failing, Madame de Klimm at 24 Plaats. In my submission that is an untrue story. If so, why is it untrue unless there is something to hide; something to endeavour to explain; something which the person accused knows is contrary to the real state of facts, as he would have the Court believe it? There is no necessity for telling falsehoods; a man does not tell such an elaborate story, an untrue story unless there is a very good reason for doing so.[17]

Buschman was found guilty and sentenced to death. He accepted his fate like a gentleman and people were impressed by his manly bearing. He asked the head of counter-espionage that he be allowed his violin to give him solace whilst waiting his last moments. This was agreed and Buschman played for hours. The execution was set for 7am on 19 October, 1915,[18] and he was transferred to the Tower. The night

11. Carl Frederick
Muller, shot 23
June, 1915
(see Chapter 3).

2. 'His temporary address
was 39 Amberley Street,
Sunderland' (p.45),
home of Miss Jessie
Speir (*Kieran Hegarty*).

13. 111 High Str
Deptford, th
premises of J
Hahn (see p.

14. Haicke Petrus
Marinus Janssen,
shot 30 July, 1915
(see Chapter 4).

15. (*left*) Willem Johannes Roos, shot 30 July, 1915 (see Chapter 4).

16. (*below left*) Ernst Waldemar Melin, shot 10 September, 1915 (see Chapter 5).

17. (*below*) 23 Upper Park Road, Hampstead, the guest house of Flora Milligan (see p.82), where Melin stayed from 12 January, 1915.

18. (*left*) Augusto Alfredo
Roggen, shot 17
September, 1915
(see Chapter 6).

19. (*below left*) Fernando
Buschman, shot 19
September, 1915
(see Chapter 7).

20. (*below*) 36a Harrington
Road, South Kensington
the lodgings of Buschm
(see p.109).

before his death he played late into the night. Beautiful music drifted across the ancient towers and battlements; Buschman seemed oblivious to the death awaiting him, losing himself in the soft, dreamy music. A list of music was found in his property when he was arrested, and no doubt such pieces were played with deep feeling that dank autumn night:

1. Fantasia
2. Bach Sonaten
3. Berceuse & c.
4. Marche Nuptiale, Greig (two pieces)
5. For You Alone
6. Celebre Serenade Espagnole
7. In This Solemn Hour, Verdi
8. I Hear You Calling Me
9. Melodie
10. Berceuse de Jocelyn
11. Cavatina, by J Raff
12. Berceuse, by Gabriel Fauré
13. Serenade, Gabriel Pierne
14. La Serenata, by G Braga
15. La Bohème
16. Tosca
17. Pagliacci[19]

Nobody was sorrier than his guard when the time came to lead them forth for execution. Buschman picked up his violin and kissed it, saying, 'Goodbye, I shall not want you any more.'

He refused the bandage for his eyes and faced the rifles of the 3rd Battalion Scots Guards, sitting in the chair with a courageous smile.[20, 21]

CHAPTER 8

George Traugott Breeckow

George Traugott Breeckow, otherwise known as Reginald Rowland or George T. Parker, was born in Stettin, Germany, in 1882. His father was Russian, having been born in Riga, but was later naturalized as a German. His father was engaged in the piano trade and later George followed him into the business. Breeckow said that he did not do military service, for medical reasons – his chest measurement was too small. In 1908 he went to the USA, spending his time travelling and arranging the export of pianos. He later gave evidence that in 1909 he took out American naturalization papers and by the end of 1913 had become an American citizen. In the meantime his father had died and, wishing to see his mother and sisters, he returned to Germany on 28 May, 1914.

Breeckow's explanation of events is as follows. On 18 August, 1914, shortly after war broke out, he obtained an emergency passport in Berlin, 'to be protected against any trouble'. He had a return ticket on the Amerika-Hamburg Line which he stopped, obtaining a money refund. He became friendly with the American consul in Stettin, and they spent many afternoons together. Through this friendship Breeckow obtained a position in a bank which was situated in the same building as the consulate. At the end of February, 1915, he had a discussion with one of the bank directors in which he expressed his desire to return to the USA, as living was very hard in Germany. Having no experience in banking, he felt that it might be some years before he would earn enough to be able to afford to leave. The director told him that he knew a gentleman who was connected with the Bureau of Foreign Affairs and might recommend Breeckow to him as an Imperial Messenger – courier – to neutral states, especially the USA. Breeckow was interested and forwarded to Berlin his application and a large photograph, together with three letters of recommendation, as was customary in Germany. He received a short letter in reply, sending

118

back his passport, thanking him for his application and stating that he would be considered, hearing from them shortly. On 20 March, 1915, Breeckow received two letters: one from the Bureau of Foreign Affairs in Berlin returning his papers and another from Naval Intelligence in Antwerp, who wanted him to resign his position with the bank and report to them at his earliest convenience. He left the bank on 1 April, but offered his services free of charge to the Bureau of Foreign Affairs as he wanted to return to the USA. He said that if he was to go to Antwerp he would need a passport allowing entry, and requested assurances that any travel expenses to Belgium would be repaid. He received confirmation by wire and the passport came the next after-noon by express letter.

In Antwerp Breeckow was first introduced to Captain-Lieutenant Lassen, then left alone in an anteroom for a few minutes before Lassen came back with Rittmeister Schneitzer. They had a general conversa-tion, about the war and what Breeckow had seen, which was a sizing-up affair. After an hour or two Breeckow was told to return in the evening, as they were very busy in the afternoon. At 9pm Breeckow called again, seeing both officers. Breeckow states: 'I came to the point and asked about America. They said "Never mind, there is plenty of time. You are here now, and in a couple of days we will let you know what is what.".'

He was later told to report the next morning about midday, as they were often up very late working until two or three in the morning. When Breeckow attended again, the conversation covered the general position and military and naval questions. The next day Breeckow visited again; he was getting very nervous and uneasy, but was now told what they wanted him to do. 'We do not know yet the situation with America and Germany, which is not very pleasant. We do not know what to do.' Breeckow was given no particulars about a passage to America, but told that he must go to England. Breeckow said that he was very surprised by this suggestion. Lassen told him that his pass-port was of no use for travel to England as it had a Berlin stamp on it, but they had a different one for him in the name of Reginald Rowland. He was to make his way to The Hague, where he was to contact a Mr Dierks:

Well you see, entering England you are supposed to have a business in hand, and they asked me if I could represent an American firm that I could represent for my own sake, Of course, the piano firm that I represented in the United States I could not represent on the Continent, because there is no business with pianos in Europe from America and so he said: 'We have an agent at The Hague, Mr Dierks, No 166 Loosduinschekade,' and to go there and see him and introduce myself, they would write to him, and he would fix me up with some business cards.

Breeckow arrived at Rotterdam, taking the electric tram to The Hague. He saw Dierks in his first-floor office. Breeckow said, 'I have come from the Naval Intelligence on work, and my name is supposed to be Reginald Rowland.' Breeckow found Dierks to be a very reserved man with a cold, unchangeable face: during his conversation Breeckow saw no change of expression. Dierks, as arranged, fixed him up with a business cover.

The day before he left Antwerp Breeckow said he was told that in London he was supposed to meet a gentleman who would approach him with the name Velociter – a catch-word. Contact was to be made through a bank, the Société Générale. His task was to forward messages back to Dierks & Co. He left Rotterdam for Tilbury at 10pm on 10 May, 1915,[1] on the steamship *Batavier*.

The next day Breeckow produced to Walter Richard Perks, an Aliens' Officer based at Gravesend, a passport in the name of Reginald Rowland bearing his photograph. Giving his details (as Dierks had arranged) as a business representative in scrap iron for Norton B. Smith Co, 243 Front Street, New York, USA, he told Perks that he had been doing well and had worked hard, trading with Germany from The Hague in copper, steel, iron and in English products sent from America. He was now on his way back to America.[2] During the journey Breeckow had become friendly with a Dr Tullidge and, after docking, they travelled to London together. After trying five hotels, they booked in at the Ivanhoe Hotel, Bloomsbury Street annexe. Breeckow was seen by the reception clerk, Miss Dora Pickett. After he had completed and signed the registration form, she noted that the new arrival was a Reginald George Rowland, born in 1884 in Kinosha, Wisconsin, USA; a piano dealer with a permanent address in Washington.[3] The following day, 12 May, he left the annexe and moved into the main building.

Breeckow had written a letter to his contact, a Mrs Wertheim, making an appointment to see her on Thursday, 13 May. The letter was signed with the initials GTP. He later stated that before leaving Antwerp he been told when signing letters and telegrams to use the name 'G.T. Parker'. But according to Breeckow, Wertheim did not turn up. As a result he sent a postcard, making another appointment on Friday, 14 May at 4pm. The card said that she would know him by him wearing a lavender sweet pea.

I was sitting int the lobby of the Waldorf Hotel and had a bunch of lavender peas in my buttonhole, and a bunch of violets lying on the

120

armchair, and a lady came in. I gazed at her for a while, and did not dare – I was not sure it was her. And then presently she went up and we met half-ways and she said, 'My name is Mrs Wertheim, are you Mr . . .?'

She then produced his postcard from her bag. He gave her the bouquet of violets. They got into conversation and decided that they would not take tea there, as the heavy rain had stopped. They took a taxi-cab to Hyde Park Corner, where they had tea in a cafe. Breeckow stated that they then had a very nice general conversation, talking about mutual acquaintances, and artistes like Madam Courland, a Dutch singer. Mrs Wertheim spoke of the musical evenings that she gave at home. They talked of America, and she told him that she had been to Boston, Massachusetts. Breeckow said that he would like to see London and it was agreed that they would meet the next day at 11am in Rotten Row. She had booked to go riding. Breeckow was pleased as he was very fond of horses, riding being his only sport.[4] This small talk no doubt did take place, but the conversation must have also covered the real reason for their meeting in England, and their task on behalf of German intelligence.

Louise Emily Wertheim was born in German Poland at Stargatt, near the border, when her parents were paying a visit. However, her birth was registered in Berlin,[5] in her maiden name of Klitzke,[6] and she spent her early years and was educated there. In 1901 she came to England, and the following year married at Eton registry office Bruno Wertheim, a man she had met in Berlin. His father was a naturalized UK subject, having been born a Russian. During the first year the couple did not have a permanent home in England and moved to America. Coming back to Europe, they met her parents in Switzerland at Lausanne. Returning to London, they moved into a newly-built house at 7 Fawley Road, Hampstead, and lived there for five or six years. Bruno Wertheim was then an accountant at the Austro-Laenderbank in Bishopsgate. He was a great spendthrift, and was helped by his wealthy relations until his father died, leaving him a very good income. Indeed, he was free to leave the bank and travelled around Europe, taking in Denmark, Norway, France, Switzerland and Italy. But the marriage was not happy and they did not always travel together. He was very fond of mountaineering and she took this up to be with him, but later found it too much for her. In May, 1913, they parted in Berlin, taking out a deed of separation.

Mrs Wertheim was left with an allowance of £518 a year, and travelled back to England to be near her husband's relations. She remained on very friendly terms with them, living in several private hotels and boarding-houses around Inverness Terrace. It was not long

121

before her husband got into financial difficulties again and bankruptcy proceedings were pending, thus her allowance of £43 3s 4d a month was paid to her by the receiver. When the war was declared she was living at 22 Pembridge Gardens, having moved from across the road at 23 Pembridge Gardens after returning from Italy. She had seen newspaper articles advising people wanting to go abroad to get a passport as soon as possible. She did so on 3 August, as she wanted to visit her mother in Berlin.

> When I had my passport I went to the station, but I had not taken my luggage, because I wanted to enquire about tickets, and on getting to the station there were hundreds of people who wanted to get away, and there were wild stories circulating about that you could not take the luggage at all, and you had to walk through Holland to get into Germany, and it was much better to wait a little longer. Well, I decided to wait a little longer till things had quietened down.

In fact she was not to leave England until 3 October, 1914.[7] Wertheim stated that she got as far as Amsterdam just as Antwerp was falling, but was unable to enter Germany. She was told by the German consul that it was impossible to enter with an English passport. Having made this connection with the authorities, no doubt word of her position and situation filtered through and she was recruited by German intelligence. Well-travelled and with a German backround, she was just the type of person that would have been useful to them. A friend later said that after war was declared she seemed very excitable, almost feverish, with pro-German views.[8]

On 15 May, 1915, the day after the first encounter, the two spies met in Regent's Park, where horses were hired from the job-master John Stuckle.[9] Mrs Wertheim rode a grey. After this exercise, arrangements were made to meet again at Hyde Park Corner the next day at 11.30am, but she never turned up: there was confusion over the time, and they missed each other. Concerned, Breeckow wrote to her making an appointment for the Monday.[10] She telephoned his hotel in the evening, to be told that he had already gone to bed and to call again next morning after 9am.[11] Contact made, at noon they walked through the park together to Hyde Park Corner, taking a cab to a café in Regent Street. After that they travelled by cab again to Richmond Park. They were to see each other most days after this meeting: he found her a pleasant companion and their friendship developed.[12] They took in the Wallace Collection, Kew Gardens and the Zoological Gardens.[13] Around 21 May arrangements were made to go to Bournemouth; they were making their plans, but also enjoying their time together.

On Saturday, 22 May the couple booked in at the Grand Hotel, Bournemouth, where they saw the wife of the manager, Mrs Edith Maria Bishop. Breeckow signed the registration form as Reginald Rowland coming from the Ivanhoe Hotel, London. Mrs Wertheim signed in as Lizzie Wertheim, giving her birthplace as London! They took separate rooms. Breeckow was to say:

We arrived in the evening about eight o'clock – I am not quite sure. We had a light supper in the hotel, and went through the City for about an hour strolling, and Mrs Wertheim went to bed, and I went to the bar, and the next morning the hotel clock was late and we were the last party in the coffee room. We went about half-past ten to the beach and sat there till one o'clock, and had lunch at a restaurant close to the pier, and went back at half-past two to the hotel, and we talked and smoked.[14]

They spent the whole afternoon in the hotel garden, as it was very hot and the garden was the only cool place that they could find.[15]

On 24 May Mrs Wertheim was not very well, and she appeared very late in the breakfast room, and in the afternoon we walked through the City, and in the evening about half-past nine it was full moon – we went to the shore. On Monday afternoon we passed an Eolian place, and there was close to it an exhibition [pianos]. I had been employed by the Eolian Company in America. On Tuesday we had our breakfast about nine and I went into the City and bought post-cards which are among my belongings, and I met Mrs Wertheim coming along and I asked her what she had bought, and she said perfume and other things. We returned by the 2.10 train, and arrived in Waterloo Station.[16]

But during this visit Breeckow had also been busy; on a copy of the *Star and Echo* newspaper dated 26 May he carefully wrote in invisible ink:

On the trip to Bournemouth rather large transports of Artillery on their way from Aldershot to S. The largest troop camp at present at Wareham near Swanage but the numbers of men had decreased. At Aldershot 2 balloon sheds.[17]

This was posted to H. Flores at 127a Binnenweg, Rotterdam, along with a copy of *The Times* of 26 May and the *Evening News* of 25 May.[18] Such a postal packet set in motion alarm bells in the censorship office. It was clear that another spy was loose in Britain, who, it was hoped, if given enough rope, would hang himself.

Plans were now made that Breeckow should visit Ramsgate and Lizzie Wertheim should travel to Scotland to gather naval intelligence about the location of the First Fleet. She appears to have been unwilling to carry out such a dangerous task; Breeckow was to write to his contacts:

As soon as she is back she will live alone so that we can use her and my address. She is an absolute lady and it has cost me much work to really win and convince her. She is extraordinarily obstinate and must be treated gently . . . Never mind, gents, I am some Bear, when it comes to handle the ladies . . .

It was considered a good idea to clock her intended activities in Scotland through the company of another lady, who would travel in all innocence and would be unsuspected.[19] To this end, at 8pm on 25 May Mrs Wertheim paid a surprise visit to an American lady named Mabel Knowles, who had lived in England for 12 years. They had met when Lizzie Wertheim took English diction lessons from her, but since their last meeting Knowles had moved to 33 Regents Park Road, and was not aware that Lizzie knew her new address. 'I was surprised to see her, and I asked her to come upstairs. I asked her who had told her my address and she said Miss Maud Hoffman had given it to her.'

Knowles asked Wertheim where she had been, as she had heard that she had gone back to Germany. She also asked if she had been interned, to which Lizzie replied, 'Why should I be, when I am a British subject?' They were to meet again on 26 and 27 May, when it was decided that they should take a holiday together in Scotland.

I hesitated, and then said Yes; where would she like to go; and she asked me to suggest some places. I said Stratford-on-Avon, as I knew she was very fond of Shakespeare, and I thought she would like to see Shakespeare's home; and she was pleased; and she said she would let me know the next day – Thursday 27 May; and she decided, in talking it over, that I needed bracing air, and would I like to go to Scotland or Ireland? I was rather keen on going to Ireland, because I had been to Scotland; and I said I would like to go to Ireland. She finally decided on Scotland.

On 28 May the two women caught a train at King's Cross Station for Edinburgh. On the journey Mabel Knowles noticed that Lizzie wrote poetry the whole time.[20] The poem was addressed 'To the Stranger', who was later identified by Wertheim as Breeckow.

Mine eyes hung on thy lips – Thou spakest
more, and gavest me thine other news – news
mysterious – Thou are not what thou art – yet
why? – Why? I understand. As thou wil'st have
it – so it shall be Blame none but thee, and
thy masters. Is there no truth in all this
world? Only foul play? Thou art vile stranger –
and shrewd thy cunning. Expect not roses –
where thou gavest poison green, and not gold
– where thou hast given lead. I heard thy
message, divined thy masters – and will
obey![21]

It seems clear that Breeckow had a hold over her, and as he
confirmed later in court, 'after a few days their relationship turned into
a love affair.'[22] However, their plans now went wrong. The women
arrived in Edinburgh at about 6pm and signed the registration form at
the hotel. But being an American alien, Miss Knowles had to visit the
local police the next morning. She found that she was without necessary passport, so decided to return home at once.[23] The cover had
flown and Lizzie Wertheim was left exposed.

In the meantime Breeckow headed for Ramsgate:

Dr Tullidge had invited me for the third time to come down to
Ramsgate to visit his friends, Mr and Mrs Scarlet, at Beechcroft, a
private home out of Ramsgate, and after I had declined twice I
accepted it, and I went down on the Friday afternoon. He introduced me to the Westbourne Hotel, and he introduced me to Mr
and Mrs Richard, and he asked them to give me the same room as
he had. The next morning I went to Beechcroft, it is a private
mansion.[24]

The Westbourne Hotel is situated on the seafront at Westcliff, and the
room Breeckow asked for was on the second floor at the front. From
his window he had a view of the sea some nine miles by three; it was a
commanding position. On the first evening Breeckow asked the
proprietor Mr Ivor Richards for a spy-glass, but not having such an
article Richards suggested that he could obtain one from a local
second-hand shop. However, there was a telescope stand on the front
only about 15 or 20 feet from the hotel door.[25] On Monday, 1 June
Breeckow returned to London and the Ivanhoe Hotel. He spent the
day writing his report to Flores in invisible ink between a covering
letter. A translation is as follows:

125

Dear Sir, I hope you understand the contents of my letter of today, and also of the previous one which was posted to you. Our friend has written to me from Tay Firth that there is nothing to be seen of the Fleet. I got a message from her, saying 'En route to the North.'

At my last visit to R [Ramsgate] there were eight mine-sweepers stationed here equipped with one quick-firing gun each. On the local pier light guns and on the promenade, various searchlights. Otherwise on the sea, five miles distant only a few high sea torpedo boats on constant patrol. In the streets at the Harbour, sand bags barricades and wire entanglements ready for landing. Garrison, one company of infantry, one company of coast artillery, and a search-light division.

You must not become impatient because I had to stay in the hotel for such a long time to quieten the detectives, who were damned near me, and you would not believe how difficult travelling and living in foreign parts is. [Breeckow stated later that he made this part up to stop his contacts becoming impatient!]

As soon as the matter up here is settled I shall start travelling from here. I shall pretend to study music then I shall have my hands free. If it is possible please send your messages on similar paper and only written on one side as I was unfortunately not able to develop them. [Breeckow had lost some thin rice paper when trying to develop a message with a candle.]

For short journeys to the coast I shall take our lady with me as it is really better if two persons look at the Harbour. We do not agree particularly well, but she will work for the cause.[26]

Lizzie Wertheim did indeed work for the cause. On Sunday, 30 May she made her way to Dundee on the Tay Firth. She then moved on to Carnoustie, about 11 miles from Dundee.[27] In the yard of a hotel Lizzie found three men working in the garage, busily cleaning cars. They saw a tall lady dressed in black, who approached them and asked if there were any coastguard stations in the district. She found that there were two, one at Westhaven, Arbroath, and the other at Auchmitie. She checked her guidebook and asked for a taxi to take her to Arbroath and round the principal parts of Carnoustie Firth. After ten minutes a taxi was obtained and she went on her way.[28] One of the men in the garage was George Robertson, a private in D Company, Third Battalion, Cameron Highlanders, who was working part-time at the hotel. He said later that she talked in quite a foreign accent, and after some consideration he came to the conclusion that she was a German spy. He took no direct action to inform the authorities, but was later questioned by the police on his evidence.[29] Tay Firth was one of the places where the British fleet rested. By going to Dundee, Carnoustie,

Arbroath and later Perth, Lizzie was able to ascertain that the fleet was not there. Such negative information would have been useful to the Germans, as there were not many places where the big ships of the fleet could shelter, and eliminating one location reduced the options of where the ships could be found.[30]

Wertheim then made her way to Inverness, not far from Cromarty Firth, another location of the fleet. Cromarty was also a naval base. She booked into the Station Hotel, Inverness, on 1 June and stayed until 3 June.[31] On 2 June she called upon Charles Charker, a clerk employed by Messrs McCrae & Dicks, Motor Liners. She had returned from a journey in one of the firm's hire cars and he asked her if she had enjoyed the drive; she replied, 'Very much'. Lizzie now wanted to make arrangements for a two-day trip to Dornoch, and requested a price. He quoted the price; then she asked him if there was a place called Cromarty, as she believed it was a very nice place to see. He agreed that it was and she asked what the extra charge was to go to Cromarty on her way to Dornoch.

> I quoted her the extra charge that it would cost her; but she said this extra charge was too much. After a considerable talk, which I just cannot remember, she said that she would take the car to Cromarty, and there make up her mind whether she would continue her journey to Dornoch, or dismiss the car after paying the chauffeur there. I booked the car.

Charker knew that, as a naval base, Cromarty was a prohibited area for aliens. He came to the conclusion, after considerable conversation with her, that she was German. Immediately after she left he telephoned the police, expressing his suspicions.[32] John McNaughton, the Chief Constable of Inverness borough police and also the registration officer under the terms of the Aliens Act, arrived at the Station Hotel in the evening at about 9pm. He first inspected the registration form that Lizzie Wertheim had completed on her arrival. What he found surprised him: the visitor had entered her name as 'Wertheim' but signed it 'Wertham'. This was a blunder which shows the amateur way that she went about her activities. It was an attempt to conceal her nationality, no doubt done in a fluster and the tension of the moment. There are a number of German names ending in 'heim', but there are not many such names in Britain – Blenheim, named after a place abroad, but little more. Wertheim is obviously a German name, and would be a disadvantage if one was engaged in spying.

The Chief Constable asked the hotel manager if he could interview his guest, and the two of them went to her room. He found a slightly stout, well-dressed, attractive woman.

I explained to her I was the Chief Constable of the Borough and also registration officer, and I had the form with me. I said I wanted to know the reason why it was not properly filled up. 'You notice the surname is spelt in one way and the signature is in another way.'
Wertheim replied, 'It was a slip of the pen, it should be h-e-i-m.' The Chief Constable said, 'I want to satisfy myself that you are of British nationality.' Wertheim said she could do that and produced her passport, which showed that she was the wife of Bruno Wertheim, a naturalized British subject of Prussian origin, born in Moscow. McNaughton asked where her husband was, as he had not noticed any entry in the registration book. She told him that she was travelling alone and for pleasure; she had come to Scotland to get away from her divorce proceedings and past troubles. He asked her where she was going from Inverness, and pointed out that it was a prohibited area. It was necessary that he should know her movements, and he was not satisfied that she was there on legitimate business. She told him she was going to Cromarty, Invergordon and Dornoch. (Cromarty Firth was between Cromarty on the south side and Invergordon on the north. They are in view of each other and command any shipping in the Firth.)

McNaughton told her that her travels did not harmonize with her statement that she was in Scotland to forget her troubles, as she was going into places where she would have trouble. He pointed out that there were large naval and military camps in the area, and that he would not allow her to proceed further. At this point she broke down and began to cry, and mentioned she had travelled from Edinburgh, Dundee, and Perth and had not been challenged by the police, and she thought it was very unfair that he should prevent her from going further. If he had any doubt of her honesty of purpose she would give him a seat in her car! He refused her offer and she said that she still intended going; he replied, 'Well, if you intend to go I am going to arrest you, and you will be detained until I communicate with the Metropolitan Police, and until I have satisfied myself of your bona fides.'

With that Lizzie changed her mind and asked if she might be allowed to return to London. He agreed, but said she would have to take the inland route, and observation would be kept on her to make sure. She gave her address in London as 62 Hammersmith Road. McNaughton agreed that she could leave at 9am on 3 June. However, very unhappy with the situation, he immediately commmunicated with the Metropolitan Police, as he was sure she was German.[33] Just before she left the Station Hotel Lizzie gave instructions to Miss Annie Macaskill, the bookkeeper, asking her to post a letter for her to 62 Hammersmith Road, London, and to forward on to this address any letters received for her at the hotel.[34]

Whilst this was taking place Breeckow had written to Flores at 127a

128

Binnenweg, Rotterdam. The envelope was intercepted by the postal authorities; it was not stuck down, which was becoming common practice to help the censor. When it was examined and treated they found that between the lines of the letter in black ink was a message in German. But Breeckow showed how very inept he was as a spy – amazingly, he had written on the back of the envelope the sender's details: 'George T. Parker, Imperial Hotel, London'![35] It did not take long for enquiries to be made and instructions to be issued by Major Drake of MO5 for Rowland to be arrested. On the morning of 4 June Herbert Fitch, a detective inspector at New Scotland Yard, arrived at the hotel. He found Rowland and told him that he was a police officer and that he intended to arrest him and convey him to New Scotland Yard pending enquiries. Rowland replied 'No'. Fitch found that the man could speak English fluently, covering his German accent with Americanisms. He did not appear to be the type one would associate with the normal run of spies, being long-fingered and thin-faced, more the type to be found on a concert platform; he seemed to have a sensitive nature.[36] Fitch instructed his prisoner to take him to his bedroom, where Breeckow was searched and the false passport was found. There was clothing hanging up, and Fitch saw two bags. On the washstand he found a glass bottle with a glass stopper, containing yellow fluid, which the prisoner confirmed was his. All the property was collected and handed over to Detective Inspector Edmund Buckley at New Scotland Yard.[37]

Buckley started to examine and list Breeckow's property. He found a steel nib in the case of a safety razor set, a visiting card of 'Reginald Rowland, 4049 Washington Avenue', and a copy of a telegram to H. Flores, 127a Binnenweg, Rotterdam, dated 3 June: 'Tell sister not to mind former letters and card. Liz met nearly all her friends at P., tender feelings will meet rest Dora's birthday. George Parker.' There was also a certificate of posting of a registered packet of 1 June with the name Wertham, Inverness, written on it. (This was highly suspicious, as Lizzie had used the changed spelling of Wertham when she registered at the hotel, so Breeckow must have been fully aware of the plan.) In the top of a shaving brush he found, in the lower part of the case, a piece of thin rice paper, folded round so as to go inside and underneath the top of the shaving brush. It contained a considerable amount in Breeckow's handwriting in English and German, detailing British warships. There was also a typewritten introductory letter on the paper of Norton B. Smith, but no evidence that any business had been done. In a notebook were the addresses of Flores in Rotterdam, Dierks in The Hague and the Westbourne Hotel, Westcliff, Ramsgate. Finally, there was a book called *Fleets of the World, 1915*. In short, the evidence against Rowland was damning![38]

129

On Friday, 4 June Gertrude Elizabeth Sophia Brandes, the private secretary to the Baroness Bruno Schroder, was surprised at the return of Mrs Wertheim. She lived at 62 Hammersmith Road with her father, and Lizzie had lived with them on and off since January, 1915.

> She told me that she had just arrived after a very rough crossing from Holland where she had been staying with my brother-in-law in the same Apartment House, and that my brother-in-law had told her that I would probably be able to put her up for the night if she called on me and brought greetings of my sister.

During her stay she left the house on a number of occasions for periods of a few days or more, but never said where she was going. At the beginning of June Lizzie told her that she would be away for a fortnight, so when she returned unexpectedly they were surprised. On Sunday, 6 June, matters came to a head, when Brandes' brother asked her to leave. He had heard that she was under suspicion and was being watched, and for that reason, and in the position that they found themselves they did not think that it was fair for her to remain at the address as it would be prejudical to their position. She replied that she did not care at all whether she was being watched. On the contrary, if people watched her, they would see she was only travelling about visiting her friends and relations, and was doing nothing wrong whatsoever. Lizzie did move out, but left some luggage. On Tuesday, 8 June a letter came for her, re-directed from Inverness. This was their first clue that their former guest had been to Scotland.[39]

In the meantime, early on Friday, 4 June, Lizzie called at 33 Regent's Park Road, the home of Mabel Knowles who had left her in Scotland. This visit was also unexpected. Mabel saw that she had two bags and two dress suitcases with her. Lizzie asked if she could leave the two bags there while going to see her solicitor. The following day Lizzie called again and took her friend's dog out, saying she had been motoring in Scotland but giving no details. In the late evening of Monday, 7 June, Mabel Knowles returned home finding her friend there again.

> She was sitting in the passage and my dog barked at her; I heard her laugh and I brought her in. I asked her what she was doing and she said she came for her bags and that she was going to Brighton that same night. When she came for her bags I was astonished she should go out at all . . . saying, 'Why, how dare you go to Brighton alone and at night!' It was bad enough for English-speaking people to go to the coast, let alone anyone who spoke with a German accent. I was very worried about it. She said, 'Oh very well; I suppose I have

130

lost the train; may I come in?' And she came in and we talked for some time until it got very late, and she asked if she could stay. I said, 'We have not got very much room; I will wait until I see my friend Miss Burnside.' And she said she would not mind sitting up in a chair. I said no, I would see Miss Burnside, and she agreed to give up her room.

Lizzie stayed the next night, but the relationship was coming to a head. On 9 June Mabel begged her to go, as she was still taking her friend's bed and there was no room for visitors. Lizzie said she would arrange to stay in a private hotel in Hammersmith, but before any action could be taken the police arrived![40]

Detective Inspector Edmund Buckley had just called at the home address of Miss Brandes and collected the luggage left by Mrs Wertheim. He and Detective Inspector Herbert Fitch moved on to 33 Regent's Park Road, arriving at about 10.30pm. On the top floor landing they knocked on the door and Buckley saw that Mrs Wertheim was with two other ladies. He said 'Mrs Wertheim, I want to speak to you on a serious matter.' He was asked into the sitting room, and then told her who he was: 'I am going to take you into custody as I believe you are engaged in espionage.' She replied, 'I am not nervous; I am not afraid.'

During this conversation Miss Knowles was present, and pointed out to the officer Mrs Wertheim's luggage, a purple dressing case, a leather suitcase and a wrist bag. These were gathered together and Mrs Wertheim suddenly said, 'There is a poem there that I want.' The officer told her that she could not have it and must not touch her luggage. Inspector Buckley left his prisoner with Inspector Fitch and Miss Knowles while Miss Burnside accompanied him for a search of the bedroom.[41] While in the room Miss Burnside told the Inspector she thought she had seen Mrs Wertheim give the curtain a little push and wave a white handkerchief or paper out of her bedroom window. Concerned, Miss Burnside got a lantern and together they went downstairs and searched the back garden, but found nothing.[42] Lizzie was then taken by cab to Cannon Row police station. On the journey she asked Buckley, 'How did you find out where I was? It does not matter either way now to my case, but I should like to know.' The Inspector would not tell her, but said it might come out in the course of the inquiry.

Her property was searched and Buckley found an envelope addressed to Reginald Rowland Esq. Ivanhoe Hotel, London, and Rowland's business card with the false American address. There was also the letter signed 'Your devoted G.T.P.' in Rowland's handwriting concerning their first meeting in England; a postcard, postmarked The

131

Hague, giving the address as 'Loosduinschekade, 166' – the address of Dierks; a draft telegram in her hand to Althuis, at the same address, from 'Wertheim, 62 Hammersmith Road'; a list of motor trips published by Macrae & Dicks of Inverness, which contained a pencil mark in Wertheim's handwriting – 'To Cromarty new Naval Base'; a list of places in Scotland – 'Edinburgh, Dundee and Carnoustie', and so on; fourteen postcards of eleven British ships; a London, Tilbury & Southend railway guide, and another poem entitled 'Eyes that smiled'. Mrs Wertheim had some explaining to do![43]

The next morning, in daylight, Ada Elizabeth Burnside, still filled with excitement and curiosity, looked out of her bedroom window where she had seen Mrs Wertheim standing. She saw pieces of a letter on the window sill. These she recovered, then went downstairs to the garden and verandah below, where she found more pieces. These she gathered up and took to Buckley.[44] He saw that it was a letter in Rowland's writing dated 3 June. It started 'My Dear Madam, Thanks ever so much for your news, etc,' and ended 'your devoted . . .'. However, much was missing.[45]

Sir Basil Thomson writes:

The artistic temperament of Breeckow was not equal to the ordeal. His pretence of being a rich American broke down immediately, and he was aghast to find how much the police knew about his secret movements. Though he made no confession, he returned to Cannon Row in a state of great nervous tension. Lizzie Wertheim, on the other hand, was tough, brazen, and impudent, claiming that as a British subject she had a right to travel where she would. She declined to sit in her chair, but walked up and down the room, flirting a large silk handkerchief as if she was practising a new dancing step.

Breeckow had maintained throughout that he knew no German, but his assurance began to break down in the loneliness of a prison cell. He had a strong imagination; no doubt the thought that his female accomplice might be betraying him worked strongly on his feelings. One morning I went over with a naval officer to see how he was. There was a question about signing for his property, and he was sent into the room for the purpose. When he found himself alone with us he said suddenly, 'Am I to be tried for my life?' 'I understand that you are to be tried.' 'What is the penalty for what I have done?' (Up to this point he had made no confession.) 'Is it death?' 'I do not know,' I said. 'You have not yet been tried.' 'I can tell from your face that it is death. I must know. I have to think of my old mother in Stettin. I want to write a full confession.'

I told him that of course he was free to write what he pleased, but that anything he did write would almost certainly be used against him at his trial. 'Never mind,' he said, 'I have carried the secret long enough. Now I want to tell the whole truth.'[46]

The statement was taken down in the presence of Inspector Buckley by Detective Constable Algernon Sprackling, who states:

I was about to read it to him, and he said: 'I would rather read it myself.' He read it over: he made alterations in his own handwriting and before he signed it I said to him: 'I have to caution you that this statement will be used in evidence against you.' He replied: 'I understand.' Then as he was about to sign he said: 'I will sign it in my correct name,' and he signed it in the name of 'George T. Breeckow'!

On 14 June Breeckow was interviewed in the presence of the American consul, as he claimed he was an American citizen, but after extensive enquiries by them this was rejected out of hand.[47] Enquiries were made into the background of Mrs Wertheim, resulting in a report dated 25 June, 1915, which finished with the comment that the claim by her to be a British subject was open to the gravest possible doubt.[48] Directions were received from the Attorney General that, as she claimed to be British, she should be tried by a jury as the legal questions could amount to considerable difficulty if her claim could not be disproved.[49] She was held in Holloway prison; Breeckow was at Wandsworth detention barracks.[50]

The two were tried together by civil court on 14 September, 1915, at the Old Bailey, the Central Criminal Court, before three judges. The trial lasted for four days. Both pleaded not guilty; during the trial Mrs Wertheim admitted little, but Breeckow admitted much and attempted to protect her. Each was found guilty of the charge of having the intention of assisting the enemy, after the jury were out for just eleven minutes.[51]

Lizzie Wertheim had nothing to say when invited to address the court, but Breeckow was loquacious:

I want to confess, my lords, that I have never received a word of information of Mrs Wertheim about the Fleet or Navy of England. It is merely a coincidence that I could fit her in my reports to the German Naval Intelligence, and I am very sorry for the miserable unfortunate position she is now in. I would like to call your attention again to this: that the German Naval Intelligence wanted to know the information with regard to the movements of the Fleet.

133

My report of the Fleet being in the Tay Firth was fictitious, because it was proved that Mrs Wertheim was not in the Tay Firth, nor did she ever reach Dornoch Firth.

I am sorry indeed that I was forced to injure England. It was not my intention to do damage to the country or the nation. The reports I have given in my letters and the newspapers gave them no intelligence which was of any value to the enemy. When I met Mrs Wertheim I confess that I took a very great advantage towards her. We became friendly; in fact in a few days it turned into a love affair. I am very sorry I used her in my reports as a kind of tool towards the Naval Intelligence to get another draft – to cover the expenses – as I intended to leave on 12 June on the *Minnehaha* to the United States and would have gone right away; but when I arrived here I was told that my ship would not go till the end of the first week. If I had stayed here and gone all alone I should have gone by that ship; but I came into contact with Mrs Wertheim, and being attracted by her personality I stayed here a little longer. Of course my expenses would not manage, and I tried to get money by writing those reports, which are great deal fictitious and untrue, not with the idea of doing any damage or harm to the country.

I was preparing for the last letter to the Naval Intelligence by writing about the police – that the police was coming after me or was after me. In another letter I said I preferred to come back to Holland for the business I was engaged for. I am very sorry that the last letter was not stopped by the post or the mail because it would show that what I said in my statement was both plain and true – that I was not here to break my neck. In the secret writing I used strong English words telling them to hell with his business – that he might do it with some other people but not with me. But fearing that I should be stopped then for the sake of £30 I tried to make up again by the secret writing about Ramsgate facts which are photographs seen in the last Fall in Germany about the Harbour, and so on, and the sand-bag barricades; and as Mrs Wertheim had gone up to Scotland I of course – I am sorry I put her in my reports. I again confess that I expected a card letter from her telling me that she was going up to Inverness and giving me the hotel, but she did not give me any information about Inverness. I am sorry that I treated her in this way; but there was the very hard and serious position I was in since this last year. I wanted to get back to the United States and by all means I had to accept any propositions made to me by the Naval Intelligence.

But I again want to remark that I did not know what was wanted – not until the 17th – the first Monday I was in London; I knew what was contained in the book and what was wanted. I repeat again they only want me to report the formation of the first Fleet and the transports from the south to France or the Dardanelles. If I had been a soldier in the German Army it would be a different proposition. I might have been ordered to come here and I might have done so; but I have nothing to do with the army; because I am an American citizen. If I had the slightest doubt that my papers of naturalization could not be traced I should have presented them here, and I am sure you would have verified my statement and everything.

The court was thrown open to the public, Wertheim was brought up, and Mr Justice Bray addressed her:

The jury have found you guilty of the offence of attempting to obtain information in relation to the disposition of his Majesty's ships, and that that information was calculated to be directly useful to the enemy. They have further found you guilty, that you did that act with the intention of assisting the enemy.

Now we have had to consider under those circumstances and under all the circumstances in this case what is the proper sentence that we ought to award. The offence is a very grave one and properly punishable by death or any less punishment. And it is a grave question that we always have to consider in these cases whether we should impose the full penalty or not. We have come to the conclusion that although the offence was extremely grave – it is difficult to suggest any information that would be of greater value to the enemy than information as to the position of his Majesty's Fleet – although we are strongly impressed with the great importance of the information which you attempted to obtain, and with the gravity of the offence you have committed, we have come to the conclusion there are circumstances which prevent the necessity of our being obliged to sentence you to death. The ground upon which we think we may dispense with that sentence is this: that you have been overpersuaded by Rowland to attempt to obtain information. There is nothing to show that before you committed this offence you had done any act of spying, and according to him, and according to the letters he wrote, and according to the view we take, you for a long time refused to do what he asked you to do, and it was with reluctance on your part that you at last consented to do what you did do. Those circumstances we think justify us in saying that we ought not to impose the full penalty. But the punishment must be severe – very severe. You must go to penal servitude for ten years.[52]

With that Mrs Wertheim just smiled bitterly and permitted the wardress to conduct her away without a word.[53] It seems that she had got off somewhat lightly in view of the evidence against her, such as her own communication with Dierks. No doubt Breeckow had pushed her to go without him to Scotland, but she was without doubt an agent in her own right. It might well be significant that in the papers of this case at the Public Record Office is a cutting from *The Times* in which Sir John Simon outlined the German treatment and execution of Nurse Cavell and the treatment of women who spy in Britain: 'No woman who had been tried for any military offence in this country has suffered the death penalty since the war began, or has even been sentenced to death.' Is this cutting in the file significant? Sir John's comment was made during a conversation with a representative of the Associated Press of America in London,[54] so was there a policy that females should not suffer the ultimate fate for political reasons? The USA was very important to both the Germans and British, and American public opinion was a key factor in which side that nation would finally support. We will never know, but such sensitivity was not to touble the court when Breeckow was brought up for his sentence.

Mr Justice Bray addressed the prisoner:

The jury have convicted you of procuring, aiding and abetting the other prisoner in attempting to collect information regarding the disposition of His Majesty's ships; they have found that the information was calculated to be directly useful to the enemy; they have further found (what was the most material part of their verdict) that this was done by you with the intention of assisting the enemy. Now the court desire to say that they agree with the verdict of the jury, both as regards yourself and the other prisoner. They consider the case to have been completely proved. The offence in your case – because you were the author of the whole scheme – is an extremely serious one. As I said with regard to your fellow prisoner, it is impossible to imagine any information which would be more useful to the enemy than information with regard to the British Fleet. Now, the law puts in our hands the discretion as to whether we shall award the sentence of death or any less punishment. In our opinion there are no circumstances whatever which would justify us in giving other than the full sentence in this case. We have in the case of your fellow prisoner awarded her a less punishment, because, as you yourself have written and admitted, it was you who caused her to commit this offence. But as regards yourself it was done for money and for money only, as far as the evidence goes. Under those circumstances, the Court having found that the offence was committed with the intention of assisting the enemy, the sentence of the Court upon you is that you suffer the penalty of death; such sentence to be executed by shooting; and the Court directs that you

136

be handed over to the competent military authority for the execution of such sentence, as if it had been passed by a Court Martial. This sentence will not be carried into execution until after such time as is allowed by the Ciminal Appeal Act, 1907, for giving notice of appeal or notice of application for leave to appeal under that Act. In the meantime you will be imprisoned in His Majesty's prison at Brixton; and the Sheriff of the County of London is hereby charged with the safe custody and with the duty of handing you over at the expiration of such time to the competent military authority.[55]

Breeckow was a pitiful spectacle as he left the dock in a state of semi-collapse.[56] He appealed against his conviction and sent a petition to the Home Office for consideration by the Army Council.[57] The Army Council dismissed it; assuming there were no legal grounds for further consideration, they saw no reason for clemency.[58] The appeal was heard before the Court of Criminal Appeal on 18 October but was dismissed, as was a petition to the King.[59]

Home Office
Whitehall
21 October, 1915.

Sir,
I am directed by the Secretary of State to acquaint you that, having had under his consideration the Petition addressed to him by George T. Breeckow @ Rowland @ Parker, now lying under sentence of death in Pentonville Prison, and having inquired fully into all the circumstances of the case, he regrets that he fails to find any sufficient ground to justify him in advising His Majesty to interfere with the due course of the law.
I have to request you be good enough to acknowledge the receipt of this decision by Bearer or by Telegram and letter.
I am, Sir
Your obedient Servant
The Governor,
HM Prison, Pentonville.[60]

The General Officer Commanding London district wrote to Major General Pipon on 23 October, 1915:

Sir, I have the honour to inform you that I have received instructions from the Army Council to carry into effect the sentence of death passed upon the prisoner George. T. Breeckow @ Rowland @ Parker, who was found guilty of espionage.

137

I have accordingly ordered that he be shot within the precincts of the Tower of London on 26 October, 1915, at dawn, under the directions of my Assistant Provost-marshal.[61]

The last scenes in Breeckow's life will live for ever in the memory of those compelled to witness them. During the five weeks between his condemnation and execution the spy broke down completely and passed his time in a state of apathetic existence which might have interested a psychologist but certainly disgusted the hardened military officials entrusted with his care. On the morning of his execution he was led out in a state of collapse. When placed in the death chair he produced a lady's silk handkerchief, evidently a relic of some past love affair, and requested that it might be placed around his eyes instead of the usual bandage. But when the sergeant-major tried to meet his wishes, it was found that the handkerchief was not large enough, so it was knotted to the bandage and then tied.

Breeckow was by this time in a dreadful state of agitation. He was literally shivering with fright and it was difficult to keep him in the chair, so the officer in charge told those strapping him in to hurry up. The last preparations were quickly made: Breeckow's chest was bared to the cold morning air and the waiting firing-party came to the aim. The order was given to fire, and simultaneously with the crack of the rifles the figure in the chair gave one tremendous, sickening bound.[62]

It was thought that he died of heart-failure before the bullets hit him, but on his death certificate the cause of death is given as violent gunshot wounds of the chest.[63] Major Blake wrote to the Resident Governor at the Tower.

Sir, I have the honour to inform you that the state prisoner handed over to me by the A.P.M., London District, on the 25th inst was this morning, by sentence of General Court Martial, shot by a detachment of the 3rd Battalion, Scots Guards at 7am.

All the Officers required by law were present, and a coroner's inquest was afterwards held.[64]

As for Lizzie Louise Wertheim, she was sent to Aylesbury convict prison, but on 17 January, 1918, she was certified as insane by the Secretary of State, who directed that she be removed to Broadmoor criminal lunatic asylum.[65] Reports stated that she has subsided into apathy, silence and delusions; she seemed entirely pre-occupied with one sole idea, that Prussians control Prussians, and that she was an important person in contact with consuls and legislations, and that nobody could leave England without her signature. Sadly, her experiences seemed to have affected her deeply. She was unable to dress and sat scratching her body all over. She become very suspicious of her food and could be seen smelling each spoonful when she was unaware that she was under observation.[66] In Broadmoor her health deteriorated and she would not talk to other patients, who began to regard her with feelings of deep aversion. She had great hatred of everybody and everything connected with England.[67] According to a report of 7 June, 1920, she had been confined to her bed for many months with lung disease at an advanced stage, in addition to chronic persecutory delirium. She was treated towards the end with whisky and brandy,[68] but to no avail, and she died of pulmonary tuberculosis during the morning of 29 July, 1920, aged 36 years.[69] Her funeral took place a few days later in the cemetery adjoining the asylum, but today no trace can be found as the site has been grassed over without markers.[70] But the Germans had not forgotten her: on 26 October, 1920, their Embassy asked for a copy of her death certificate.[71]

Both Breeckow and Wertheim paid a terrible price for the high life that they enjoyed for such a short time.

CHAPTER 9

Irving Guy Ries

Irving Guy Ries was a pseudonym: this spy's real name remained unknown to the British authorities until the time of his death, when Basil Thomson stated that he had made a full confession and given his true name. He travelled under the name of Ries, born in Chicago. He was described as a man of 55 years, five feet four inches tall, with a small face, high forehead, blue eyes, fair complexion, and greyish-brown hair.[1]

On 4 July, 1915, he arrived from New York and landed at Liverpool, making his way to London where he stayed at the Hotel Cecil in the Strand, well known to Americans.[2] He entered England under the guise of a representative for the hay and corn business of two firms, Charles Schaefer & Sons and Eidt & Wayand of New York,[3] establishing trading connections for selling hay and oats. Suspicion against him was aroused by the postal interception of a telegram for £40 sent from Rotterdam on 9 July by one N.M. Cleton of 72a Prevenier Stracht, to the payee, Irving Guy Ries, at the Strand Hotel. The well-known Rotterdam address put the British on guard. The telegram was cashed at the Strand, Southampton Street post office the following day, against his signature on the pink form.[4, 5] From this it was clear that Ries must have either communicated his address at the Hotel Cecil to the sender or arranged it before he arrived. Still the British took no direct action.

Ries later stated that he did not do any business in London. However, on 15 July he went to the St George Hotel, Liverpool, staying there under 48 hours and leaving on 17 July[6] for the Station Hotel, Newcastle-on-Tyne. Here he had to register as an alien and was interviewed by the police, producing his passport. He said that he was a merchant and intended to travel to Glasgow on business, but had broken his journey from Liverpool. He was asked to give names of any firms with whom he was in business or intended to do business with.

He said he could not give any names, but from an American citizen this was accepted. On 20 July he journeyed on to Glasgow, once again registering with the police. The next day he moved to Edinburgh, following the well-known route of the German spy, staying at the Crown Hotel.[7] Registering again, he stated that he had come to call on corn dealers, and he was going to look up their names in the directory.[8] He did call on a James Harper Paterson of Messrs Cochrane Paterson & Co, but did no business.[9] He also called on Mr Argyle Lindsey of 138 Constitution Street, Leith, a local JP, but once again no business was done and Lindsey was of the opinion that Ries knew little of the hay and oats trade.[10] A third call was on George McClellan at his business address of 34 North Bridge, Edinburgh, but Ries did not impress and did not seem very keen to close a deal.[11] On 25 July he called again at the Aliens' Registration Office and said that he was going back to Liverpool, and then intended to return to the Hotel Cecil, London. After that he wanted to cross to Rotterdam as a person there, a Mr Meisner, owed him a sum of $600 which he wished to collect. He mentioned to the police that he had visited a number of firms in the city. The next day, 26 July, he was again in Liverpool, staying once more at the St George Hotel, and on 28 July he booked in again at the Hotel Cecil, London.[12]

A second telegram arrived from N.M. Cleton for the payment of monies to Ries, this time £20, which was cashed on 3 August at the same post office.[13] Ries also prepared to go to the continent by calling at Bow Street police station on 7 August, when he again produced his passport and registered.[14] On 9 August he went to the American consulate in London, and produced his passport to get a visa. Mr Ripley Wilson, the vice-consul, dealt with the matter, and directly he saw the passport he began to examine it very carefully. The printing of the eagle was very poor and the watermark on the reverse side did not look as if it was inlaid in the paper but put on afterwards by some mechanical process. In Wilson's own words, 'It came over me that it was not right, that there was something the matter with it.' He was sure that it was a forgery, so he took it to the consul general's office. This official questioned Ries about the passport, asking where he had got it; Ries replied, 'In New York'. The Americans allowed the suspect to leave the building, then handed over the passport to New Scotland Yard.[15]

At 12 noon on 10 August, 1915, Inspector Joseph Sandercock of New Scotland Yard went to the Hotel Cecil to detain Ries. He and his men had a long wait. It was not until 10.45pm that the suspect approached the reception clerk to get the key to his room. Sandercock called him into a quiet corner, finding Ries considerably under the influence of drink but not yet drunk. The Inspector told him that he

141

had reasons to doubt that he was an American citizen, and that he should accompany him to his room which would be thoroughly searched, as would he himself. Afterwards they would convey him to New Scotland Yard where he would be detained during the investigation. Ries replied, 'All right, you are too late I expected you last night, I quite expected this as I knew there was some misunderstanding about my passport at the American consulate.'

He was then taken up to his room by lift. A search was made and a notebook was found containing names and addresses of firms in Edinburgh, plus visiting cards and a large number of copy letters of business introduction. He was taken to New Scotland Yard, and kept in custody at the adjoining Cannon Row police station. It was not long before Ries wanted to put his side of the story; on 12 August he wrote a note which he handed to the police officer in charge of the cells, requesting that Inspector Sandercock call to see him.[16] That same day Ries was seen by Sir Basil Thomson and Major Drake; shorthand notes were taken by PC Algernon Sprackling. Ries stated:

Irving Guy Ries is not my correct name. I cannot say what my name is as my people on the other side are respectable and I would not like to give them away. I am an American. My father was Dutch and my mother was Scottish. The copy letters in the books represent genuine business. You can buy forged American passports in the streets of New York. I was standing in a bar of a saloon in New York one day, when two fellows approached me. I got into conversation with them, and they were boasting that they had been on the Continent travelling with false passports. There were four of us present, and the outcome of our conversation was that a wager was made that one of us should travel on the Continent with a false passport, and we tossed up and I had to go. Milner and Wilson supplied me with a passport. I think they live along The Broadway, New York, but I do not know their address. I believe they went to another man who forged the passport, but I do not know who he is. I live in Chicago.

I landed in Liverpool and came to London by the boat train on 4 July last. I put up at the Cecil and have been waiting for cables, but have not yet received any. I did not see anybody here in London on business. I am representing two firms in New York. I had some money sent to me from a friend of mine who is in Rotterdam. His name is Cleton and he is an American. I do not know whether he is married. I do not know his Christian name, but his initials are 'NM'. I know that a money order was sent to me in the name of Madame Cleton. I spent the money here. I did not know that he was married. I cannot account for it why she should send me money.

142

I did not see anybody when I was in Liverpool. I cannot say what day I went there but I duly registered myself. From Liverpool I went to Newcastle but I had no particular reason for going there. I got there about 17 July and stayed there two or three days. I could not see any one on the Saturday or Sunday, but saw some people on the Monday. From there I went to Glasgow and stayed at the Blythswood Hotel. I think that was on 20 July. I looked up several people in Glasgow including Messrs A. Albrethson & Co, 41 Anne Street; Mongo Gray & Co, 94 Hope Street, and Angus Brothers Ltd, 73 Robertson Street. I also wrote to them. My business with them was relating to corn. I stayed there two or three days, then went to Edinburgh, and stayed there from Friday to Monday. I visited several people there. From Edinburgh I went back to Liverpool and stayed there about two days, and then I returned to London. I have not been anywhere else. I did not like to do any more business there. I came to London and then had a rest, nothing else.

I booked a passage from Hull to Copenhagen on the SS *Flore* but afterwards found that I could not get a visa on my passport. When I got to Copenhagen, I intended to go back to the States. Since I returned to London, I have not been doing anything except sight-seeing. I had no letters of introduction to anyone over here, and the persons with whom I had been drinking on the night that I was arrested were strangers. I had cards printed with the name of Ries, because I came over with this passport. It was all through this bet that I travelled with this passport. It strikes me now that it was a very dangerous thing to do. I am not either a German or a German-American.

Asked if he was willing to give his real name and place of birth in order that his identity might be established he said:

I do not like to give away my people. I have not been doing any-thing wrong. I have many good connections in America, and I cannot give you my name. I was expecting to be arrested because the vice-consul kept the passport. The American consul told me it was a fraud. I did not send any acknowledgement when I received the money order. I gave a receipt to the post office, that was all. I have not sent any telegrams or letters. Only letters to the States. I do not know what happened to the persons who travelled on the same boat on which I crossed. I came over on the SS *New York*. I have not met any of the acquaintances I have made on the ship since. I landed in Liverpool on 4 July. When coming across, I dam-aged my knee and I was laid up at the hotel for some time as I could hardly walk. I used to go to Kensington Gardens and read. I have

143

never been to sea. I have worked my way up in the States, doing all kinds of work. I will not tell you where I was born as it might be used against me. I do not know who filled in the description on my passport. I do not know the consul general for Germany at Rotterdam. I have visited Germany six or eight years ago but have never been to Wesel. I know nothing about what you mean. I have had nothing to do with such people. If you think I am a German spy, you must have got scared. I will think it over as to whether I shall disclose my right name.[17]

Ries was next questioned on 19 August. This time, in addition to Sir Basil Thomson and Major Drake, Captain Hall and Lord Herschell of the Admiralty were present. Ries stated:

I wanted my fare to New York and I was expecting to receive about $200 or $300 from the States. I do not know who would send me money from Europe. I thought I should receive the money from the States and did not expect it from Holland. I had nothing to do with a lady named Cleton, and it is funny if she should have sent me money. I cannot give any explanation. I know a man named Cleton, whose real name is Hogan. He is an American, and is a very tall thin man. I have no friends in Brighton. I was not expecting Cleton to meet me in Copenhagen, and I do not know why he should want to meet me. I cannot understand it. I have not been to Brighton, and I have never addressed any letter to Cleton from Brighton.

At this point Sir Basil Thomson read out a letter, in English, dated 9 August, postmarked Rotterdam, and addressed to Irving Guy Ries Esq, Hotel Cecil, Strand, London. It was stamped as opened by the censor in London on 12 August, 1915.

Dear Friend, Thanks very much for your letter from Brighton of July 31st. That was indeed very nice for you to have met such nice people. As for the settlement of your affairs it is awfully difficult for me to give an advice from here. You are surely in a position to judge better than I can what will be the best. I need not tell you that I find good that you act as you think best. If you cannot manage to go to Copenhagen before you leave for the States let me know and I shall give the necessary instructions to the Bank to remit to London instead of Copenhagen the necessary funds for your journey home. As I intend to go to Copenhagen shortly I can easily talk things over in your place. Let me hear from you soon. Never mind the long letters, I am quite content with a postcard now and then. I know it's a bother to write letters when one's away for his holiday. It'll interest

144

you to hear that Fred has left town for Switzerland. As soon as I know his address I let you know. Kindest regards to you and all the friends from the States.
Yours sincerely
N M Cleton

Ries's explanation was as follows:

I have never been in Brighton. I do not think Hogan is still in Rotterdam. I have never told him about nice people I have met. Will you kindly make enquiries at the Hotel Cecil and people will know that I used to go out at 9 o'clock and come back at 11.30. The letter may refer to someone else, but certainly not to me. He knew I was coming under a wrong name. He sent be £20. I came over under my wrong name for a bet. It is true that the police wanted me. It was not for a crime, but something wrong in business. I have told you the truth and nothing else. I do not like to tell you my proper name, because of the disgrace to other people.

Thompson then read to the prisoner another letter postmarked Rotterdam on 16 August, 1915, some days after Ries's arrest, but addressed in the same way as the first:

Dear Friend, From your postcard of the 9th I learned with great regret that you are not feeling as well as we all should like to hear. As I wrote you on the 9th inst. it does not matter at all to me to have the money sent to England instead of Copenhagen. In fact I thought it better to remit to London. The interests the banks here are paying are not so remunerative anyhow in comparison with what we have to pay for taking up money on stocks. The money is due to you anyhow and I think it is better to let you have part of it now, the rest I can have remitted to the States or wherever you wish to have it. You know I shall carry out your wish to the letter, you've only got to say how you want to have do it. For investment England and the States are the best countries, at present anyway. I spoke with the Bank yesterday about the costs of sending the money. As it is just as cheap to do it by telegraph direct I prefer to do it this way and am sending you by cable £40. About the rest due to you I await your answer by telegraph if you want it, else by letter. I do hope that your next card will bring news about your health, my best wishes anyway. It is too bad to feel queer when you are away from home.
Very sincerely yours
N M Cleton

Ries continued:

I did not write to say I was not feeling well. I cannot understand the whole story. I should say Hogan must have left Rotterdam. I have not got any communication from him. I did not know that Hogan is passing under the name of Saunderson. The money I received from Hogan is for some business we have done together. I did not think I should have any further money out of it. It was some queer business, but I should not like to say what it was. I do not think anyone else was in the business, only Hogan and myself. If I had received that letter at the Hotel, I should have explained matters to Hogan. I would not have refused any money. I first met Hogan in the States, and have known him for years. He has been in the electrical business, and many adventures. He is a 'schemer'. He used to buy and sell cattle and horses from Canada and the Argentine to be delivered after the war. I cannot understand why he should send me money. I was dealing in oats. Perhaps he sold some cattle and so sent me £40. Cleton's address is Pioneer Street, or something like that. It may be 72 Prevenier Stracht. My father was Dutch, but I do no know the Dutch language. I cannot account from where Hogan received the money. I have nothing to do with the Germans and nothing to do with Wesel. I would not have done anything for the German Government. I came over here with a forged passport it is true, and it looks very strange, but I have not done anything here. I have no mission to carry out here. I have nothing to do with Germans, as God is my witness. Cleton was not present when the bet was made, but came later. I wrote to Hogan from New York.

With that Sir Basil Thomson told Ries he would be charged, and he was removed.[18, 19]

The court martial took place at Westminster Guildhall on 28 and 29 September, 1915. Again the President was Lord Cheylesmore, with eleven members of the court ranging in rank from brigadier-general to major. The judge advocate was Kenneth Marshall, Mr Bodkin appeared for Lieutenant Peevor as prosecutor, and Mr Huntley Jenkins as counsel for the prisoner, under the instructions of Messrs Percy Robinson & Co.[20]

Ries faced four charges under the Defence of the Realm (Consolidation) Regulations 1914: that on or about 4 July, 1915, he came to England for the purpose of collecting information that might be useful to the enemy; that he was in communication with a spy, N M Cleton of 72a Provenier Stracht, Rotterdam; that he was in possession of a false passport; and that he registered himself at Bow Street police station as an alien and as an American who had a genuine pass-

146

port, with intent to assist the enemy. He pleaded not guilty to all charges.[21]

Ries's defence was anything but plausible. He agreed that he went by the name of Irving Guy Ries, aged 55 years, and stated that he was connected with other men in smuggling diamonds into the United States for the purpose of avoiding duty. He could give no reasonable explanation of the communications with Cleton. Prevenier Stracht was classed as a residential street, in a good area, the houses being mostly three storeys high and let out in tenements; 72a consisted of two upper floors with a shop on the ground floor. The ground floor was called 72b and was occupied by a mining engineer; 72a was used by a Madame Cleton, ostensibly as a boarding-house.[22] She was a middle-aged Dutch woman who had the reputation of being a widow and purported to be one. She had a grown-up daughter and a boy of about 12 years.

Under cross-examination by Mr Bodkin, it became clear that Ries's explanations were hardly credible.

> Q. Why could you not get a passport in your own name?
> A. It takes a longer time.
> Q. This did not take long?
> A. Yes.
> Q. Oh, come; how many days after the bet, the wager, did you have that thing in your hand; they can be bought in the streets of New York, you say?
> A. Certainly.
> Q. Did you buy it?
> A. Yes.
> Q. How much did you pay for it?
> A. Nothing to do here.
> Q. Tell me how much you paid.
> A. I paid five dollars.
> Q. Five dollars?
> A. Yes.
> Q. Really?
> A. Yes.
> Q. You can pick them up as cheap as that?
> A. Sure.
> Q. New, or second-hand?
> A. New.
> Q. Brand new?
> A. Yes.
> Q. Where did you get it; where did you buy it?
> A. There are certain men connected with it.

147

Q. I wnat to get where these things are obtained in New York. Where did you get this now, Mr Ries?

A. There it was; a man Mulliner, and Wilson, obtained it for me.

Q. Mulliner and Wilson?

A. Yes.

Q. What is the address?

A. I do not know.

Q. Oh, come.

A. I do not know; it may be somewhere abroad; I do not know.

Q. It may be, or may be not; where was it?

A. I do not know.

Q. This is a serious matter. Do not tell this court you do not know where you got that passport.

A. No.

Q. You do not know where you got it?

A. I gave the money, the order, and I paid him the money, and he brought me the passport; that is all.

Q. How did you know where to go for it?

A. There was a talk about them – the false passports.

Q. Were these strangers you spoke to about false passports?

A. Oh no, not strangers, they were men to be seen in bars there.

Q. That may be; were they strangers to you?

A. Not quite.

Q. And how much was the bet?

A. A few thousand dollars.

Q. How much?

A. A few thousand dollars.

Q. Two thousand dollars?

A. A few thousand dollars.

Q. I wonder if they were Germans you had the bet with?

A. Oh no.

Q. You would know a German if you saw him, I suppose?

A. Certainly.

Q. As you talk German?

A. I do a bit.

Q. Oh! – very well.

A. I do not know.

Q. Do you mean to say that is not your tongue?

A. Eh?

148

21. George Breeckow, shot 26
    October, 1915
    (see Chapter 8).

22. Louise Emily Wertheim
    when a prisoner at
    Broadmoor (see p.121).
    (*Dr David Mawson*).

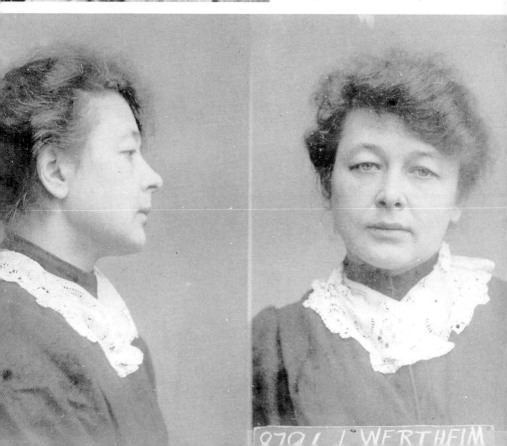

23. The Westbourne H‹
    Ramsgate, Kent, wl
    Breeckow stayed in
    May, 1915.

24. 33 Regent's Park
    Road, where
    Lizzie Wertheim
    was arrested on
    9 June, 1915
    (see p.131).

25. Irving Guy Ries,
shot 27 October,
1915
(see Chapter 9).

26. Albert Meyer, shot
2 December, 1915
(see Chapter 10).

27. Ludovico Hurowitz-y-Zender, shot 11 April, 1916
(see Chapter 11).

28. Today there is a car port where the rifle range once stood.

Q.	Do you mean to say that is not your tongue – German?
A.	Yes, but I have been travelling a great deal.
Q.	In Germany?
A.	No, I have not been in Germany for six or eight years.
Q.	Where did you pick it up?
A.	I was educated in Switzerland and brought up there as a boy.
Q.	These were not Germans you had the bet with?
A.	No.
Q.	When was this bet?
A.	It was about the beginning of June.
Q.	As long ago as that?
A.	Yes.
Q.	The beginning of June?
A.	Yes.
Q.	Was that when you adopted the name Ries?
A.	Yes.
Q.	The beginning of June. And then it took how long to get the passport?
A.	Oh, a few days.
Q.	Yes, a few days. Why did not you start at once?
A.	I had to arrange matters of business first.
Q.	Where?
A.	In New York.
Q.	What business?
A.	About the corn trade, and my own affairs.
Q.	But you were a diamond smuggler at that time?
A.	Oh yes.
Q.	Had you temporarily suspended that business for the corn trade?
A.	Oh no; it goes on all the year round – the diamond trade.
Q.	There are no seasons for smuggling diamonds, are there?
A.	No.
Q.	So then, when you wanted to arrange business; what business?
A.	I tried to get in the corn trade.
Q.	Why did you go to Schaefer and to Eidt & Wayand; had you ever known them before?
A.	No.
Q.	Were you an absolute stanger to them?
A.	Yes.

149

Q.	Did you have any communication with them before you left New York?
A.	No – oh yes, certainly.
Q.	Yes, I thought so. Did not they want to know who you were?
A.	Yes.
Q.	What did they say?
A.	I put it something else.
Q.	What did you say?
A.	I came across a man.
Q.	Oh, these unnamed men. What did you say to Schaefer, and what did you say to Eidt & Wayand? What did you say to them as to who you were?
A.	I represented myself as Mr Ries from Chicago.
Q.	That is all?
A.	That is right.
Q.	That is all, is it?
A.	Yes.
Q.	Had they ever heard of you before?
A.	No, but I told them I knew the late American Hay Company, and I knew the people.
Q.	You knew what?
A.	I knew the people, the late American Hay Company.
Q.	Of the late American Hay Company?
A.	Yes.
Q.	Is that where you picked up about hay, as much as you did know?
A.	Yes.
Q.	So that these two firms did not know who they were employing?
A.	No.
Q.	An absolute stranger, who gives the name of Ries, a man from Chicago, walks in, and says. 'Please will you let me be your agent?'?
A.	Quite so.
Q.	What were they going to pay you?
A.	That is commission.
Q.	What were they going to pay you?
A.	Only the commission on top of their prices.
Q.	Do you mean you travelled 3,000 miles to England without any money from your principals?
A	Oh no.
Q.	What were they going to pay you?
A.	If there was any business then it is good.

Q.	Was that the only business you came over on?
A.	I had the diamond business to back me up.
Q.	Do you say you were travelling in diamonds?
A.	Yes.
Q.	You left New York in diamonds?
A.	No, my people.
Q.	About coming here to England as representing these firms, did you get any money at all to come with?
A.	No.
Q.	You came on your own?
A.	Certainly.
Q.	Your own expenses?
A.	Certainly.
Q.	Do you really say you paid your own expenses for coming to this country?
A.	That is not so much.
Q.	Did you do it?
A.	Certainly.
Q.	And, when you got here; when you got here you went to pretty good hotels?
A.	Yes.
Q.	St. George's, the Hotel Cecil, the Crown, and so forth?
A.	Yes.
Q.	You did yourself pretty well?
A.	Oh yes, I did.
Q.	On your own expenses?
A.	Yes.
Q.	From first to last, have you ever got a farthing from those two firms?
A.	No.
Q.	Never?
A.	Not anything.
Q.	Did you write any letters to any persons before you left New York?
A.	Not that I am aware of.
Q.	Did you ask Schaefer and Eidt & Wayand to give you some introductions?
A.	No.

Later in the cross-examination Mr Bodkin returned to the question of the bet.

Q. Just about this bet, once or twice is this what you said about it, and I will ask you if it is true: 'I was standing in a bar of a saloon in New York one day when two fellows approached me.'

A. Yes.

Q. Now is that right?

A. Yes.

Q. Now kindly give me their names.

A. I do not know the names.

Q. Was there anybody appointed stakeholder.

A. Yes.

Q. Who?

A. I cannot say now.

Q. And how much was deposited as stake?

A. One thousand dollars.

Q. You put down 1,000 dollars?

A. Yes.

Q. And he put down 1,000 dollars?

A. Yes.

Q. Who?

A. The other man.

Q. You do not know his name?

A. No, not his name.

Q. Did not you make just a memoranda of it? Did not you?

A. No; I have not got it here.

Q. And the stakeholder; did he not just put down his name and address?

A. Yes.

Q. Where is that? What is it? What is his name and address?

A. I have not got it here.

Q. You do not know his name?

A. Not to my memory now.

Q. You do not know his address?

A. No.

Q. Do you mean to tell the court that you put your name down for a bet of 2,000 dollars, and you put down 1,000 dollars, and you cannot give the name and address of anybody? You are coming to England in fear and coming with a forged passport. Do you say that you did that for a bet, and you cannot give any more particulars than that about it?

A. It does not matter about a bet.

152

Q.	'It does not matter about a bet.' Suppose you had got out of this country, as you tried to do, where would you get the money from your bet?
A.	Oh, that is in safe keeping.
Q.	Now what is the story: that you got this passport for a bet, or to get out of America, because you had been doing some diamond smuggling – which is the story?
A.	That is right; to get out of the States.
Q.	Is it because of the bet or that you were afraid of the police and wanted to get out of America?
A.	It is both.
Q.	So that the bet just came at the right time?
A.	Yes.
Q.	That was a stroke of luck, was not it?
A.	It was.
Q.	So the bet cost you 1,000 dollars?
A.	That does not matter.
Q.	You seriously say that the bet came along just at the time you wanted to get away from the States?
A.	Yes.[23]

The Judge Advocate, Kenneth Marshall, directed the court in the following terms:

With regard to the last two charges there is no question that the accused is guilty, having been found in possession of a false passport, and of having falsely represented himself as a person to whom the passport had been issued, because he has himself admitted that, and the sole question you will have to consider with regard to those charges is whether he did it with intent to assist the enemy or not.

Now, the accused has put forward two distinct reasons why he had that false passport. One is that it was the result of a somewhat curious bet which he made with two apparently unknown men in New York. Anyhow, he has been unable to give us their names or addresses, or the name or address of the stakeholder. A curious bet for $2,000 that he would come over to this country, and travel under a false passport, and, at the same time he says that he was wanted by the police of the United States for his smuggling in diamonds, and that therefore in any case it was convenient for him to come abroad under a false name. You will have to consider whether you can accept either of those stories, or both of them in combination, as a reasonble explanation of why he came to this country. And you will have to bear the fact of his coming with that false passport before your mind when you are considering whether or not he is guilty of the first charge.

Now, Mr Huntly Jenkins has urged upon you that no evidence of any sort has been put before you to show that in fact any information was collected by the accused while he was here, of such a nature that it might be useful to the enemy, or that any attempt was made by him to collect such information, and he says if it had been able to be proved, evidence would have been brought before you; but in this case, as in others which have been brought before this court, the charge is not that of collecting information, or of attempting to collect information, but of doing an act preparatory to collecting information, and the act preparatory alleged is coming to this country and proceeding to those various towns which have been mentioned. It is impossible, of course, to give definite evidence of what a man's intention in doing anything is; that is an inference the court has to draw from all the circumstances.

Mr Huntly Jenkins has said to you that this man came here as the agent of two American firms, and to show he did come on genuine business he refers you to that exhibit No 16, the book, which he says contains genuine letters. There is no doubt that the accused did go to those two firms, and he did get himself appointed as some sort of agent, and when he came to this country he visited various firms and made enquiries about selling oats and hay, and he wrote to, I think, certainly one or both of the firms in connection with that business, and Mr Huntly Jenkins asks you to accept that as showing that it was a genuine business. I do not know how it will strike you at all, but it seems to me that that business was in fact merely a nominal business for this reason, that we have been told by the accused that he did not in fact transact any business; he did not get any orders, and he did not transact any business, and though he had that nominal business, do not you think that either for carrying out his bet of travelling here on a false passport, or of disguising his identity, or for the purpose of coming here as a spy to collect any information, it would have been a wise precaution for him to have some business which he could refer to as his object in coming here?

Now, as to whether the business was the real object of his visit or not, Mr Huntly Jenkins says that it was natural for him to go to Newcastle, Liverpool, Glasgow and Edinburgh, as being places where he was likely to do good business. It is perfectly obvious, gentlemen, to all of you, that they were also likely places where he could collect information which might be of a nature useful to the enemy, and you have to consider to what the circumstances must point in his going there. Mr Bodkin has pointed out to you it is rather remarkable, if he was really there on business, that his visits

154

to those various places were of such very brief duration, and that after calling on firms who were unable to see him, he did not think it worthwhile, as he was not in any particular hurry, and he has told you he was not in any particular hurry – he did not think it worthwhile to remain to see those firms, but he merely wrote to them subsequently, pointing out to them he had called on them in the hope of doing business, and regretted he had not found them in. Gentlemen, those are the considerations, I think, of what you have to bear in mind with regard to the first charge.

The second charge is: 'Without lawful authority or excuse having been in communication with a spy, in that you in the United Kingdom had been on or about 31 July, 1915, in communication with a spy, that is to say, with a person named N.M. Cleton of 72a Provenier Strasse, Rotterdam.' With regard to that charge I should like to draw your attention to the Regulation under which that charge is framed. It has been proved, beyond all doubt, that he was in possession of the name and address of this N.M. Cleton. Now the Regulation makes it an offence to be in communication with a spy, and it then lays down that: 'For the purposes of this Regulation (a) a person shall, unless he proves to the contrary, be deemed to be in communication with a spy if the name or address or any other information regarding a spy is found in his possession.' And then it goes on to explain that by saying what is meant by that term. 'Any address, whether within or without the United Kingdom, reasonably suspected of being an address used for the receipt of communications intended for the enemy shall be deemed to be the address of a spy, and communications addressed to that address to be communications with a spy.' As I say, the accused was admittedly in possession of this address, 72a Prevenier Strasse. We have had here Major Drake, who is in charge of the Espionage Branch at the War Office, who has told you that in consequence of communications which were intercepted going to and from that address, orders were given that all correspondence to that address should be sent to the War Office for examination. Gentlemen, do you think that Major Drake's evidence satisfies you that it was a reasonable suspicion that that was an address used for the receipt of communications? If you think on those communications which Major Drake saw it was reasonable to suspect that address was used for the receipt of such communications, and the accused was in possession of that address, the Regulation does not say that for a person to be guilty of this offence the prosecution must prove that he knows that address to be the address of a spy, but, on the contrary, it says, 'A person shall, unless he proves to the contrary, be deemed to be in communication with a spy if the name and address, or any other

155

information regarding a spy is found in his possession.' Has the accused, Ries, satisfied this court that he did not know he was in communication with a spy? That is the onus that is cast on him, to satisfy the court he did not know that this was the address of a spy that he was communicating with.

I do not think, gentlemen, there is any other point that I have to put before you. Your decision will have to be arrived at separately in regard to each charge, and you will have to say on each charge, not only is he guilty of the offence set out in the charge, but also if he committed that offence, if you find him guilty of that, with intent to assist the enemy or not.[24]

The court retired at 3.22pm and returned just eight minutes later. Lieutenant Peevor was asked by the President if he had any information to give the court by way of the prisoner's character. In view of his incorrect name there was nothing to add; Ries declined to make any statement and was removed. Lord Cheylesmore then thanked the counsel for the courteous manner in which they had conducted the case and the assistance they had been to the court.[25] Irving Guy Ries was found guilty of all charges. The sentence was death by shooting.[26]

On a submission dated 21 October, 1915, His Majesty the King was pleased to confirm the finding and sentence of the court and to command that the sentence be carried into effect. On 25 October the Major-General Pipon:

I have the honour to inform you that I have received instructions from the Army Council to carry into effect the sentence of death passed upon the prisoner IRVING GUY RIES, who was found guilty of Espionage.

I have accordingly ordered that he be shot within the precincts of The Tower of London on 27 October, 1915, at daybreak, under the directions of my Assistant Provost-Marshall.[27]

Sir Basil Thompson wrote:

There was no doubt whatever that he was a spy, but his case differed from the others in the fact that it could not be shown that he had ever sent information to the enemy. In fact, it seemed clear that the Germans were adopting new tactics, and that they intended in future to send spies on flying visits to England, and get them to come and report the result of their observations verbally . . . He took his condemnation with perfect philosophy. He spent all his time in reading, and he gave his guards the impression that he was a man who had divested himself of all earthly cares and felt himself to lie

156

under the hand of Fate. If he expected that the American Government would press for a reprieve and would be successful he never showed it.

On 26 October he was removed to the Tower, and as soon as he knew that a date was fixed for his execution he asked for writing materials and made a full confession, giving his true name. He was permitted to shake hands with the firing party, and said, 'You are only doing your duty, as I have done mine.'[28] After taking one glance at the chair which was soon to hold his dead body, he gave a grave smile.[29] He was shot by a detachment of the 3rd Battalion, Scots Guards at 7am[30] and died like a brave man.

The present files and papers contain nothing of his correct name and confession. Thomson kept his word and Ries's aged parents never knew of his fate and dishonour. Time heals, and ignorance can be better than knowledge!

CHAPTER 10

Albert Meyer

Albert Meyer has been described as a despicable character,[1] but unfortunately his court-martial file is missing, most likely destroyed, and it is impossible to discover much about his personality. The British postal censorship authority was alerted to the likelihood of another spy operating in London when, checking letters addressed to Holland, they came across one to a suspect address: Mr Goedhardt, 147 Van Blankenburgstraat, The Hague. Chemists carried out tests, finding invisible ink, and developed a message between the lines, translated as follows.

I hope that you have received my first letter. I have been to Chatham. The Royal Dockyard is closed entirely, but I got in in spite of all. There are a few cruisers there and a lot of guns and [...] as well as destroyers, for instance, *Duncan*, 2nd class, 14000 tons, *Lowestoft*, 3rd class, *Boadicea*, *Lance*, *Pembroke*, *Wilder* and *Actaeon*, etc.

The mouth of the Thames is guarded by steel like the Humber, but even more so. The opening [...] ships pass at night and this is indicated from a watch boat through three vertically arranged red lanterns.

I have described to you the state of affairs here in London. A wounded Territorial told me in the course of a conversation that one German is worth twelve of Kitchener's men. It is mostly [...]. There are many boys of 16 and 17 amongst them. They make enough effort and advertise in order to get soldiers. At every street corner, theatre and cinema, people are challenged to join.

The Government appeals to woman and young girls to persuade their fiancés and husbands. Ammunition is made everywhere. At Dartford (Thames) a large metal factory has been turned into an ammunition factory and here every small metal workshop is making ammunition.

In order to get soldiers, the proprietors of shops have been asked to dismiss certain people and when the employees try to find positions somewhere else they are refused and they are asked, why do you not join the Army? People are forced in this country.

So far I have not been able to find out anything important, but it will come in time.

Yours truly,

(Signed) Svend Person[2]

Upon enquiry, the name and address of the sender were shown to be false. The letter was not allowed to go through and was retained. It was now just a question of playing a waiting game. All port officers were warned to look out for persons having papers with the Dutch name and address in their possession.[3]

As suspected, a number of other letters and postcards were intercepted, all in the same handwriting, with different false addresses. The second item, found after the heat treatment, was a postcard of 12.30pm, 13 July, 1915, signed 'Lopez'.[4]

Wounded sailor of torpedo boat 18. They were in a battle last week, for boats sunk, torpedo boat 18 now at Sheerness. HMS *Pembroke* at Plymouth.[5]

Then a letter posted in west London at 8.30pm on 20 July was found, addressed 28 Greek Street and signed 'Belmonte'. It asked if information had been received from Lopez and said that business was bad and that the writer expected to shortly go to Spain. The original letter was retained and a tracing of the envelope kept. On the back of this letter in invisible writing was found the following.[6]

I was taken for a Turk. Transport with Canadians left London at 9.45pm. There were engineers who had arrived at the beginning of June with many guns. Some sailors of HMS *Dominion* are walking about here. Transports are leaving again today. Have you received a block with 9 pages of writing from the Frontier?[7]

There was little to go on, apart from the fact that the spy was foreign, but extensive enquiries and detective work were put in hand. Eventually the British had a piece of luck. A typewritten letter posted in west London at 3pm on 27 August, 1915, was intercepted by the post office at 8pm. Heating and other tests failed to disclose secret writing. The letter was photographed, had the censor's label attached to it by Second Lieutenant Cooke, and was allowed to go on. It was thought from the nature of the letter that at last the real address of the spy had been obtained.[8]

London W., August 29, 1915
1 Margaret Street,
Oxford Circus

Dear Friend,
As I made my mind up to do business with the Amsterdamsche Sigarrenfabrik so I intend to buy for 80 cigars to sell on my own account. I would kindly ask you to advance me 50 pounds to pay 30ps duty and expenses. After agreement to pay a deposit for me about 20ps.
    Hoping you will favour my demand and hear soon from you, I remain
Yours very truly,
(signed) TOMMY[9]

The Metropolitan police were now instructed to search for and arrest the suspect. Calling at 1 Margaret Street, a dingy lodging house in Soho, they examined the registration forms supplied by the landlady, Mrs Waack. These did not disclose any similarity in handwriting with the intercepted mail. But upon questioning the landlady, it was found that there were two people staying who were yet to register. Checking one of their trunks, the police found a luggage label in similar writing to the suspect letters, with the words 'Albert Meyer'. He was arrested: the police found him[10] to be a man aged 22, and five feet seven inches in height.[11] He was staying with his wife, whom he called 'Kitty' (he had married Catherine Rebecca Godleman at St Pancras registry office on 20 May, 1915); she was also taken into custody. He protested that he knew nothing of the letters, but on searching his address, invisible ink and writing materials were discovered, and a pen which had been in contact with lemon juice.[12] Also discovered was a small cheap typewriter, which was found to have typed the letter signed 'Tommy'. Meyer had told his landlady that he was in the tailoring business. She stated that he posted his own letters but that, strangely, his laundry and parcels had been sent to him in other names.

From enquiries and testimonials it appeared that Meyer had been employed in Hamburg from September, 1910, to August, 1911. He then made his way to Spain, staying in Seville and later Pamplona. In June, 1914, he came to England and worked as a cook at Cabins Ltd, in Oxford Street, London, then moved to the Imperial Hotel,

Blackpool, as a waiter. Both employments were of short duration. On 9 August, 1914, when trying to cross to Holland, he had been detained at Folkestone as a prisoner of war. He was sent to the detention barracks at Queensferry, Flintshire, until the British released him on 29 September, 1914, seemingly because he was a Turkish subject. Returning to London he moved into 40 Albany Street, near Regent's Park. At the beginning of April, 1915, he was on the move again, making his way to Holland.[13]

On 22 March he had applied at the Permit Office to go to Copenhagen via Flushing and Germany, giving his nationality as Dutch, having been born of Dutch parents in Constantinople. His reason for leaving the country was that, owing to the war, he was unable to get a job with sufficient remuneration, and had only been in work for about five weeks. He said that he did not want to take the sea voyage to Denmark as he was a poor sailor.[14] His application was referred for enquiry but later granted, with the remark that he was Danish. On his return to Britain in the second week in May, he went back to 40 Albany Street, moving on at the end of the month to number 134. On 20 July he moved again, to 1 Margaret Street. Postcards were found addressed to the prisoner at 96 Shaftesbury Avenue: an accommodation address owned by a Mr William Marshall. Letters to Mrs Marciella, a name used by Meyer's wife, were also sent to this address.[15]

After arrest Meyer and his wife were detained at Cannon Row police station on suspicion of espionage.[16] However, she was released shortly afterwards as no evidence was found of any complicity. On 1 September he was moved to Wandsworth detention barracks.[17] He maintained a defiant defence, stating that the letters had been written by another man who had left the writing materials at his address; the letter giving his correct address was the work of his friend, who had done it maliciously. To help prove matters, Meyer was asked for a specimen of his own handwriting: he became very indignant and, putting on an injured attitude, asked the interrogator if he thought he was lying.

Enquiries into his lifestyle revealed his habit of moving from one lodging house to another, always in debt and promising his landladies that he would settle his account once remittances had arrived from his parents, who lived abroad. When he had money he spent it freely, lunching and dining in the most fashionable and expensive restaurants. Living for the moment, when his money was gone he would be found cadging a meal at different foreign restaurants in the Soho area. Or he could turn to the immoral earnings of his woman. He had no consideration for his German spy-masters: he cheated them, sending masses of fictitious material which he coloured dramatically, and would do nothing but harm to the cause of the Central Powers.[18] He was not

161

adverse to lying outrageously, and was shameless in attempting to take any opportunity to divert guilt to innocent people. He stated that the typewriter found at his premises was bought by him from a fellow lodger and that the pen and paper had been left there by a man named Bridges, who had also borrowed the machine.[19]

He was court-marshalled at Westminster Guildhall on 5 and 6 November, 1915.[20] Facing six charges, he was found guilty and sentenced to death.[21] On 25 November Major-General Lloyd, commanding London District, wrote to Major-General Pipon stating that the Army Council had instructed him to carry out the execution of Meyer, found guilty of espionage; accordingly, he was ordering that the prisoner was to be shot within the precincts of the Tower of London on Saturday, 27 November, 1915, at daybreak.[22] The next day Pipon was informed that the execution had been postponed until further orders were received,[23] as a petition had been received from Meyer's solicitor, Mr Percy Robinson.[24] After review it was considered that there was absolutely nothing in this petition to warrant any interference with the findings or sentence of the court.[25] The Danish authorities would not recognize Meyer as a subject, and the British came to the conclusion that he was either a Turk or a German, but it was doubtful which.[26] Finally, on 1 December Pipon received orders that Meyer was now to be shot at daybreak on Thursday, 2 December.[27]

From The Officer Commanding Troops, Tower of London
To The Resident Governor, Tower of London, E.C.
2nd December 1915

Sir,
I have the honour to inform you that the state prisoner handed over to me by the A.P.M., London District on the 25th ultimo., was this morning, by sentence of General Court Martial, shot by a detachment of the 3rd Bn. Scots Guards at 7.45a.m.

All the Officers required by Law were present and a Coroner's Inquest was afterwards held.
Lieut Colonel,
Commanding 2nd. (Res) Bn. Welsh Guards,
O.C. Troops. (28)

An account of the execution is as follows.

It was fully expected, judging by his demeanour during the period he was waiting to be shot, that he would prove awkward, but nothing untoward happened until the morning of the execution. When the dread summons came in the cold dawn he was then in an hysterical state and when escorted from his cell suddenly burst into a wild effort to sing 'Tipperary.' His guard attempted to silence him, but all in vain.

He stopped on reaching the miniature rifle range where he was to be shot and cast a raving eye at the chair standing in the middle. Then he burst into a torrent of blasphemous cursing, reviling his Maker and calling down the vengeance of Heaven on those who had deserted him. Struggling fiercely with his stalwart guard, he was forcibly placed in the chair and strapped tightly in. Before the bullets of the firing party could reach him he had torn the bandage from his eyes, and died in a contorted mass, shouting curses at his captors, which were only stilled by the bullets.[29]

CHAPTER 11

Ludovico Hurwitz-y-Zender

Ludovico Hurwitz-y-Zender was born in Lima, Peru, in the year 1878. His father was Peruvian, but his grandparents were of Scandinavian extraction; according to Zender his grandfather was a Scandanavian captain who came to Peru with a sailing vessel after guano, but the ship was lost and he settled in that country. Unfortunately, once again the court-martial file cannot be found, but sufficient papers remain to tell his story.

Ludovico received a first-class eduction and could speak French and English well. He also had a smattering of the language spoken by the natives in the mountains of Sierra del Peru. Until August, 1914, he traded as a merchant selling goods along the coast from Callao to Tumbles, and into the interior between the coast and the Marasion River.

In August, 1914, he left Peru for Europe, by way of the United States. His explanation was that he intended to trade in paper, handkerchiefs and various foods. His journey took in New York, Bergen, Christiania (Oslo) and Copenhagen.[1] The British were to form the opinion that it was in Christiania that he was recruited by the German secret service.[2]

The British, in early June, 1915, were very concerned about five telegrams sent from various highly sensitive areas on 15, 20, 22, 24 and 25 May to August Brochner, 11 Toldbodgade Christiania. These, from experience, bore a decidedly suspicious appearance. Brochner was found to be German and in daily touch with the German consulate at Bergen. He had no ostensible business, being merely a 'post box' for the German secret service. The telegrams were all sent by a man signing his name as Ludovico Hurwitz or Hurwitz Zender, giving an address of 59 Union Street, Glasgow. A telegram was dispatched to the Chief Constable of Glasgow giving instructions for the arrest of this man. However, they were just too late, and information was sent to

London that the suspect had gone to Newcastle and had probably re-embarked for Norway towards the end of May. It was found that this was indeed the case: he had sailed on 28 May from Newcastle to Bergen on the ship *Haakon VII*.

The security services felt that, as the man had carried on his work with impunity, he would in all probability return to complete his task. His description was therefore circulated to all port officers at places where aliens were allowed to enter the country, with instructions that he be arrested, his personal belongings seized and sent under escort to New Scotland Yard. On 2 July the SS *Vega* arrived in Newcastle from Bergen and Zender was arrested. He was transported to London and detained at Cannon Row police station. In his possession was £84 in notes and £5 in gold, a list of handkerchief manufacturers in Glasgow, and a dozen white handkerchiefs, which appeared to be samples as they were unused and unwashed. There was also a bill from the Palace Hotel, Copenhagen, for 23 and 24 June, which showed he had been in Denmark. Another bill from the Grand Hotel, Christiania, dated 25 to 29 June, showed that he had then returned to Norway. The British suggested that his visit to Denmark followed his return from Germany, as he had ample time to go there, and it was suspicious that immediately after spending a few days back in Christiania he should leave again for Britain.[3] On 6 July the War Office instructed that he be handed over by the civil police to the commandant at the detention barracks, Wandsworth, with a warning that Zender was suffering from venereal disease.[4]

The telegrams that were the substance of the investigation were worded as follows.

15 May. 'Buy immediately 180 cases 100/2 tins smoked herrings as guaranted good quality. Ludovico Hurwitz.'

20 May. 'Ship 140 cases 100/2 tins Concord Canning Anchovies guaranted good quality. Ludovico Hurwitz.'

22 May. 'Offer immediately appetite anchovies best quality cases 200/2 tins. Hurwitz Zender.'

24 May. 'Ship immediately 160 100/2 tins Concord Canning Anchovies guaranteed good quality. Ludovico Hurwitz.'

25 May. 'Buy 600 cases 100/8 tins Norwegian sardines. Ludovico Hurwitz.'

From their knowledge of codes the British intelligence service were sure that these contained information as to the activities of units of the fleet. The telegrams gave four different phrases for the same thing: 'Buy immediately', 'Ship', 'Ship immediately', and 'Buy'. They read this as 'the arrival', 'departure', 'lying at anchor', and 'coaling' of British ships. The telegram of 15 May was read as conveying the message that there were 18 large cruisers coaling or about to depart from the Firth of Forth. That of 20 May was interpreted as saying there were 14 destroyers lying in the Firth of Forth. They thought the telegram of 22 May referred to 20 or two of the same class of vessel – represented by 'appetite' and 'anchovies' – which were doing something or other at some port or estuary, shown by the words 'best quality'; and that the telegram of 24 May conveyed the information that 16 destroyers ('Concord Canning Anchovies') are doing something – probably arriving in the Firth of Forth, which was represented by 'guaranteed good quality'. By the telegram of 25 May they understood that six vessels of a class represented by 'Norwegian sardines' were departing from some port which they were unable to specify.[5]

Zender was interviewed at New Scotland Yard on 15 July and extensively questioned by Major Drake.

Drake	You sent off telegrams on 15, 20, 22, 24 and 25 May. About every four days you sent off a telegram ordering tinned fish?
Zender:	No, I did not always.
Drake:	There was one on 15 May. Is that your telegram?
Zender:	Yes, on 15 May.
Drake	(read telegram from Glasgow dated 15 May, 'Buy immediately 180 cases, 100 half tins smoked herrings, guaranteed good quality'): What was to be done with them when he bought them?
Zender:	To be shipped as soon as possible to Peru.
Drake:	Why did you not say 'Ship 180 cases immediately'?
Zender:	Just the same.
Drake:	It seems to me rather different. Is that your telegram?
Zender:	Yes.
Drake	(read telegram of 25 May to the same address, 'Buy 600 cases, 100/8 tins Norwegian sardines): What was to be done with these?
Zender:	To be shipped to Peru.
Drake:	When you say 'Buy' you mean 'Ship'?
Zender:	If they bought, they must be shipped.
Drake:	Is this your telegram?
Zender:	Yes sir, that is my telegram.
Drake:	It is dated Glasgow, 24 May, to the same address.

'Ship immediately 160 cases half tins Concord Canine Anchovies guaranteed good quality.' In that telegram you say 'Ship immediately'?

Zender: It has just the same meaning.

Drake: There is no different meaning in 'buy', 'buy immediately' or 'ship immediately'?

Zender: There is no difference because if they are bought, they must be shipped.

Drake: What do you pay a word for telegrams to Norway?

Zender: It is not very expensive, about two-and-a-half pence, I think.

Drake: When sending telegrams you don't generally send more words than are necessary, do you?

Zender: No.

Drake: Then what would you say if I suggest there is another meaning when you say 'buy' to what there is when you say 'buy immediately'? Also when you say 'ship' and 'ship immediately'?

Zender: No different meaning at all.[6]

Zender had not done his homework. It was the wrong season for supplying sardines and experts in the tinning of such fish scorned that such an order could be genuine, as no fish were available.[7] For cover for his work in Britain, the Germans had supplied him with 16 sample tins of fish, a price list, and a copy letter from Brochner.[8]

AUGUST BROCHNER.
Telegramadresse: 'Augbrochner'
Telefon 14084
Kristiania 25th June 1915
Toldbodgd. 11
Mr Ludovico Hurwitz y Zender,
p.t. Chritiania.

Dear Sir,

Enclosed I hand you a copy of your account with a balance of Kr. 6873.25 in your favour, which I trust you will find correct. As soon as the new remittance, which you mentioned, arrives from your firm in Peru, I shall be pleased to put the net amount to the credit of your account.

Re Drafts: You can make your drafts from England against me either in English or Scandanavian money, as convenient for you.

Re Interest: I am sorry that I cannot pay you more than 3% p.a. on the balance of your account, but as you are entitled to draw checks against me, the money is always ready and cannot earn a higher interest.

Shipment: Due to your instructions I shall continue to send all the goods I bought for you to New York for re-shipment to Peru.

Enclosed the latest price list for fish – conserves. I hope to receive your favoured orders soonest possible as the delivery takes a long time and prices are increasing.

I am, dear Sir,

Yours faithfully,

(signed) AUGUST BROCHNER.[9]

Price list for fish – Conserves.

La Macutenea		in oil 250 grams		Kr.	23. –	pr% boxes.
Buque	"	150	"	"	14.25	"
Mercedes	"	140	"	"	14.00	"
Marietta	"	125	"	"	13.25	"
Gyda	"	125	"	"	13.25	"
El Gallo	"	125	"	"	13.25	"
Carmen in Tomatos		125	"	"	13.25	"
Ship	"	150	"	"	14.25	"
Stella	"	125	"	"	14.25	"
Marietta in Tomatos		160	"	"	15.50	"
Mercedes	"	140	"	"	14.00	"
Lydia	"	125	"	"	13.25	"

Prices are without engagement.[10]

Zender agreed that he had stayed in Glasgow from 12 April to 24 May in order to buy coloured handkerchiefs. Enquiries revealed that he had told his landlord that he was an agent for a Peruvian tinned fish company. However, he did no business at all, following the pattern of other German agents. Leaving Glasgow on 24 May, he made his way to Carlisle, staying until the night of 26 May, moving on to Newcastle on 27 May where he embarked for Norway the next day.[11]

In part of his interrogation on 15 July, 1915, he was questioned about his time in Berlin.

> *Drake*:   Your last visit was on 11 April?
>
> *Zender*:   Yes sir, I arrived in Newcastle.
>
> *Drake*:   And went to Glasgow on 12 April?
>
> *Zender*:   Yes sir, on the next day.
>
> *Drake*:   What did you do in Glasgow?
>
> *Zender*:   I did not do anything in the way of business, but went several times to play golf.
>
> *Drake*:   Did you go to any other place?

Zender:	Yes sir, I went to Inverness.
Drake:	Did you go to Edinburgh?
Zender:	I went to Edinburgh one afternoon.
Drake:	Then you stayed there and left on 28 May for Bergen?
Zender:	From Newcastle, yes. I cannot say if the date is right, but my passport would show that.
Drake:	Then you stayed ten or 12 days in Glasgow?
Zender:	A month about. From 24 April to the end of May.
Drake:	And you did nothing all that time?
Zender:	I was waiting for my mail, and I could only get a copy of a letter over from Christiania.
Drake:	Did you write any letters?
Zender:	I have written letters to Norway. I sent postcards.
Drake:	Did you do any other business, beside buying tinned fish?
Zender:	I expected to get instructions to buy iron and steel knives from Sheffield, but my firm wrote me not to buy them.
Drake:	What firm?
Zender:	In Peru.
Drake:	Is that the only business you are interested in?
Zender:	I am also interested in buying stuff in Scandinavia for Peru.
Drake:	While you were in Glasgow did you get any mails at all?
Zender:	No mails from Peru. I received several letters from Norway.
Drake:	Who is your agent?
Zender:	A.C. Brochner.
Drake:	What is his business?
Zender:	He is a general agent and lives in Christiania.
Drake:	You were to buy iron goods in Sheffield?
Zender:	I received instructions not to buy them.
Drake:	Later you were told not to buy the iron goods but to buy something in Norway?
Zender:	To buy fish. I got instructions to buy them before I left Peru.
Drake:	Did you order any?
Zender:	Yes sir, from Mr Brochner. I ordered several lots when in Norway and in Glasgow.
Drake:	Why did you go to Inverness?
Zender:	I asked Mr Terry, the owner of the hotel, which was the best trip, as my mail did not arrive, and he recommended me to go to Inverness, and return via Oban,

169

	but I could not do so as there was no steamer running.
Drake:	Did you go to any other place?
Zender:	I went up to Aberdeen and Inverness and returned to Glasgow. I stayed in Aberdeen one night. That was the day before I arrived in Inverness.
Drake:	Where did you stay?
Zender:	In the Temperance Hotel near the station.
Drake:	When you stayed at the Temperance Hotel, did you write you name in the visitors' book?
Zender:	Yes, my whole name.
Drake:	Did you send any telegrams from Inverness or Aberdeen?
Zender:	I do not think so.
Drake:	And you visited no other place in Scotland.
Zender:	Glasgow and Edinburgh one afternoon.
Drake:	Did you register in Edinburgh?
Zender:	No sir, because I went to lunch and returned the same day.
Drake:	What did you do there?
Zender:	I had a little walk along Prince's Street.
Drake:	How long were you there?
Zender:	Maybe an hour or two.
Drake:	Did you go anywhere outside Edinburgh?
Zender:	No sir.
Drake:	When you walked along Prince's Street, did you go up the hill?
Zender:	From the station, I walked along the main street. I only went along where the gardens are.
Drake:	Do you know what date that was?
Zender:	No.

Later in the interview Major Drake returned to the subject.

Drake:	How long were you in Inverness?
Zender:	Two or three days.
Drake:	I thought you said only one day?
Zender:	I should think it was two or three days. You can see it on the registration paper.
Drake:	What did you do there?
Zender:	Nothing. I had a walk round the place.
Drake:	One walk, or one walk every day?
Zender:	I was just walking round about the town. I also bought a pair of glasses (pince nez) there.
Drake:	Did you go anywhere else in the neighbourhood?

170

Zender:	No sir.
Drake:	Did you take any motor trips?
Zender:	No sir.
Drake:	You did not go there for business?
Zender:	No, I went there on the recommendation of Mr Terry. Mr Terry put it on paper how to go.
Drake:	What did he write down?
Zender:	He wrote the way to go. From Aberdeen to Inverness, and then to Oban by steamer.
Drake:	He suggested you should go there?
Zender:	He suggested I should go.
Drake:	You did not go to Inverness to look at the fleet?
Zender:	No.
Drake:	Did you expect to see the fleet there?
Zender	No sir.
Drake:	Or Aberdeen?
Zender:	No sir.
Drake:	Did you see the fleet?
Zender:	No sir.
Drake:	Not at all?
Zender:	I have not seen anything at all.
Drake:	Nor at Aberdeen?
Zender:	No sir.
Drake:	Nor at Edinburgh?
Zender:	I did not even see the sea at Edinburgh.
Drake:	Nor at Glasgow?
Zender:	No sir.
Drake:	When you walked about the golf links at Glasgow, did you see any ships?
Zender:	No sir.
Drake:	And for five weeks you stayed at Glasgow and walked about the golf links?
Zender:	I was not looking at Mr Terry playing golf, but waiting for my mail.
Drake:	What was it costing you a week?
Zender:	For staying at the hotel and for breakfast, I paid 28 shillings a week. My lunch and tea I got outside.
Drake:	And all the time you were doing no business, because your mail did not arrive?
Zender:	No mail arrived from Peru.
Drake:	Who were you going to sell the tinned fish for?
Zender:	I should have sold for my own account.
Drake:	Does your firm allow that?
Zender:	Yes.[12]

171

On 27 July the Consul General for Peru called at the War Office asking for permission to interview Zender. He was informed that if he made a written application facilities would be granted.[13] The court martial was to take place on 28 September, but on 20 September the Peruvian legation requested its postponement until November. Documents required for Zender's defence were to be obtained from Lima through the offices of the London consulate.[14] So that there could be no grounds for complaint by the prisoner, this request was agreed.[15] Time went by, and it was not until 22 December that MO5 were informed by the Consul General that the letter to Peru requesting the evidence had gone astray![16] He told the British that he did not want to delay matters, and would expedite them by sending a cable. It was proposed to have affidavits made before either a British minister or the British consul, and he wished to know which the British would prefer.[17] MO5 were of the opinion that it was not for the prosecution to say how the defence should conduct their case.[18] It seemed clear to them that, as nearly two months had passed since the postponed trial, the prisoner was endeavouring to obtain a more or less indefinite postponement. Furthermore, it was thought that the affidavits would not be of much value in criminal proceedings.[19] It was then a question as to whether the prosecution, having once allowed a postponement, were as a result more or less committed to granting another.[20] It was found that letters from Peru took on average from 26 to 28 days to reach London. Upon consideration it was decided that the trial could be put back another six weeks. But Messrs Crosse & Sons, the defence solicitors, were informed, 'It must be clearly understood that no further delay will be allowed and the trial must proceed as soon after 19 February as possible.'[21]

The general court martial took place at Caxton Hall, Westminster, on 20, 21 and 22 March, 1916. Zender faced four charges, was found guilty and sentenced to death by shooting.[22] On the morning of 7 April the prisoner was taken from Wandsworth detention barracks to the Tower of London and informed of his fate: the execution would take place on 11 April.[23] A petition was received from the minister for Peru, dated 8 April, outlining the facts as they saw them.[24] However, it was considered that there was nothing in it to interfere with the findings of the court or the sentence, and the matters should proceed as arranged.[25] Zender died at 7am on 11 April, 1916, showing a fair amount of calm,[26] under the bullets of the 3rd Battalion, Scots Guards.[27]

Years later, an advertisement appeared in 1975 in *Exchange & Mart*

Curios

.303 brass cartridge case, used in Execution First World War Spy,

172

Tower of London, inscribed. 8 only issued, offers. Box (Surrey) 7803. SP99. [28]

The cartridge had been found on the Thames beach below the Tower promenade, and was engraved 'H. Zender, The Tower of London, 22nd January 1916'.[29]

CHAPTER 12

Remember

Who remembers the spies today? Few even know that such executions took place; even fewer where the bodies were laid to rest. For years it was said that the spies were interred within the grounds of the Tower of London; the *Official History* said so. But between 1914 and 1916 discreet journeys had taken place to the East London Cemetery, Plaistow. The garrison of the Tower were often used to provide funeral parties for British soldiers who had died in London hospitals. This gloomy duty was regularly done by troops of the Honourable Artillery Company. In words of an HAC private, 'More often than not these victims of war had no friends to follow them to the grave, and our little groups of artificial mourners alone made the journey behind the hearse to some outlying cemetery, there to fire a volley over an unknown comrade.'[1] And so it would have been with the spies: without friends, and aliens in the land of the enemy. They were interred quickly and silently, and then forgotten, a closed chapter and a disagreeable memory.

You can still see the grave of Carl Hans Lody today by taking the District Line to Plaistow, from where a good walk will lead you to the grave. At the exit of the station turn sharp right at the side of the building and go down some steps to the street below. This brings you to Settle Road: look to your right, and high up on the station wall you will see the street nameplate. Ahead and to your left is the Curwen Community Centre: take the alleyway to its left. A few yards on you will see the nameplate for Juliette Road; turn right here into Hartsworth Close, leading to Whitelegg Road. Follow this along a very long row of grey-doored garages, which run along the side of the railway line. Ahead are more steps, taking you up to a grass-edged pathway called Wilson Walk. Turning left, you will see a playing field on your right, with rugby posts reaching towards the sky. Behind this is the East London Cemetery, your destination.

When you arrive opposite the edge of the cemetery you will see a line of about half a dozen larger trees, where two kestrels nest each year. Use these as a direction sign to Carl Hans Lody's grave. Cast your eye just past the large tree, extending your gaze a further 20 yards. You will see a single black headstone. This is the grave of Lody, the spy. And behind the grave is a vision of the Britain of the booming 1980s: Canary Wharf, our tallest office building at some 35 storeys and 800 feet.[2]

Looking into the cemetery you will see the chapels; use these as a marker when you enter the cemetery. Continue along a high walkway, where the locals exercise their dogs. At the gate turn right into Grange Upper Road. Turn right at the junction, walking past a line of small terraced houses, until you reach the cemetery, on your right.

There is much to see. To your left, a short distance past the entrance is the Air Raid Memorial, Hackney, 1939–1945, which contains air raid casualties: grave one contains some 83 people and grave two another 22. Ahead is the stone cross commemorating those who died in the First World War, behind which are the two chapels. Even today, one can still occasionally see a shining black horse and hearse carriage, with the driver magnificent in his livery, as it slowly makes its way towards another interment. A single bell will toll its mournful message across the gravestones. It is an area where the traditions of London's East End are still upheld: death is too final to be modernized.

Walk on between the chapels, and ahead your eye falls upon a large, grey-painted anchor, part of a memorial 'In memory of those who perished launching HMS *Albion*, June 21st 189?' (the last digit is unclear). This memorial was raised by subscription. Look up and you will see beyond the line of large trees you viewed from the walkway. You are almost there. Lody's grave (number 257), in black with gold lettering, is plain and different to the others. Its lies close to its neighbours, but it is as if it is set apart from the other commemorative stones. It is stark and to the point: no sentiment here, just remembrance. Lody's grave is the only spy's grave one can find. It was not until 26 November, 1974, that the present stone was placed at its head. Two ladies, one of whom had a father who had been a friend of Lody, ordered and paid for it after visiting the cemetery and finding just grass and the grave's number marker.[3] Each April money comes from Germany to pay its upkeep.[4] Tulips push their way upwards in spring – appropriate, in their Teutonic regimental way, among the English clutter of graveyard.

> Here tulips bloom as they are told;
> Unkempt about those hedges blows
> An English unofficial rose. . .[5]

However, there is much history connected with the Lody grave. Back in October, 1924, an enquiry was received by the War Office from the German Embassy concerning the site of his grave. The War Office confirmed that the grave was located in the cemetery. As a result the War Graves Commission's inspector visited and arranged with the cemetery superintendent for a wooden cross to be erected, as there was no marker on his grave. Once this was done the German Embassy were informed, as were MI5. At this time Lody's relations were visiting his grave once a year, and had put it in good order. However, they were concerned and enquired through the German Embassy whether the grave could be regarded as being permanent? The War Graves Commission sought the advice of the War Office and Foreign Office about the possibility of exhuming and reburying his remains in a private grave. The War Office had no objection to this, providing only that the body could be identified. The Foreign Office stalled, stating that they had no information on German practice in burying spies, and suggested that if the matter were raised subsequently, the case could then be considered on its merits and in accordance with precedent at the Home Office, as they would have to grant any licence for exhumation.

When the War Graves Commission made their next visit to Lody's grave in November, 1934, they found that the family had placed a white headstone and kerb on the grave. The cemetery superintendent's office informed the Commission that this area of common graves was unlikely to be used further in the foreseeable future, and that the removal of existing burials was impossible as each coffin had been cemented down. But still the Germany Embassy raised the question of permanence, and the British informed them that Lody's grave was unlikely to be disturbed for the reasons stated. In September, 1937, the German chargé d'affaires met the War Graves Commission's vice-president after submitting another request for exhumation and reburial. There was some agreement and a meeting of minds, in that the vice-president stated that the Commission would have no objection provided there was no publicity. The Germans agreed and said they would be satisfied with reburial in a single grave in the same cemetery. Still there was known to be a legal doubt as to whether Lody's grave was a war grave. In view of the circumstances the War Office recommended that the grave should be left as it was, as Lody's body was not the only remains buried in it, and with the lapse of time there would be great difficulty in making a positive identification.

The British view was passed to the German Embassy with a suggestion by the War Graves Commission that they might acquire another site in the cemetery for a memorial to bear the names of all the German civilians buried there. The Germans were in agreement and the suggestion was taken up.[6]

A new headstone was required in 1974 because the white headstone provided by the Lody family was destroyed by bombing in the Second World War. The field was relaid in the 1960s and the bomb craters were filled, the area being recovered and the corpses reburied. Many graves were rearranged using a new numbering system (graves 1,000–1,500). Lody's grave was one of a number retaining their original numbers, and was certainly replaced in its original position.[7]

To find the memorial to the other spies, face the HMS *Albion* memorial and take the path to your left. Next to the pathway, after about 100 yards, you will find a small stone commemorating the other spies buried in nearby unmarked common graves, over which other burials have taken place several times. Apart from the ten other executed men, there are the names of seven prisoners who died of ill health or accident.[8] At the base is an inscription in German which reads: 'Here rest in God the above mentioned German men who died during the World War in civil captivity'. So Germany took those of German extraction, and Ludovico Hurwitz-y-Zender, who was not, to its bosom. When I first visited this memorial on 8 December, 1993, I found at the base a wreath of green leaves, with white plastic flowers and red ribbon. It appears that they are not forgotten.[9]

But the Germans were not to be stilled. When a German cemetery was established at Cannock Chase following an agreement in October, 1959, it was initially planned by the Volksbund Deutsche Kriegsgräberfürsorge eV to move the graves of the eighteen war dead registered in the East London Cemetery. But as they state, regrettably, due to lack of efforts on the English side, the move was never carried out.[10] However, the Commonwealth War Graves Commission has no record of this request. It appears to be a clouded issue.

In May, 1969, the miniature rifle range at the Tower of London was demolished, and later a prefabricated office building was erected between the towers.[11] Today a simple carport covers the site. There is no memorial to the dead, and no visitor is allowed to view the scene; apart from a limited view of the carport roof from Northumberland Walk, it is in an area skirted by the Casemates restricted for use as offices and the homes of the Yeoman Wardens.

And what of the future? Over 80 years have passed. Will the first light of dawn again be disturbed by a firing squad? Who are we to know, in this volatile world? If the balance of events becomes unstable, the lonely walk over the cobblestones to death might be seen again.

The history of the Tower will then move on; another chapter to be written. The Tower of London has lasted almost a thousand years: it could last another thousand, and in that time there will be much to tell.

Josef Jakobs

Josef Jakobs was the only spy to be executed in the Tower of London in the Second World War. At 8.20am on Saturday, 1 February, 1941, two farm-workers were walking across Dovehouse Farm, Ramsey Hollow, Huntingdonshire, when they heard what appeared to be three pistol shots. They found a man, Jakobs, lying on his back, covered by a camouflaged parachute – he had broken his leg. The man threw the weapon into a steel helmet, saying that he came from Hamburg and was in no war. But he had torn up a code and had buried an attaché case under his body. The case contained a wireless transmitter that could work both short and long waves. Jakobs also had in his possession a small torch with a flashing device, and a map that was marked in positions corresponding to the RAF aerodrome of Upwood and the satellite airfield of Warboys.

Jakob went before a court martial on 4–5 August, 1941, at the Duke of York Headquarters, Chelsea. He was found guilty and sentenced to death by shooting. He was executed in the Tower of London on 15 August, 1941.

References

Note: IWM = Imperial War Museum; NLC = Newspaper Library, Colindale; PRO = Public Record Office. Unless otherwise specified, full publication details are given in the Bibliography.

INTRODUCTION

1. *The Tower of London From Within*, Major General Younghusband, pp37–40.
2. *The Tower of London From Within*, Appendix A, p307.
3. *The Tower of London From Within*, Appendix B, p310.
4. *The Tower of London From Within*, Appendix D, p311.
5. PRO, Kew. WO138/38. Ref. 76110/28 (R Record), dated 1 March, 1934.
6. *Who Was Who 1916–1928*, p194.
7. Lord Chancellor's Department. Letter to L G Sellers dated 11 July, 1994, ref MS54/1994/50.
8. Letters from L. G. Sellers to the Prime Minister, John Major, dated 17 April, 1995, and acknowledgement from Deputy Press Secretary at 10 Downing Street dated 21 April, 1995.
9. Security Service, London, for Director General. Letter to L G Sellers dated 24 May, 1995.

CHAPTER 1 – GERMAN SPIES IN BRITAIN

1. *German Spies In England*, William le Queux, p30.
2. NLC. *The Evening News*, Friday 30 October, 1914, p 2. A poem called 'Chivalry' by CEB. (From The Poetry Library, Royal

Festival Hall, London. CEB is Claude Edward Burton; his pseudonym was Touchstone.)

3. IWM, Department of Documents. *Secret Well Kept*, an unpublished account of the work of Sir Vernon Kell, by his wife GRK, Chapter 18, pp117–43. Ref pp/MCR/120, Reel 1.

4. NLC. *The Times*, 9 October, 1914, p3, col 1.

5. *Behind The Scenes of Espionage – Tales of the Secret Service*, Winfrede Ludecke, pp90–1.

6. PRO, Chancery Lane. Crim 1.151/2. Deportation Order Register Number 9024.

7. *The German Spy System From Within*, Sir G. Gaunt, Chapter X1, pp155–72.

8. *German Spies In England*, pp 159–62. (Kronauer was also a barber and an agent of Steinhauer – see *Steinhauer, The Kaiser's Master Spy*, p51.)

9. *Queer People*, Sir Basil Thomson, pp 34–5. (Otto Weigals was engaged in the foreign fruit trade, according to *Steinhauer, The Kaiser's Master Spy* p16.)

10. *German Spies At Bay*, S. T. Felstead, Chapter 1, pp1–9.

11. PRO, Chancery Lane. Crim 1.151/2. Deportation Order Register Number 9024.

12. IWM, Department of Printed Books. *Journal of the Royal Artillery*, 'Military Intelligence and Incidents Connected Therewith During the War', a lecture delivered at the Royal Artillery Institute on 15 November, 1921, by Lieutenant-General Sir G. M. Macdonogh (Adjutant-General to the Forces), vol XLV111, 1921–22, pp399–408.

13. *Stand To*, no 41, 'The Old Contemptibles', John Terraine.

14. *The Fighting Nation*, Major Smithers, p79.

15. *What Fools We Were*, Brigadier-General Cockerill, p42.

16. *40 OB*, Hugh Cleland Hoy, Chapter 2, p23.

17. House of Lord's Record Office. Diplomatic Papers. Examination of Parcels and Letters. Mails. Memorandum of HM Governmental and French Government to Neutrals, 1916, CD 8223 XXX1V 47, Miscellaneous no 9.

18. *German Spies At Bay*, pp71, 82.

19. *The Invisible Weapons*, J. C. Silber, pp39, 62, 105.

20. *German Spies At Bay*, p77.

21. *The Invisible Weapons*, p 105.

22. *German Spies At Bay*, pp74–5.

23. *The U-Boat War, 1914–1918*, Edwyn Gray.

24. *The Blockade, 1914–1919*, W. Arnold-Forster, pp24–5.

25. *German Spies At Bay*, p12.

26. *The Invisible Weapons*, pp40–1, 60–1, 107–10.

27. *German Spies At Bay*, p31.
28. *The Invisible Weapons*, pp60–1.
29. *The Man of Room 40*, E. W. Ewing, p174.
30. *40 OB*, pp24–7.
31. IWM, Department of Printed Books, ref K6140. *Picture Post*, 26 November, 1938, article by C. Olsson, p67.
32. *The Scene Changes*, Sir Basil Thomson, pp236–7.
33. *German Spies At Bay*, pp159–65.
34. House of Lord's Record Office. Lloyd George papers, Series C/Box 18, Aliens, Folder 2. Document printed for use of Cabinet, 3 October, 1914, ref T/4 – (29).
35. House of Lord's Record Office. Lloyd George papers, Series C/Box 18, Aliens, Folder 2. Document printed for use of Cabinet, 17 October, 1914, ref T/4 – (30) C/18/2/3 (previous CID paper 181–B).
36. House of Lord's Record Office. Lloyd George papers, Series C/Box 18, Aliens, Folder 2. Document printed for use of Cabinet, 9 December, 1914, Scottish Office, ref T/4 – (33) C/18/2/6, pp1–3.
37. NLC. *The Evening News*, Friday 30 October, 1914, p2.
38. House of Lord's Record Office. Lloyd George papers, Series C/Box 18, Aliens, Folder 2. Document printed for use of Cabinet, 7 December, 1914, ref T/4 – (32) C/18/2/5. 11810, pp1–5.
39. House of Lord's Record Office. Accounts and Papers XV 1916, Miscellaneous Reports No 30 (Cd 8324), Visits of Inspection by Officials of the United States.
40. House of Lord's Record Office. Lloyd George papers, Series C/Box 18, Aliens, Folder 2. Document printed for use of Cabinet, 5 January, 1915, R McK, ref T/4 – (34) C/18/2/7, pp1–3, Curfew For Alien Enemies.
41. *The German Secret Service*, Colonel W. Nicolai, pp252–3.
42. PRO, Kew. HO45/10727. Paper marked 254753/99, 8 January, 1916.
43. *German Spies In England*, pp223–4. (In *Steinhauer, The Kaiser's Master Spy*, Steinhauer states that through the negligence of one of his Admiralty staff the British came into possession of information about the spy system he maintained. He writes that Berlin received news that the German spy system had been unmasked and knew that letters were being opened. He states, 'Let them go on thinking we know nothing about it.' He asks us to believe that he used this knowledge to send out rubbish, but this appears very strange for he confirms (p6) that after the arrest of his spy ring he had no spies at all in Britain! He made no

attempt to replace them. Also, just before Britain entered the First World War he visited a number of these spy contacts himself, which he would not have done if he thought they were compromised as it would have been too dangerous. Is this simply an attempt to justify his efficiency? If so, it does not stand up to examination!)

CHAPTER 2 – CARL HANS LODY

1. PRO, Kew. WO71/1236. Court Martial Papers, evidence by Carl Hans Lody, p149.
2. PRO, Kew. WO71/1236. Exhibit 12, Emergency Passport Number 01572.
3. NLC. *Daily Express*, Saturday 31 October, 1914, no 4545, p1.
4. NLC. *New York Times*, Wednesday 11 November, 1914, vol LX1V, no 29745, p1, col 3.
5. PRO, Kew. WO71/1236. Evidence by Carl Hans Lody, pp150–2, 154–8.
6. *Spy and Counter Spy*, Emanuel Victor Voska and Will Irwin, George G Harrap & Co, 1941, pp69, 77.
7. PRO, Kew. WO71/1236. Evidence by Carl Hans Lody, pp159, 163, 189.
8. *Queer People*, pp 122–3.
9. *Secret Service*, Sir George Aston, p85.
10. PRO, Kew. WO71/1236. Evidence by Carl Hans Lody, pp165, 168.
11. PRO, Kew. WO71/1236. Exhibit 38, telegram marked 98.
12. PRO. Kew. WO71/1236. Deposition of William Mills, p21.
13. PRO, Kew. WO71/1236. List of exhibits index, p1.
14. *The Invisible Weapons*, pp40–1.
15. PRO, Kew. WO71/1236. Deposition of Malcolm Brodie, p22.
16. PRO, Kew. WO71/1236. List of exhibits index, p2.
17. PRO, Kew. WO71/1236. Evidence by Carl Hans Lody, p175.
18. *German Spies At Bay*, p30.
19. PRO, Kew. WO71/1236. List of exhibits, p30, undated police report.
20. PRO, Kew. WO71/1236. Evidence by Carl Hans Lody, pp 175–6.
21. *German Spies At Bay*, p30.
22. PRO, Kew. WO71/1236. Examinations of Mary Downie, pp39–40
23. PRO, Kew. WO71/1236. List of exhibits, statement by Mary Downie, p41.

24. PRO, Kew. WO71/1236. List of exhibits, statement by Julie Brown and her examination, p38.

25. PRO, Kew. WO71/1236. List of exhibits, p13, translation of letter to editor, translation no 1187.

26. PRO, Kew. WO71/1236. Examination of Mrs Julie Ann Frances or Brown, p36.

27. PRO, Kew. WO71/1236. Evidence by Carl Hans Lody, p182.

28. PRO, Kew. WO71/1236. Examination of Ida McClyment, pp47–8.

29. PRO, Kew. WO71/1236. Evidence by Carl Hans Lody, pp178–80.

30. PRO, Kew. WO71/1236. Examination of Mary Downie, p41.

31. PRO, Kew. WO71/1236. Evidence by Carl Hans Lody, pp170, 181.

32. PRO, Kew. WO71/1236. List of exhibits index, p3, envelope containing letter to Herrn J Stammer dated 26 ??month, 1914.

33. PRO, Kew. WO71/1236. List of exhibits index, pp4–6, translation Edinburgh dated 27 September, 1914.

34. PRO, Kew. WO71/1236. Evidence by Carl Hans Lody, pp201–2.

35. PRO, Kew. WO71/1236. Examination of Ruth Routledge, pp49–50.

36. PRO, Kew. WO71/1236. Examination of Miss Jean Frost, pp50–1.

37. PRO, Kew. WO71/1236. Examination of Alfred Hussey, pp70–2.

38. PRO, Kew. WO71/1236. List of exhibits index, pp24–7, statement of Dr John Lee dated 3 October, 1914 (Dublin).

39. PRO, Kew. WO71/1236. List of exhibits index, pp7–9, translation of letter.

40. PRO, Kew. WO71/1236. List of exhibits index, p27, statement of Dr John Lee.

41. PRO, Kew. WO71/1236. Examination of James Cameron, pp91–2.

42. PRO, Kew. WO71/1236. List of exhibits index, letter from CID Edinburgh to MO5(g) dated 2 October, 1914, pp10–11.

43. PRO, Kew. WO71/1236. List of exhibits index, letter 2/x, War Office to RIC, p53.

44. PRO, Kew. WO71/1236. List of exhibits index, letter to War Office from RIC, p55.

45. PRO, Kew. WO71/1236. List of exhibits index, statement of District Inspector Cheesman, RIC, p19; and examination of Charles Cheesman, pp78–85.

46. PRO, Kew. WO71/1236. List of exhibits index, statement of

John W Lee, MD, p28.

47. PRO, Kew. WO71/1236. List of exhibits index, letter from RIC to Colonel Kell dated 4 October, 1914, p23.
48. PRO, Kew. WO71/1236.List of exhibits, police report, p31.
49. PRO, Kew. WO141/82. Minute Sheet, entry no 3 dated 7 October, 1914.
50. PRO, Kew. WO141/82. Minute Sheet, entry no 4.
51. PRO, Kew. WO141/82. Minute Sheet, entry no 5 by Kenneth Marshall, Acting DJA for JAG.
52. PRO, Kew. WO141/82. Minute Sheet, entry no 9 dated 8 October, 1914.
53. PRO, Kew. WO141/82. Minute Sheet, entry no 18 dated 21 October, 1914.
54. PRO, Kew. WO141/82. Minute Sheet, entry no 22 dated 23 October, 1914.
55. NLC. *New York Times*, Saturday 31 October, 1914, p3.
56. NLC. *Daily Express*, 31 October, 1914, no 4545, p1.
57. NLC. *Daily Mail*, 31 October, 1914, p3.
58. NLC. *Daily Express*, 31 October 1914, no 4545, p1.
59. NLC. *Daily Mail*, 31 October, 1914, p3.
60. NLC. *Daily Express*, 31 October, 1914, p1.
61. NLC. *Daily Mirror*, 31 October, 1914, no 3439, p2.
62. NLC. *Daily Mail*, 31 October, 1914, p3.
63. NLC. *Daily Mirror*, 31 October, 1914, p2.
64. NLC. *Daily Mail*, 2 November, 1914, p3.
65. NLC. *Daily Express*, 31 October, 1914, p1.
66. NLC. *Daily Mirror*, 31 October, 1914, p2.
67. NLC. *Daily Mail*, 2 November, 1914, p3.
68. PRO, Kew. WO71/1236. Evidence by Carl Hans Lody, pp171-3.
69. NLC. Daily Mail, 2 November, 1914, p3.
70. NLC. *The Times*, Sunday 1 November, 1914, p3.
71. NLC. *The Times*, Sunday 1 November, 1914, p3.
72. PRO, Kew. WO71/1236. Statement in court.
73. NLC. *New York Times*, Saturday 14 November, 1914, p2, col 8.
74. NLC. *Daily Mail*, 3/11/94. p3.
75. PRO, Kew. WO71/1236. Speech for defence by Mr George Elliott, p235/238.
76. NLC. *Daily Mirror*, 3 November, 1914, p4.
77. NLC. *Daily Mail*, 3 November, 1914, p3.
78. PRO, Kew. WO141/82. Report marked 'Secret', 63/1656 (AG3).
79. PRO, Kew. WO94/103. Handwritten letter dated 5 November, 1914.

80. *Sixty Years In Uniform*, John Frazer, p220.
81. PRO, Kew. WO141/82. Handwritten letter by Lody dated 5 November, 1914. (This is clearly Lody's letter. On minute sheet no 36 is a letter from Lody to OC 3rd Grenadier Guards dated 5 November, 1914 (29/Xi/14). The AG's directions were to place the letter in this file and not send it to the regiment, 2 January, 1915. PRO, Kew, WO94/103 contains a letter in different handwriting, not Lody's, and written on lined paper. It states, 'If it is within the frame of reglements I wish this may be made known to them.' This appears to have been written from memory and is not the same.
82. *Queer People*, p124.
83. *The Tower of London From Within*, p128.
84. The 3rd Battalion Grenadier Guards was the only regular battalion left at home. Later, when the Guards Division was formed, it was decided to send out the 3rd Battalion.
85. *Sixty Years In Uniform*, pp220–1.
86. NLC. *New York Times*, Wednesday 25 November, 1914, p5, col 6.
87. NLC. *New York Times*, Sunday 22 November, 1914, p4, col 1.
88. *Steinhauer The Kaiser's Master Spy*, Steinhauer, p38.

CHAPTER 3 – CARL FREDERICK MULLER

1. PRO, Kew. WO141/2/2. Examination of Carl Muller, p15.
2. *Secret Service*, p103.
3. PRO, Kew. WO141/2/2. Examination of Carl Muller, pp15–18.
4. PRO, Kew. WO141/2/2. Evidence by Arthur Francois Brys, p14.
5. PRO, Kew. WO141/2/2. Evidence by Edmond Herinex, p19.
6. PRO, Kew. WO141/2/2. Examination of Car Muller, p19.
7. PRO, Kew. WO141/2/2. Evidence by Edmond Herinex, p22.
8. PRO, Kew. WO141/2/2. Examination of Carl Muller, pp20–8.
9. PRO, Kew. WO141/2/2. Evidence by Minor Taylor, p22.
10 PRO, Kew. WO141/2/2. Evidence by James Dalton, p 3.
11. PRO, Kew. WO141/2/2. Evidence by Miss Jessie Speir, pp24–39.
12 PRO, Kew. WO141/2/2. Evidence by Walter James Dalton.
13. PRO, Kew. WO141/2/2.Evidence by Mary Elizabeth Tansley.
14. PRO, Chancery Lane. Crim 1/684. Exhibits, postcard postmarked 12.45pm, 15/Jan/15, London SE.
15. PRO, Chancery Lane. Crim 1/684. Exhibits, in envelope marked 25.50.

16. PRO, Chancery Lane. Crim 1/684. Exhibits.
17. PRO, Kew. WO141/2/2. Evidence by Edward Abraham, pp48–9.
18. PRO, Kew. WO141/2/2. Evidence by Robert Addison Scott p50.
19. PRO, Kew. WO141/2/2. Evidence by Mary Elizabeth Tansley, p46.
20. PRO, Chancery Lane. Crim 1/684. Exhibits, postcard postmarked 10.30am 30/Jan/15, London WC.
21. PRO, Chancery Lane. Crim. 1/684. Exhibits.
22. PRO, Kew. WO141/2/2. Evidence by Mr Pratt, pp51–3.
23. PRO, Chancery Lane. Crim 1/684. Exhibits, letter in German, translated for author by Johnathan Hill.
24. PRO, Kew. WO141/2/2. Copies of translation of letters, marked A.
25. PRO, Kew. WO141/2/2. Examination of Ada Perdaux, taken at the Tower of London, 17 March, 1915, p34.
26. PRO, Kew. WO141/2/2. Examination of Josiah Edward Mitchell, taken at the Tower of London, 11 March, 1915, p17.
27. PRO, Kew. WO141/2/2. Copies of translation of letters, marked B.
28. PRO, Kew. WO141/2/2. Evidence by Arthur Francis Brys, pp14–17. (I was surprised to learn that this meeting took place outside Leadenhall House, 101 Leadenhall Street, London, as I was employed there during the 1960s!)
29. PRO, Kew. WO141/2/2. Evidence by Cuthbert Edward Farrar, pp50–1.
30. PRO, Kew. WO141/2/2. Evidence by Mary Elizabeth Tansley, p46.
31. PRO, Kew. WO141/2/2. Evidence by Edmond Buckley (second day), pp4–7.
32. PRO, Kew. WO141/2/2. Copies of translations of letters, marked C.
33. PRO, Kew. WO141/2/2. Statement from Elizabith Gemmell, taken in the Tower of London, p19.
34. PRO, Kew. WO141/2/2. Third day of hearing, summing up by Mr George Elliott, p60.
35. PRO, Kew. WO141/2/2. Statement of evidence taken of Christine Emily Hahn on 19 March, 1915, at the Tower of London, pp42–3.
36. PRO, Kew. WO141/2/2. Continuation of summing up, p61.
37. PRO, Kew. WO141/2/2. Continuation of Mrs Hahn's evidence.
38. PRO, Kew. WO141/2/2. Evidence by Carl Muller, p111.
39. PRO, Kew. WO141/2/2. Continuation of Mrs Hahn's evidence.

40. PRO, Kew. WO141/2/2. Copies of translation of letters, marked D.
41. PRO, Kew. WO141/2/2. Evidence by Edward Mugridge, p67.
42. PRO, Chancery Lane. Crim 1/684. Exhibits, 8 February, 1915.
43. PRO, Chancery Lane. Crim 1/684. Exhibits, 18 February, 1915.
44. PRO, Chancery Lane. Crim 1/684. Exhibits, 24 February, 1915.
45. PRO, Kew. WO141/2/2. Third day of hearing, summing up by Mr George Elliott, p62.
46   PRO, Kew. WO141/2/2. Statement of evidence taken on 11 March, 1915, from Robert Tilbury in the Tower of London, pp16–17.
47. PRO, Kew. WO141/2/2. Copies of translation of letters, marked E.
48. PRO, Kew. WO141/2/2. Statement of evidence taken on 8 March, 1915, from John Barr Fetherston at the Tower of London.
49. *Queer People*, p132.
50. IWM, Department of Printed Books. Ref K 6140, *Picture Post*, 26 November, 1938, article by C. Olsson, pp61–71.
51. PRO, Kew. WO141/2/2. Statement of evidence taken on 8 March, 1915, from George Riley in the Tower of London, pp10–12.
52. PRO, Kew. WO141/2/2. Statement of evidence taken on 8 March, 1915, from Inspector Edward Parker at the Tower of London, p13.
53. *German Spies At Bay*, p48.
54. PRO, Kew. WO141/2/2. Evidence by George Riley, continued.
55. PRO, Kew. WO141/2/2. Evidence by Edward Parker, pp67–77.
56. PRO, Kew. WO141/2/2. Evidence by Sergeant MacDonald, pp77–8.
57. PRO, Kew. WO141/2/2. Evidenec by Carl Muller, second day, p59.
58. PRO, Kew. WO141/2/2. Statement of evidence taken on 17 March, 1915, from Inspector Edward Parker at the Tower of London, p27.
59. PRO, Kew. WO141/2/2. Statement of evidence taken on 11 March, 1915, from Inspector Edward Parker at the Tower of London, p16.
60. PRO, Kew. WO141/2/2. Statement of evidence taken on 17

March, 1915, from Charles Ainsworth Mitchell at the Tower of London, pp36–7.

61. PRO, Kew. WO141/2/2. Evidence by Charles Ainsworth Mitchell, second day, pp2–4.
62. PRO, Kew. WO141/2/2. Report of 2 March, 1916 by B.B. Cubitt, ref 63/2418(AG3), marked 'immediate and secret'.
63. PRO, Kew. WO141/2/2. Report by Major R. Drake, MO5(g) IP, ref 12125/A.
64. *Secret Service*, pp98–9.
65. PRO, Kew. WO94/103. Report of 17 March, 1915, by Inspector A Goatley.
66. PRO, Kew. WO141/2/2. Third day, p36.
67. PRO, Kew. WO141/2/2. Evidence by Muller, second day, p93.
68. PRO, Kew. WO141/2/2. Evidence by Muller, second day, p116.
69. PRO, Kew. WO141/2/2. Evidence by Muller, second day, p112.
70. PRO, Kew. WO141/2/2. Evidence by Muller, second day, p111.
71. Third day, p53.
72. PRO, Kew. WO141/2/2. Third day, p66–8.
73. PRO, Kew. WO94/103. Letter of 9 June, 1915.
74. PRO, Kew. WO94/103. Notes 2 and 3, 11 June, 1915.
75. PRO, Kew. WO141/2/2. Cutting from *Morning Post*, 22 June, 1915.
76. PRO, Kew. WO141/2/2. Minute no 9, 22 June, 1915, register no 63/2418.
77. *Queer People*, pp132–3.
78. PRO, Kew. WO141/2/2. Report of 23 June, 1915, marked 'Confidential', from Brigade Major, Brigade of Guards.
79. PRO, Kew. WO141/2/2. Report by W. Culver James, Surgeon-Colonel, Honourable Artillery Company.
80. *Queer People*, p133.
81. IWM, Department of Printed Books. Ref K 6140, *Picture Post*, 26 November, 1938, article by C Olsson, pp61–71.

CHAPTER 4 – HAICKE PETRUS MARINUS JANSSEN AND WILLEM JOHANNES ROOS

1. PRO, Kew. WO141/1/7. Evidence by Richard Cleveland, p17.
2. PRO, Kew. WO141/1/7. Evidence by Alfred Percy, pp14–16.
3. PRO, Kew. WO141/1/7. Evidence by Richard Cleveland, pp17–18.
4. PRO, Kew. WO141/1/7. Evidence by Rose Pauline Crocker, pp18–19.

5.   PRO, Kew. WO141/1/7. Evidence by Miss Nancy Rouse, pp21-3.
6.   PRO, Kew. WO141/1/7. Report of 5 June, 1915, by Major R Drake, MO5(g).
7.   PRO, Kew. WO141/1/7. Proceedings of general court martial, charges read by Judge Advocate, pp3–5
8.   PRO, Kew. WO141/1/7. Evidence by Inspector John Thomas McCormack, pp23–6.
9.   PRO, Kew. WO141/1/7. Evidence by Bertram Sumpton, pp27–8.
10. PRO, Kew. WO141/1/7. Edmond Buckley, pp28–33.
11. PRO, Kew. WO71/1312. Examination of Fred Combigne Cook, p7.
12. PRO, Kew. WO71/1312. Mr R D Muir, opening address, p4.
13. PRO, Kew. WO71/1312. Examination of Jennie White, p11–12.
14. PRO, Kew. WO71/1312. Examination of James Sutherland, pp9–10.
15. PRO, Kew. WO71/1312. Examination of Malcolm Brodie, pp36–8.
16. PRO, Kew. WO71/1312. Examination of John Wightman, pp14–15.
17. PRO, Kew. WO71/1312. Examination of Donald Mann, pp19–20.
18. PRO, Kew. WO71/1312. Examination of William Gunn, pp15–18.
19. PRO, Kew. WO71/1312. Examination of Albert Fitch, pp22–3.
20. PRO, Kew. WO71/1312. Edmond Buckley, pp23–8.
21. PRO, Kew. WO71/1312. Examination of Charles Ainsworth Mitchell, pp33–5.
22. PRO, Kew. WO71/1312. Examination of Kate Knight, p35.
23. PRO, Kew. WO71/1312. Examination of Algernon Sprackling, p47.
24. *Queer People*, pp135–6.
25. PRO, Kew. WO71/1312. Examination of Algernon Sprackling, pp45–50.
26. *Queer People*, p136.
27. PRO, Kew. WO94/103. Two letters, ref 63/2842(AG3) and 63/2843(AG3).
28. PRO, Kew. WO94/103. Memorandum, army form C348, from OC Troops, dated 7 May, 1915.
29. PRO, Kew. WO94/103. Letter dated 9 June, 1915.
30. PRO, Kew. WO141/1/7. Proceedings of general court martial, pp1–5.

31. PRO, Kew. WO141/1/7. George Evans, pp52–9.
32. PRO, Kew. WO141/1/7. John Louis Van Gelder, pp59–67.
33. PRO, Kew. WO141/1/7. Eustace Fulton, p87.
34. PRO, Kew. WO141/1/7.
35. PRO, Kew. WO71/1312. Proceedings of general court martial, pp1–3.
36. PRO, Kew. WO71/1312. Examination of George Evans of Evans & Evans, trading as Fribourg & Treyer of 34 Haymarket, London, pp28–30.
37. PRO, Kew. WO71/1312. Examination of John Louis Van Gelder, director of John Hunter, Morris & Elkin Ltd of 55 St Mary Axe, City, London, pp30–2.
38. PRO, Kew. WO71/1312. Examination of Major Reginald Drake, pp39–41.
39. PRO, Kew. WO71/1312. Examination of Captain William Reginald Hall, pp44–6.
40. PRO, Kew. WO71/1312. Mr Eustace Fulton, pp50–5.
41. PRO, Kew. WO71/1312. Judge Advocate, pp56–7.
42. PRO, Kew. WO71/1312. Prisoner's verbal statement, pp57–9.
43. PRO, Kew. WO71/1312. Army form section F, sentence and minute of confirmation.
44. PRO, Kew. WO141/1/7. Report of 27 July, 1915, ref 63/2842(AG3), extracted from WO file 63/2842, marked 'Confidential'.
45. PRO, Kew. WO141/1/7. Minute no 5A.
46. PRO, Kew. WO141/1/7. Minute sheet 6A, AG3, Major R. Drake.
47. PRO, Kew. WO141/1/7. Minute no 13, AAG.
48. PRO, Kew. WO141/1/7. Report of 27 July, 1915, ref 63/2842(AG3), Marked 'Secret'.
49. PRO, Kew. WO141/1/6. Letter dated 30 July, 1915, from H.S.J. Maas, ref 859.
50. PRO, Kew. WO91/103. Letter dated 30 July, 1915, marked 'Secret', to Resident Governor and Major of the Tower of London.
51. PRO, Kew. WO141/1/6. Letter dated 30 July, 1915, ref 32A.
52. German Spies at Bay, pp107–8.
53. Queer People, pp136–7.

CHAPTER 5 – ERNST WALDEMAR MELIN

1. PRO, Kew. WO71/1237. Melin's statement of 27 July, 1915, pp1, 9.

2. PRO, Kew. WO71/1237. Evidence by Ernst Melin, pp50–7, 69–71.
3. NLC. *The Daily Telegraph*, 12 January, 1915, p14, col 5.
4. PRO, Kew. WO71/1237. Examination of Flora Milligan, pp14–19, 21.
5. PRO, Kew. WO71/1237. Examination of Henri David Holtzman, p28.
6. PRO, Kew. WO71/1237. Examination of Flora Milligan, pp17–19.
7. PRO, Kew. WO71/1237. Evidence by Ernst Melin, pp59–60.
8. PRO, Kew. WO71/1237. Hubert Ginhoven, summary of evidence taken on 26 July, 1915, at Wellington Barracks, p5.
9. PRO, Kew. WO71/1237. Exhibit 12B.
10. PRO, Kew. WO71/1237. Exhibit 12D.
11. PRO, Kew. WO71/1237. Exhibit 12E.
12. PRO, Kew. WO71/1237. Exhibit 13B.
13. PRO, Kew. WO71/1237. Examination of John Barr Fetherston, second day, pp2–7.
14. PRO, Kew. WO71/1237. Reginald John Drake, summary of evidence taken on 26 July, 1915, at Wellington Barracks, p7.
15. PRO, Kew. WO71/1237. Exhibit 15, small notebook.
16. PRO, Kew. WO71/1237. Examination of Thomas Duggan, pp33–6.
17. PRO, Kew. WO71/1237. Exhibit 16, portion of a leaf believed to have been torn out of exhibit 15 (small notebook) and bearing writing believed to be in the handwriting of the accused.
18. PRO, Kew. WO71/1237. Thomas Duggan, summary of evidence taken on 26 July, 1915, at Wellington Barracks, and examination, p35.
27. PRO, Kew. WO71/1237. Examination of Charles Ainsworth Mitchell, p36.
20. PRO, Kew. WO71/1237. Exhibit 20, statement by Melin taken at New Scotland Yard on 15 June, 1915, pp22–3.
21. PRO, Kew. WO71/1237. George Charles Peevor, Second Lieutenant, 10th Battalion, Essex Regiment, summary of evidence taken on 26 July, 1915, at Wellington Barracks, and examination, p13.
22. PRO, Kew. WO71/1237. Exhibit 23, note dictated by Second Lieutenant Peevor of a statement made by the accused on 28 July, 1915, p28.
23. PRO, Kew. WO71/1237. Exhibit 24, statement by Ernst Waldemar Melin, p29.
24. PRO, Kew. WO71/1237. Exhibit 25, statement by Ernst Waldemar Melin on 27 July, 1915, pp5–10.

25. PRO, Kew. WO71/1237. Proceedings, pp1–4.
26. PRO, Kew. WO71/1237. Address by Mr Elliot, pp47–8.
27. PRO, Kew. WO71/1237. Examination by Mr Bodkin, pp72–4.
28. PRO, Kew. WO94/103. Letter dated 8 September, 1915, refs CRLD 59010 and 59013.
29. PRO, Kew. WO94/103. Letter dated 10 September, 1914, marked 'Secret 2'.
30. *Queer People*, p147.
31. *German Spies At Bay*, p184.

CHAPTER 6 – AUGUSTO ALFRED ROGGEN

1.   *German Spies At Bay*, pp125–9.
2.   PRO, Kew. WO141/61. Statement by Roggen on 11 June, 1915, marked C.
3.   *Queer People*, p144.
4.   PRO, Kew. WO141/61. Evidence by Edmund William Spalding, p29.
5.   PRO, Kew. WO141/61. Examination of Walter Richard Perks, p18.
6.   PRO, Kew. WO141/61. Evidence by Henry Beeton Brown, pp21–3.
7.   PRO, Kew. WO141/61. Introduction of evidence by Mr Bodkin, p9.
8.   *German Spies At Bay*, p127.
9.   PRO, Kew. WO141/61. Evidence by Edmund William Spalding, p26.
10. PRO, Kew. WO141/61. Report of 15 July, 1915, by Major Drake, p1.
11. PRO, Kew. WO141/61. Evidence by Mabel Irene Livingstone or Bissett, pp31–4.
12. PRO, Kew. WO141/61. Evidence by Robert Mackenzie, pp37–41.
13. PRO, Kew. WO141/61. Evidence by Mabel Irene Livingstone, continued.
14. PRO, Kew. WO141/61. Report of 15 July, 1915, by Major Drake, pp2–3.
15. PRO, Kew. WO141/61. Copy of postcard to H. Flores Esq, marked A.
16. PRO, Kew. WO141/61. Copy of postcard to A. Grund Esq, marked B.
17. PRO, Kew. WO141/61. Evidence by Jane Walker, pp34–7.
18. PRO, Kew. WO141/61. Evidence by John Wright, pp42–6.

19. PRO, Kew. WO141/61. Evidence by Edmund Buckley, pp53–5.

20. PRO, Kew. WO141/61. Evidence by Charles Aynesworth Mitchell, pp56–8.

21. PRO, Kew. WO141/61. Evidence by Major Reginald John Drake, p57.

22. PRO, Kew. WO141/61. Report of 15 July, 1915, by Major Drake, pp5–6.

23. *Queer People*, p144.

24. PRO, Kew. WO141/61. Statement by Roggen, marked C, p3.

25. PRO, Kew. WO141/61. Report 63/3062(AG3) of 7 September, 1915, marked 'Secret'.

26. PRO, Kew. WO141/61. Four-page 'Petition' written in ink by Roggen at Wandsworth detention barracks on 21 August, 1915, according to minute 10B received on 25 August for consideration.

27. PRO, Kew. WO141/61. Minutes 11A, 12, 13, 14, 15, 16, 17, 18.

28. PRO, Kew. WO141/61. Letter dated 7 September, 1915, ref 63/2971(AG3), to General Officer Commanding, London District, Horse Guards.

29. PRO, Kew. WO141/61. Letter marked 'Secret', ref 63/29(AG3).

30. PRO, Kew. WO141/61. Minute 21, register no 63/3062, minute sheet 4.

31. PRO, Kew. WO141/61. Letter marked 21A, from Legacion del Uruguay.

32. PRO, Kew. WO141/61. Minute 21, continued.

33. PRO, Kew. WO141/61. Letter marked 24A, three pages.

34. PRO, Kew. WO141/61. Letter dated 10 September, 1915, signed R H Brade.

35. PRO, Kew. WO141/61. Minute 25, ref 63/30062., dated 11 September, 1915.

36. PRO, Kew. WO141/61. Report marked 'Immediate and Secret', signed B B Cubitt.

37. PRO, Kew. WO141/61. Minute 29, ref AG3, 14 September, 1915.

38. PRO, Kew. WO141/61. Letter to the Minister of Uruguay dated 15 September, 1915.

39. PRO, Kew. WO141/61. Letter dated 15 September, 1915, ref GRLD 50910.

40. PRO, Kew. WO141/61. Account submitted by solicitors dated 20 September, 1915.

41. PRO, Kew. WO141/61. Minute note 31.

42. PRO, Kew. WO141/61. Handwritten note in pencil by Roggen.
43. PRO, Kew. WO141/61. Account submitted by solicitors dated 20 September, 1915.
44. *Queer People*, p145.
45. PRO, Kew. WO94/103. Letter dated 17 September, 1915, letter 2.
46. *Queer People*, p145.
47. *German Spies At Bay*, pp130-1.

CHAPTER 7 – FERNANDO BUSCHMAN

1. PRO, Kew. WO71/1313. Examination of Herbert Ginhoven.
2. PRO, Kew. WO71/1313. Evidence of Fernando Buschman, p1–10.
3. PRO, Kew. WO71/1313. Evidence of Fernando Buschman, second day, p19.
4. PRO, Kew. WO71/1313. Examination of Emil Samuel Franco, pp57–8.
5. PRO, Kew. WO71/1313. Evidence of Fernando Buschman, pp13–14.
6. PRO, Kew. WO71/1313. Examination of Emil Samuel Franco, pp57–68.
7. PRO, Kew. WO71/1313. Examination of John Barr Featherston, pp32–40.
8. PRO, Kew. WO71/1313. Examination of Major Reginald John Drake, pp71–89.
9. PRO, Kew. WO71/1313. Examination of Sergeant Hubert Ginhoven, pp91–4.
10. PRO, Kew. WO71/1313. Examination of George Riley, pp40–7.
11. PRO, Kew. WO71/1313. Exhibit 28, 'General Impressions of London'.
12. PRO, Kew. WO71/1313. Exhibit 24, statement dated 5 June, 1915.
13. PRO, Kew. WO71/1313. Exhibit 25, statement dated 24 June, 1915.
14. PRO, Kew. WO71/1313. Court martial, army form A47; army form A9.
15. PRO, Kew. WO71/1313. Court martial, army form, part B.
16. PRO, Kew. WO71/1313. Evidence by Fernando Buschman, second day, pp22–3, 35, 47–8.
17. PRO, Kew. WO71/1313. Mr Bodkin, second day, pp60–2.

18. PRO, Kew. WO94/103. Letter to Major General Pipon, ref CRLD 59012/BM.
19. PRO, Kew. WO71/1313. Exhibit 18, property found on prisoner.
20. *German Spies At Bay*, pp123–4.
21. *Behind the Scenes of Espionage – Tales of the Secret Service*, pp142–3.

CHAPTER 8 – GEORGE BREECKOW

1. PRO, Kew. WO141/3/1. Evidence by George Breeckow, third day, 16 September, 1915, pp128–34.
2. PRO, Kew. WO141/3/1. Evidence by Walter Richard Perks, first day, pp7–8.
3. PRO, Kew. WO141/3/1. Evidence by Miss Dora Pickett, first day, p12.
4. PRO, Kew. WO141/3/1. Evidence by George Breeckow, pp137–8.
5. PRO, Kew. WO141/3/1. Evidence by Louise Emily Wertheim, pp71–6.
6. Unpublished article by John Maclaren, Huddersfield, p1.
7. PRO, Kew. WO141/3/1. Evidence by Mrs Wertheim, pp71–6.
8. PRO, Kew. WO141/3/1. Evidence by Mable Knowles, p23.
9. PRO, Kew. WO141/3/1. Evidence by John Stuckle, pp13–14.
10. PRO, Kew. WO141/3/1. Evidence by George Breeckow, pp138–9.
11. PRO, Kew. WO141/3/1. Evidence by Mrs Wertheim, pp87–8.
12. PRO, Kew. WO141/3/1. Evidence by George Breeckow, p139.
13. PRO, Kew. WO141/3/1. Evidence by Mrs Wertheim, p88.
14. PRO, Kew. WO141/3/1. Evidence by George Breeckow, pp139–40.
15. PRO, Kew. WO141/3/1. Evidence by Mrs Wertheim, p89.
16. PRO, Kew. WO141/3/1. Evidence by George Breeckow, p140.
17. PRO, Chancery Lane. Crim 4. 1366.
18. PRO, Kew. WO141/3/1. Evidence of Colonel Alfred Walter, Warden, p37.
19. PRO, Kew. WO141/3/1. Summing up by Mr Justice Bray, p202.
20. PRO, Kew. WO141/3/1. Evidence by Mabel Knowles, pp16–18.
21. PRO, Kew. WO141/3/1. Summing up by Mr Justice Bray, pp194–5.
22. PRO, Kew. WO141/3/1. Breeckow's address to the court before sentence, p207.
23. PRO, Kew. WO141/3/1. Evidence by Mabel Knowles, p18.

24. PRO, Kew. WO141/3/1. Evidence by George Breeckow, pp152–3.
25. PRO, Kew. WO141/3/1. Evidence by Ivor Richards, pp15–16.
26. PRO, Kew. WO141/3/1. Evidence by George Breeckow being examined regarding exhibit 66, pp152–3.
27. PRO, Kew. WO141/3/1. Summing up by Mr Justice Bray, p196.
28. PRO, Kew. WO141/3/1. Evidence by William Beattie Bruce, pp34–5.
29. PRO, Kew. WO141/3/1. Evidence by George Robertson, pp23, 32–4.
30. PRO, Kew. WO141/3/1. Summing up by Mr Justice Bruce, p5.
31. PRO, Kew. WO141/3/1. Evidence by Bella Peattie, p24.
32. PRO, Kew. WO141/3/1. Evidence by Charles Charker, pp26–7.
33. PRO, Kew. WO141/3/1. Evidence by John McNaughton, pp27–31.
34. PRO, Kew. WO141/3/1. Evidence by Annie Macaskill, pp24–5.
35. PRO, Kew. WO141/3/1. Evidence by Colonel Alfred Walter Warden, pp36–8.
36. *Queer People*, p137.
37. PRO, Kew. WO141/3/1. Evidence by Herbert Fitch, p38.
38. PRO, Kew. WO141/3/1. Evidence by Edmund Buckley, pp38–41.
39. PRO, Kew. WO141/3/1. Evidence by Gertrude Elizabeth Sophia Brandes, pp2–8.
40. PRO, Kew. WO141/3/1. Evidence by Mable Knowles, pp18–19.
41. PRO, Kew. WO141/3/1. Evidence by Edmund Buckley, pp41–2.
42. PRO, Kew. WO141/3/1. Evidence by Ada Elizabeth Burnside, p59.
43. PRO, Kew. WO141/3/1. Evidence by Edmund Buckley, pp43–7.
44. PRO, Kew. WO141/3/1. Evidence by Ada Elizabeth Burnside, p59.
45. PRO, Kew. WO141/3/1. Evidence by Edmund Buckley, p42.
46. *Queer People*, pp138–9.
47. PRO, Kew. WO141/3/1. Evidence by Edmund Buckley, pp48, 57.
48. PRO, Kew. WO141/3/1. Evidence by report of 25 June, 1915, by Edmond Buckley to Superintendent P Quinn.
49. PRO, Kew. WO141/3/1. Minute marked 4 to DPS.
50. PRO, Kew. WO141/3/1. Report marked 'Secret' of 24 July, 1915, ref 63/2855(AG3).
51. PRO, Kew. WO141/3/1. Fourth day of trial, p201.

52. PRO, Kew. WO141/3/1. Fourth day of trial, pp206–9.
53. *German Spies At Bay*, p118.
54. PRO, Kew. WO141/3/1. *The Times*, 25 October, 1915, 'British and German Methods'.
55. PRO, Kew. WO141/3/1. Fourth day of trial. pp209–10.
56. *German Spies At Bay*, p118.
57. PRO, Kew. WO141/3/1. Letter from Home Office 19th October 1915, marked immediate.
58. PRO, Kew. WO141/3/1. Letter marked Secret and Immediate of 19th October 1915. Reference 63/2855. (A.G.3.)
59. PRO, Kew. WO141/3/1. Report by Leonard W. Kershaw. Registrar of the Court of Criminal Appeal of 18 October, 1915.
60. PRO, Kew. WO141/3/1. Letter of 21 October, 1915, from the Home Office to the Governor, HM Prison, Pentonville.
61. PRO, Kew. WO94/103. GRLD 67690/BM, marked 'Secret'.
62. *German Spies At Bay*, pp118–19.
63. Certified copy of an entry of death, application no. WOO8237 DXZ 210791.
64. PRO, Kew. WO94/103. Marked 'Secret'.
65. Broadmoor Hospital. File 879, notice Criminal Lunatics Act 1884. 47 & 48, Vict c64 S2, stamped 29 January, 1918, prisoner no 281, 179/17.
66. Broadmoor Hospital, File 879. Statement respecting Criminal Lunatics to be filled up and transmitted to the medical Supt with every Criminal Lunatic.
67. Broadmoor Hospital. File 879, small unsigned and undated report dated 28 November, 1917.
68. Broadmoor Hospital. Treatment sheets and notes, item 23 of 7 June, 1920.
69. General Register Office, Southport. Certified copy of an entry of death, no DXZ 349165, application no B002926, registration district Easthampstead, sub-district Sandhurst. (Death recorded after an inquest held on 30 July, 1920.)
70. Broadmoor Hospital. File 879, copy letter from deputy medical superintendent to solicitor dated 29 July, 1920.
71. Broadmoor Hospital. File 879, letter ref C614/20, dated 26 October, 1920.

CHAPTER 9 – IRVING GUY RIES

1. PRO, Kew. WO71/1238. Exhibit 3, p3, no 52607.
2. PRO, Kew. WO71/1238. Exhibit 5, registration form, Hotel Cecil Ltd, Strand, London WC.

3. PRO, Kew. WO71/1238. Evidence by Irving Guy Ries, p46.
4. PRO, Kew. WO71/1238. Exhibit 7, Post Office telegraph, ref R59.533/2383.
5. PRO, Kew. WO71/1238. Exhibit 8, telegraph money order, ref 2383 S4446.
6. PRO, Kew. WO71/1238. Exhibit 1, registration form, Hotel St George (Liverpool) Ltd.
7. PRO, Kew. WO71/1238. Exhibit 11, registration form, Crown Hotel, Edinburgh.
8. PRO, Kew. WO71/1238. Exhibit 12. Register of aliens, first report.
9. PRO, Kew. WO71/1238. Examination of James Harper Paterson, pp14–17.
10. PRO, Kew. WO71/1238. Examination of Argyle Lindsey, pp17–21.
11. PRO, Kew. WO71/1238. Examination of George McClellan, pp22–7.
12. PRO, Kew. WO71/1238. Opening address by Mr Bodkin, pp5–7.
13. PRO, Kew. WO71/1238. Exhibit 9, Post Office telegraph, ref S4446.596/248.
14. PRO, Kew. WO71/1238. Opening address by Mr Bodkin, p8.
15. PRO, Kew. WO71/1238. Examination of Ripley Wilson, second day, pp12–13.
16. PRO, Kew. WO71/1238. Examination of Joseph Sandercock, second day, pp3–12.
17. PRO, Kew. WO71/1238. Exhibit 14, transcript of shorthand notes, New Scotland Yard, 12 August, 1915.
18. PRO, Kew. WO71/1238. Exhibit 15, transcript of shorthand notes, New Scotland Yard, 19 August, 1915.
19. PRO, Kew. WO71/1238. Examination of Algernon Sprackling, second day, pp15–26.
20. PRO, Kew. WO71/1238. Courts martial army form 47, and form of order for the assembly of a general or district court martial, army form A9.
21. PRO, Kew. WO71/1238. Army form 9, and list of charges, pp1–4.
22. PRO, Kew. WO71/1238. Examination of Hubert Ginhoven, second day, pp27–9.
23. PRO, Kew. WO71/1238. Evidence by Irving Guy Ries, second day, pp45–63.
24. PRO, Kew. WO71/1238. Judge Advocate, second day, pp83–7.

25. PRO, Kew. WO71/1238. Lord Cheylesmore, p87.
26. PRO, Kew. WO71/1238. Army form 9, section F.
27. PRO, Kew. WO71/103. Letter ref CRLD 61745/BM, marked 'Secret'.
28. *Queer People*, pp156–7.
29. *German Spies At Bay*, p151.
30. PRO, Kew. WO71/103. Letter from Officer Commanding Troops, Tower of London to Resident Governor.

CHAPTER 10 –ALBERT MEYER

1. *Queer People*, pp160–1.
2. PRO, Kew. WO141/83. Translation of letter in invisible ink, 20 June, 1915.
3. PRO, Kew. WO141/83. Report marked 'Secret' by Captain Carter, dated 10 September, 1915.
4. PRO, Kew. WO141/83. Captain Carter's report, continued.
5. PRO, Kew. WO141/83. Translation of message in invisible ink written on a postcard, 13 July, 1915.
6. PRO, Kew. WO141/83. Captain Carter's report, continued.
7. PRO, Kew. WO141/83. Translation of message in invisible ink, dated 20 July, 1915.
8. PRO, Kew. WO141/83. Captain Carter's report, continued.
9. PRO, Kew. WO141/83. Copy of letter dated 29 August, 1915.
10. PRO, Kew. WO141/83. Captain Carter's report, continued.
11. PRO, Kew. WO141/83. Form E, permits no 2947.
12. PRO, Kew. WO141/83. Petition by Percy Robinson & Co, solicitors, dated 26 November, 1915, 18A, p2.
13. PRO, Kew. WO141/83. Form E, permits, no 2947.
15. PRO, Kew. WO141/83. Captain Carter's report, continued.
16. PRO, Kew. WO141/83. Minute no 1, register no 63/3342.
17. PRO, Kew. WO141/83. Letter dated 1 September, 1915, 1A, marked 'Secret', by V J M Gattie.
18. *German Spies At Bay*, p157.
19. PRO, Kew. WO141/83. Marked 18a, petition by Percy Robinson & Co, solicitors, dated 26 November, 1915, p2.
20. PRO, Kew. WO141/83. Minute 7, 11 November, 1915.
21. PRO, Kew. WO141/83. Minute 16B, marked 'Secret', ref 63/3342(AG3).
22. PRO, Kew. WO94/103. Letter dated 25 November, 1915, ref GRLD 65511/BM.
23. PRO, Kew. WO94/103. Letter dated 26 November, 1915, marked 'Pressing', ref GRLD 65511/BM.

24. PRO, Kew. WO141/83. Minute 18 (received 1pm, 26 November, 1915).
25. PRO, Kew. WO141/83. Minute 19.
26. PRO, Kew. WO141/83. Copy of report marked 25B, 29 November, 1915.
27. PRO, Kew. WO141/83. Ref 30A 63/3342(AG3), dated 30 November, 1915, sent by special messenger.
28. PRO, Kew. WO91/103. Letter dated 2 December, 1915, to Resident Governor.
29. *German Spies At Bay*, p158

CHAPTER 11 – LUDOVICO HURWITZ-Y-ZENDER

1. PRO, Kew. WO 141/2/4. Copy statement by Zender, p 1 & 2.
2. *German Spies At Bay* by S.T. Felstead, published by Hutchinson in 1920, p140.
3. PRO, Kew. WO 141/2/4. Report by R.J. Drake, Major, G.S. Dated 27th July, 1915.
4. PRO, Kew. WO 141/2/4. Letter for the Director of Personnel Services from the War Office, marked Secret. dated 6th July 1915. 63/2973. (A.G.3.)
5. PRO, Kew. WO 141/2/4. Report by R.J. Drake, Major, G.S. Dated 27th July 1915.
6. PRO, Kew. WO 141/2/4. Interview at New Scotland Yard of 15th July 1915.
7. *Queer People*, p148.
8. PRO, Kew. WO 141/2/4. Report by R.J. Drake, as above.
9. PRO, Kew. WO 141/2/4. Typed copy marked B.
10. PRO, Kew. WO 141/2/4. Typed copy marked C.
11. PRO, Kew. WO 141/2/4. Report by R.J. Drake, as above.
12. PRO, Kew. WO 141/2/4. Interview at New Scotland Yard of 15 July, 1915.
13. PRO, Kew. WO 141/2/4. Letter from Brigadier General, Director of Personnel Services, of 28th July 1915. Marked Secret. 63/2973. (A.G.3) To the Commandant Detention Barracks, Wandsworth.
14. PRO, Kew. WO 141/2/4. Margin note 10. And letter marked 10B, from Peruvian Legation, London 20th September 1915.
15. PRO, Kew. WO 141/2/4. Letter to R.H. Campbell Esq at Foreign Office, marked 'Secret', dated 23rd September 1915.
16. PRO, Kew. WO 141/2/4. Margin note marked 14. M.O.G. 5G. 28th December 1915.

17. Public Record Office, Kew. WO141/2/4. Minute note 15. Register number 26931. By J.P. Shelly, Captain. 21/12/15.
19. PRO, Kew. WO 141/2/4. Minute 18. To J.A.G. F.C. Beason D.P.S. for A.G. 30/12/15.
20. PRO, Kew. WO 141/2/4. Minute 20. M.O.G. 5. 4/1/16.
21. PRO, Kew. WO 141/2/4. Draft for the Director of Military Intelligence, to Messrs Crosse & Sons, 7, Lancaster Place, Strand.
22. PRO, Kew. WO 141/2/4. Letter of 5th April 1916. Marked Confidential 63/2973 (A.G.3.)
23. PRO, Kew. WO 141/2/4. Report of 11th April 1916. Marked Secret. G.R.L.D. 59009/B.M. To the Secretary of the War Office from Major General Commanding London District.
24. PRO, Kew. WO 141/2/4. Five p letter to His Excellency E.de.la Feunte, Minister for Peru. From W.S.M. Knight. 1 Garden Court, Temple. Dated 8th April 1916.
25. PRO, Kew. WO 141/2/4. Minute Note 36. To D.P.S.
26. *German Spies At Bay*, by S.T. Felstead. Published by Hutchinson in 1920. P142.
27. PRO, Kew. WO94/103. Letter to Resident Governor, Tower of London, dated 11 April, 1916, from Lieutenant Colonel commanding 2nd (Res) Battalion Welsh Guards, OC Troops.
28. *Exchange and Mart*, 25 September, 1975. 'Collecting', p35.
29. *After The Battle*, Number 11, 1976, pp3–4.

CHAPTER 12 – REMEMBER

1. *The Great War I Was There*, Part 22, 'I Guarded Spies in the Tower' by J.B. Sterndale Bennett. P 860.
2. *Daily Mail*, Friday, 10 March, 1995, p62,'Canary Wharf gets its head in the clouds'.
3. Letter to L.G. Sellers from Gisela Rehrike, Hamburg, dated 12 June, 1995.
4. Conversation between the author and secretary, East London Cemetery, Plaistow.
5. *Complete Poems of Rupert Brooke*, from 'The Old Vicarage, Grantchester' p93 (Café des Westons, Berlin, May, 1912), Sidgwick & Jackson, 1939.
6. Letter to L. G. Sellers from Commonwealth War Graves Commission dated 28 June, 1995. ref CEM 5470. IS 6 95.
7. Letter to L. G. Sellers dated 10 May, 1995, from Volksbund Deutsche Kriegsgraberfursorge cv from Stiel, Head of Section, Grave Identification and Information of Relatives.

8. *After The Battle*, no 11, German spies in Britain, p3.
9. Conversation between the author and Ron, gardener at the East London Cemetery, on 8 March, 1995. (Ron cares for the memorial and places flowers there from time to time.)
10. Letter to L.G. Sellers dated 29 November, 1994, from Volksbund Deutsche Kriegsgräberfürsorge vE from von Lutzau, Head of Department.
11. *After The Battle*, no 11, German spies in Britain, p2.

Acknowledgements

I would like to thank all the people and organizations listed below for their help and support, without which this book could not have been written.

It has not always been possible to trace the copyright holders of all the material I have quoted, and I would be pleased to hear of any person to whom this applies.

Arnell, June
Barter-Bailey, Sarah (Librarian, Royal Armouries, Tower of London)
Bird, Maggie (Metropolitan Police Archives Branch)
Bligh, Ms K V (Assistant Archivist, House of Lord's Record Office)
Braganza, Mr
Broadmoor Hospital Authority
Cabinet Office (Historical and Records Section)
Churchill Archives Centre, Cambridge
Commonwealth War Graves Commission Maidenhead
Courtney, S (Chief Clerk, Middlesex Guildhall)
Delaney, John (Imperial War Museum, Department of Photographs)
East London Cemetery Company Ltd, Plaistow, London
Ebsworth, Mrs S.
Feather, Fred (Essex Police Museum)
Furguson, W.
German Historical Institute, London
German State Archives
Gilles, Robin (Metropolitan Police Archives Branch)
Guard's Museum, Birdcage Walk, London
Guenin, J (Superintendent, St Mary's Cemetery, Harrow Road, London)
Gunn, Alan

Harfield, Alan, FRHistS
Hegarty, Kieran
Hill, Johnathan
Hook, Ian (Keeper, Essex Regiment Museum)
Honourable Artillery Company, London
Hunt, Mr (Imperial War Museum, Department of Printed Books)
House of Lord's Record Office
Imperial War Museum, Departments of Printed Books, Documents,
    Sound Records and Photographs
Kelly, W.E.
Kent Elms Library, Leigh-on-Sea (all the staff)
Knott, Roy
The Law Society
Liddel Hart Centre for Military Archives, King's College, London
Lord Chancellor's Department, London
Lutzau, von (Head of Department of Graves Identification &
    Information of Relations at German War Graves Commission)
Maclaren, John
Mawson, Dr David C.
Metropolitan Police (Archives Branch)
Middlesex Guildhall, Crown Court
National Army Museum
Newspaper Library, Colindale, London
O'Brien, Kate (Military Archivist, King's College, London)
Palmer, T (Deputy Chief Clerk, Middlesex Guildhall)
Poetry Library, Royal Festival Hall, London
Public Record Office, Chancery Lane, London
Public Record Office, Kew (Crown Copyright is reproduced with the
    permission of the Controller of Her Majesty's Stationery Office)
Rehmke, Gisela (Hamburg)
Royal Armouries, Tower of London
Royal Commission on Historical Manuscripts, Chancery Lane,
    London
Royal Naval College, Greenwich
Scarlet, Julie
Sellers, Elaine (my wife)
Simpson, Mrs L.
Small, I C (Enquiries Section, Commonwealth War Graves
    Commission)
Smith, Mrs E (Record Office, Lord Chancellor's Department)
Southend-on-Sea Library
Steel, Nigel (Imperial War Museum, Department of Documents)
Tyler, Major General Christopher (Governor of Tower of London)
Tibbotts, Mrs Sharon (Photographic Librarian, Tower of London)

Volksbund Deutsche Kriegsgraberfursorge eV (German War Graves
  Commission)
Walker, Mrs G.M. (Secretary, East London Cemetery Company Ltd)
Wilkinson, Mary (Imperial War Museum, Department of Printed
  Books)

Bibliography

After The Battle. Number 11, 'German Spies in Britain'. 1976.

W. Arnold-Forster, *The Bockade 1914–1919*, Oxford Pamphlets on World Affairs, Clarendon Press, 1939.

Sir George Aston, *Secret Secret*, Faber & Faber, 1930.

Brigadier-General Cockerill, *What Fools We Were*, Hutchinson, 1944.

E.W. Ewing, *The Man of Room 40*, Hutchinson, 1939.

S.T. Felstead, *German Spies At Bay*, Hutchinson 1920.

John Frazer, *Sixty Years In Uniform*, Stanley Paul, 1939.

Sir G. Gaunt, *The German Spy System From Within*, Hodder & Stoughton, 1914.

Edwyn Gray, *The U-Boat War*, Leo Cooper/Pen & Sword Books, 1994.

Hugh Cleland Hoy, *40 OB*, Hutchinson, 1932.

Robert Rhodes James, *Gallipoli*, Papermac, 1989.

Journal of the Royal Artillery, vol XLV111, 1921–22.

Winfred Ludecke, *Behind the Scenes of Espionage – Tales of the Secret Service*, Harrap, 1929.

Colonel W. Nicolai, *The German Secret Service* (trans. George Renwick, FRGS), Stanley Paul, 1924.

Lieutenant Colonel the Right Honorable Sir Frederick Ponsonby, *Grenadier Guards in the Great War of 1914–1918*, vol 1, Macmillan, 1920.

William le Queux, *German Spies in England*, Stanley Paul, 1915.

Picture Post, 26 November, 1938.

J.C. Silber, *The Invisible Weapons*, Hutchinson, 1922.

A.J. Smithers, *The Fighting Nation*, published by Leo Cooper/Pen & Sword Books, 1994.

Stand to, no 41, Western Front Association.

Steinhauer, *Steinhauer The Kaiser's Master Spy*, English edition (ed. S T Felstead) John Lane/Bodley Head, 1930.

207

John Terraine, *Stand To*, no. 41, 'The Old Contemptibles', Western Front Association.

The Great War I Was There, part 22, 'I Guarded Spies in the Tower'.

Sir Basil Thomson, *Queer People*, Hodder & Stoughton, 1922.

Sir Basil Thomson, *The Scene Changes*, Collins, 1939.

Who Was Who, 1916–1928, A&C Black, 1929.

Major-General Younghusband, *The Tower of London From Within*, Herbert Jenkins, c1920.

Index

Rotterdam, (cont.) 114,
120, 129, 140, 144,
145, 146
Routledge, Ruth, 27, 30,
33
Rowland, Reginald, 123,
129, 131, 135
Royal Oak, H.M.S., 85
Roxburgh Hotel, 27, 30,
33
Ruston Proctor & Co, 96,
97

Sandercock, Inspector,
141, 142
Saunderson, Richard, 83,
89, 91, 146
Scarlet, Mr & Mrs, 125
Schaefer, Charles & Sons,
140, 149
Schneitzer, Rittmeister,
119
Schroder, Baroness, 130
Schwieger, Kapitanleutant
Walther, 10
Simon, Sir John, 136
Smith, Kate, 87, 88, 90, 91
Southampton, 12, 51, 52,
53, 59, 64, 65, 66, 71,
108, 114
Spalding, Edward William,
97
Speir, Miss Jessie Neilson,
45, 46, 47, 48, 50, 55,
58
Sprackling, Constable, 69,
133, 142
Stammer, Herr, 22, 33

Star & Echo, newspaper,
123
Steinberg, J., 32
Storse, Gottlieb, 17
Stubenwoll, Karl, 6
Stuckle, John, 122
Sumpton, Sergeant, 65
Sutherland, Sergeant,
Suttie's Hotel, Aberdeen,
66, 70

Tansley, Mary Elizabeth,
47, 52
Tarbet Hotel, Loch
Lomond, 99, 100, 103
Terry, Mr, 169, 171
Thomspon, Charlie, 57
Thomson, Sir Basil, 11,
62, 68, 70, 87, 111,
112, 132, 140, 144,
146, 156, 157
Three Nuns Hotel,
Aldgate, 96, 97
Thornton & Company,
96, 97
Thule Steamship
Company, 80
Tiger, H.M.S., 55
Tilbury, Robert, 57
The Times, 37, 123, 136
Trossachs Hotel, 98
Tullidge, Dr, 120, 125
Turk's Head Hotel,
Newcastle, 66, 77
Tyrell, Lewis & Co, 114

Ullstein Verlag, Berlin, 23
U.12 subarmine, 85

Van Dyck, Charles, 55
Vega, S.S., 165
Vernon, S.S., 86, 92
Volksbund Deutsche
Kriegsgräberfürsorge,
177
Volteria, S.S., 72

Waack, Mrs, 160
Walker, Jane, 99
War Graves Commission,
176
Wassal, John, 54
Wedderburn, Captain, 92
Weimer Hotel, 87
Wertheim, Bruno, 121,
128
Wertheim, Louise Emily,
98, 122–139
Whitby Abbey, S.S., 45
Wightman, Inspector, 67
Wilder, H.M.S., 158
Wilson, Mr, 142, 148
Wilson, Ripley, 141
Wood, Field Marshal, 61
Wright, Superintendent,
99

Yalm, River, 3
York Hotel, York, 69

Zeppelins, 12, 29, 82, 90,
111
Zimmerman telegram, 11
Zoological Gardens, 122